Let's Talk Polygamy
UNCENSORED

Modern-Day Solutions Found in This
Ancient Marital Practice

Coach Nazir
Coach Fatimah
Coach Nyla

OUTSTANDING
PERSONAL RESULTS LLC

For inquiries regarding permissions, speaking opportunities, and bulk order purchases, please email: support@outstandingpersonalrelationships.com

Authors: Coach Nazir, Coach Fatimah, Coach Nyla

Publisher: Outstanding Personal Relationships LLC

Official Website: www.outstandingpersonalrelationships.com

Cover Design: Faatimah Al-Mujaahid

Interior Design: Coach Nazir

Author Illustrations: Coach Nazir

Library of Congress Cataloging-in-Publication Data

ISBN: 978-0-9892051-1-5

Website Resources:

- Official Website: *www.outstandingpersonalrelationships.com*

- Coaching: *www.outstandingpersonalrelationships.com*

CONTENTS

PART 1

LET'S TALK POLYGAMY WITH COACH NAZIR   XII

PART 2

Let's Talk Polygamy with Coach Fatimah 120

PART 3

Let's Talk Polygamy with Coach Nyla   226

DEDICATION

We wrote this book to empower others who desire to learn about polygyny and how it can work in modern times. We didn't have many resources available and pray this helps you along your journey no matter where you are.

This is for the men who have that inner struggle yet know there is a way to live authentically but have yet to find it, the initial wives who don't understand what's happening with their hearts and the roller coaster of emotions, and any incoming wives who also ride the roller coaster of emotions and are trying to understand their place while facing social stigmas for desiring to build a family with a quality man.

Abu Qatadah reported: The Messenger of Allah, peace and blessings be upon him, said, **"The best of what a man leaves behind are three: a righteous child who supplicates for him, ongoing charity the reward of which reaches him, and knowledge that is acted upon after him."**

Source: Sunan Ibn Mājah 237
Grade: *Sahih* (authentic) according to Al-Albani

عَنْ أَبِي قَتَادَةَ قَالَ قَالَ رَسُولُ اللهِ صَلَّى اللَّهُ عَلَيْهِ وَسَلَّمَ خَيْرُ مَا يُخَلِّفُ الرَّجُلُ مِنْ بَعْدِهِ ثَلَاثٌ وَلَدٌ صَالِحٌ يَدْعُو لَهُ
وَصَدَقَةٌ تَجْرِي يَبْلُغُهُ أَجْرُهَا وَعِلْمٌ يُعْمَلُ بِهِ مِنْ بَعْدِهِ

سنن ابن ماجه كتاب المقدمة باب ثواب معلم الناس الخير 237

المحدث الألباني خلاصة حكم المحدث صحيح في صحيح ابن ماجه 199

We pray that this weigh heavily on our scale of good deeds and that people, especially our offspring find guidance in this work for generations and that you continue to pray for us and our meeting in jannahtul firdaus, ameen.

INTRODUCTION

Who Is This Book For?

This book is designed for anyone interested in exploring polygyny as a marital choice, whether you're just curious or deeply committed to this lifestyle. It's particularly aimed at those questioning the modern narrative of monogamy. This book is for you if:

- You are curious or committed to polygyny
- You are questioning modern views on monogamy

If you find yourself in either of these categories, you're in the right place. This book aims to challenge your preconceptions about marriage and its relevance in today's world.

How Not to Use This Book

The Don'ts

Before diving into how to make the most of this book, let's talk about what not to do.

Imagine you've just read a chapter on effective communication in polygynous relationships. Using that to belittle your spouse(s) in an argument is not the purpose of this book.

Words of wisdom:

- Don't weaponize the knowledge you gain
- Respect that everyone's journey is unique

The insights we share in this book are the result of years of experience and growth; they're meant to enlighten, not to be used as ammunition.

How to Use This Book

The Do's

The best way to use this book is as a guide to broaden your understanding of polygyny.

If you're facing a challenge in your polygynous relationship, refer to the relevant section in this book for advice and perspective.

Words of wisdom:

- Use this book as a guide for understanding polygyny
- Keep an open mind; you may agree or disagree, and that's okay

We'll share stories, tactics, and perspectives aimed at providing you with a well-rounded view of the lifestyle's benefits and challenges. All we ask is that you withhold judgment until you've either put our advice into practice or have found healthier, more effective alternatives. Deal?

Your Study Guide to Polygyny

Consider this book to be your comprehensive study guide on polygyny. We've packed it with training, insights, perspectives, and anecdotes that cover the full spectrum—from the highs to the lows.

If you're wondering how to navigate conflicts in a polygynous relationship, you'll find real-life stories that offer both cautionary tales and solutions.

Remember, you'll get the most out of this book when you approach it with the intent to learn, rather than just for casual reading.

We've given you the tools; now it's up to you to use them. A word to the wise is enough. Let's get started.

How to Contact Us

If you have questions, need further clarification, or are interested in media inquiries, we're just a click away.

You can reach us through our website at **outstandingpersonalrelationships. com**/contact or directly via email at **support@outstandingpersonalrelationships.com**

PART 1

Let's Talk Polygamy with Coach Nazir

Chapter 1

MY JOURNEY TO UNDERSTANDING POLYGYNY

The Book That Started It All

IN 1995, I TOOK MY FIRST STEPS INTO MARRIED LIFE AND A NEW RELIGION—the same one Malcolm X embraced 11 months before his untimely death. Eager to learn, I found myself at IQRA Books on Devon Avenue in Chicago. Among the shelves filled with books on history, Arabic, and marriage, one title caught my eye: "Polygamy in Islam."

Imagine being a newlywed and stumbling upon a book that could potentially change your entire perspective on marriage. That was me.

I was with Coach Fatimah at the time, and we were both new to this journey. While I was engrossed in this book, she was elsewhere in the store, curating our future Islamic library. I was so intrigued by the book that I decided it was a must-buy, despite my initial belief that polygamy was a practice of ancient times.

THE LEARNING CURVE – FROM THEORY TO REALITY

After purchasing the book (and discreetly placing it at the bottom of our shopping bag), I devoured its contents in only a couple of hours. However, it was more of an academic read and lacked the practical advice needed for navigating the complexities of polygynous relationships.

Reading about polygamy in religious texts is one thing; living it is another. The book was informative but didn't cover any of the day-to-day challenges.

A Cautionary Tale

Don't Use This Book as Ammunition

A friend once told me about an argument he had with his wife over polygyny. In the heat of the moment, he used my situation to challenge her views, which didn't end well.

Imagine being used as an example in someone else's marital dispute. Not a good look for anyone involved.

This book is not intended as a tool to win arguments, but as a means of knowledge to improve communication and deepen understanding.

Reflection Points

Time for Some Soul-Searching

As you go through this book, you'll find various reflection points designed to provoke thought and introspection.

Reflection Points:

- The way I plan to get the most from this book is to…
- Three things I must remember and practice with this book are…
- My intention with this book is…

We strongly recommend jotting down your answers in a journal, as these questions will appear at the end of each of my chapters.

THE LIGHTER SIDE OF POLYGYNY: A TRIP DOWN MEMORY LANE

Three's Company: My First Brush with Polygamy

"Come and knock on our door, come and knock on our door, we've been waiting for you, we've been waiting for you, where the kisses are hers and hers and his, three's company, too…"

If you recognize these lyrics, you probably remember the TV show "Three's

Company," featuring the comedic genius of John Ritter as Jack Tripper.

Imagine being a young boy, watching a show where one man lives with two women. It's like a light bulb moment, right?

"Three's Company" was my first exposure to the idea of one man living with multiple women.

The show was comedic but sparked real curiosity, or perhaps fantasy.

The show revolved around Jack living with two female roommates—first Chrissy, then Cindi and Terri, along with the ever-present brunette, Janet. To keep the landlord at bay, Jack pretended to be a gay man, a ruse that led to many crazy situations. Of course this isn't polygyny related, but bear with me.

THE CURIOUS CASE OF JACK TRIPPER

Why Not Just Marry Both?

As a young man, I was intrigued by the show. I couldn't help but wonder, why Jack didn't marry both of them. After all, they were already roommates sharing a living space, albeit in separate rooms.

I knew he was a straight guy, always trying to impress women. So, why did he not take the next, logical step?

The show presented a unique living arrangement but stopped short of exploring polygamy. It made me question societal norms around relationships.

MODERN DAY CULTURE AND INFLUENCE – FROM LARRY TO QUAGMIRE

Jack wasn't as ridiculous as Larry when it came to lusting over women; a character who seemed to inspire Quagmire from "Family Guy." But the point is, "Three's Company" was my first exposure to the idea of a man living with multiple women.

Western culture often flirts with unconventional relationship structures but rarely delves deeper, so it's important to distinguish between TV fiction and real-life possibilities.

While "Three's Company" was far from an ideal representation of polygyny, it was my first introduction to the concept of one man living with multiple women whom he liked. Even as a boy, it made me consider the possibilities of this lifestyle.

Clarity Matters: What Is Polygamy?

First things first, let's get the definition straight. Polygamy is when a person is *married* to multiple spouses. The key term here? Marriage. This isn't just about relationships; it's about a binding marital commitment.

TWO SIDES OF THE SAME COIN: POLYGYNY VS. POLYANDRY

Polygamy is a gender-neutral term, and it comes in two flavors:

- **Polygyny:** When a man is married to multiple wives
- **Polyandry:** When a woman is married to multiple husbands

Even though this book is called "Let's Talk Polygamy UNCENSORED," we're zeroing in on polygyny, the most commonly practiced form of polygamy.

Fun Fact: I first learned the term "polygyny" after becoming a Muslim. Before that, like many folks, I thought polygamy was just a man with multiple wives. And for those who mix up the terms, it's pronounced "polygyny," (poll-i-gin-y) not "polygamy" (poll-i-gam-y).

Polyamory: The Odd One Out

Don't mix up polyamory with polygamy. The prefix "poly" means "many," but polyamory involves multiple consensual *relationships*, not *marriages*. So, it's not under the polygamy umbrella, which is our main focus here.

However, for clarity, many depictions purporting to be polygyny show one man and multiple women and they are all either sleeping together, kissing each other intimately, or engaged in sexual encounters. That is not polygyny, and would be best described as polyamory.

The Marriage Factor: Why It's Crucial

Polygamy is rooted in marriage—a public, binding commitment, often celebrated with a wedding ceremony. Without this marital contract, any relationship, regardless of its form, leans more towards polyamory than polygamy, or polyandry.

Real Talk: Shows like Maury Povich and Paternity Court wouldn't be so packed with drama if we all stuck to a more moral approach in relationships. Just saying.

Reflection Points

1. When did you first learn about polygamy?
2. What were your initial thoughts on it?

We are not Anti-Monogamy; We're Pro Morals

Let's get one thing straight from the outset: We're not against monogamy. We're all for morals and ethical choices in relationships.

The TV Shows That Got It Wrong

I grew up in the '90s, a time when TV shows seemed to have a weird take on marriage. Take "The Fresh Prince of Bel-Air," for example. Will Smith, who was everyone's favorite actor pre-Chris Rock slap, once told Uncle Phil and Aunt Viv he wanted to marry Lisa. Their reaction? Panic. "You're too young," they said. "You've got your whole life ahead of you."

The same thing happened on "The Cosby Show." Vanessa wanted to get married, and instead of offering support, her parents, Cliff and Claire Huxtable, shut her down. "You're too young," they insisted. "You haven't lived life."

The Questions That Burned Inside Me

These TV moments left me puzzled. Why were parents so against their kids getting married? Wasn't marriage supposed to be a noble thing? Why not guide them toward it instead of away from it?

My Own Story: A Tale of Mixed Messages

My parents tied the knot at 21, and I was already five years old. Yep, I was born to teenage parents—a Black American dad and a Puerto Rican mom. They had six kids and stayed married for seven years.

When I told my mom I wanted to marry my girlfriend, Coach Fatimah (that's her middle name, by the way), she echoed those TV shows: "You're too young. Date around first." This left me confused, especially considering the values taught at my private Christian school.

The Problem with Extended Adolescence

I believe it's harmful to stretch out adolescence like we do in America. Travel the world, and you'll see 10 to 12-year-olds with more grit and courage than many 18 to 20-year-olds who are glued to video games. My mom's advice disappointed me, but I tried to understand where she was coming from.

The Journey to Finding My Path: The Ups and Downs of Young Love

In my early teens, my high school sweetheart and I did what most young couples do: we broke up, got back together, and navigated the rollercoaster of puberty. We lost touch for a while, especially during a period when I was searching for truth and, admittedly, misbehaving.

The Malcolm X Influence

During this time, I stumbled upon some information about Islam. Sure, I'd seen the movie "Malcolm X" and loved it. I admired the way the women in the movie dressed—they looked so dignified and respectable. But I wasn't interested in Islam. The guy who tried to introduce me to it had a sketchy past and lacked character. When he pitched Islam to me, my response was, "I'm not giving up my women, my weed, or my baby back ribs." Yep, I said it.

A New Chapter: Embracing Islam

Fast forward a bit. After delving deep into the Quran and its scientific insights, I decided to become a Muslim. The Quran introduced me to polygyny as a legitimate marital option, even though I didn't know anyone who practiced it. With my newfound faith and moral code, I knew marriage was the honorable path.

I wanted to be different from the Christians I'd grown up around—those who said one thing in church, but did the opposite in life. I didn't want to be a hypocrite or neglect my faith.

A few months after reuniting with Fatimah, it was clear we needed to get married. So we did, and started our family. I was thrilled, even though some folks still said, "hey, you're too young." I was 19, but I felt like a grown man who'd found his path—a path rooted in truth.

I knew that cultures worldwide valued marriage. It's such a sacred event that entire ceremonies and rituals are built around it. It was time for me to step up and honor that tradition.

The Importance of Morality in Family Structures

Marriage is a universal social contract, valued across cultures. This was especially important to me, coming from a city where nearly four out of five homes lack an active father and marriage rates hover below 30%. When I told friends that my father was present and married to my mother while I was growing up, they were shocked. That was extremely disheartening.

The Ills of a Broken Society

In a society rife with dysfunction, the abnormal can often appear normal. Just look at the statistics which clearly show something's not working. Families are the building blocks of society, and when they crumble, so do communities and nations. This leads to all sorts of societal ills—degradation, degeneracy, and what's termed in Arabic as "fahisha," or filth.

The Consequences of Failed Family Structures

Consider the high rates of infidelity in a society that enforces monogamy. While men cheat slightly more than women, infidelity isn't the leading cause of divorce. Single-parent homes, particularly those led by single mothers, result in a host of problems for their children, from higher rates of incarceration and substance abuse, to increased instances of suicide and molestation.

The Irony of Societal Norms

It's ironic that a society that encourages marriages where procreation isn't possible naturally looks down on polygyny, which can rapidly expand families. With over 100 million people on psychotropic drugs, it's evident that our society has a massive problem stemming from a lack of moral values.

Back in the '80s and '90s, two-parent households were the norm on TV. Representation matters, which is why we not only wrote this book, but strive to form outstanding personal relationships. We're not anti-monogamy; we're pro-morals. Irrespective of practicing monogamous or polygamous relationships, standing firm on those morals is crucial.

Reflection Points:

- Being pro-morals is important to me because…
- I can adjust my moral compass today by…

Chapter 2

WHY POLYGYNY?

IN THIS CHAPTER, I'VE BROKEN DOWN THE TOPIC INTO TWO DISTINCT categories for the sake of simplicity. The question of why men are inclined toward polygyny is a subject of great curiosity for both men and women. While I'm not a biologist, scientist, or any other kind of "ist," I firmly believe that men have a natural inclination toward polygyny.

The Litmus Test

You can gauge this inclination with a straightforward question directed at any heterosexual man. If he's honest, his answer will likely affirm the biological inclination toward polygyny. Here's the question:

"If your wife had no objections to polygyny and fully supported you having a second wife, would you be open to it?"

Notice that financial considerations are not part of this question. In my experience, I've never heard a man outright say "no" to this question. Some might say they are monogamous by choice, but they don't reject the idea outright. Others might joke about not wanting an "extra headache," implying that their current marriage is already challenging.

Two Categories of Inclination

Now, let's delve into the two categories I mentioned earlier:

1. Biological Programming: The first category suggests that men are inherently inclined, or 'pre-programmed,' if you will, toward polygyny. This inclination is not a reflection of their current marital status or relationship

satisfaction. In other words, the desire for polygyny exists independently of whether they are fulfilled in their current marriage.

2. Unrelated to Current Circumstances: This means that a man's interest in polygyny is not necessarily a quest for something missing in his current relationship. It's not about dissatisfaction or unfulfillment that he's trying to remedy by adding another wife to the equation.

In summary, the inclination toward polygyny seems to be a natural part of male biology, rather than a response to current circumstances or relationships. It's a topic worth exploring further, especially for those interested in understanding the dynamics of polygynous relationships.

The Legacy Factor

We've already debunked the myth that a man's desire for another wife must mean something is lacking in his current relationship. We'll delve deeper into that shortly. But let's shift our focus to another driving force behind this inclination: the quest for legacy.

The Drive for Greatness – The Biological Imperative

Many men are not simply content with excelling in their careers; they're also thinking long-term. They're pondering what they'll leave behind for future generations. This drive is often closely tied to their children. For many men, their kids aren't just offspring; they're team members destined to carry on the family name and legacy.

This drive for legacy is intrinsically linked to our biological urge to procreate. It's not just about having children; it's about ensuring those children thrive and continue the family lineage. This is a universal sentiment, deeply ingrained in cultures worldwide.

Historical Perspective

When we talk about legacy, the story of Prophet Jacob (Yaqub), (may peace and blessings be upon him) comes to mind. He had 12 sons through his four wives. Despite the trials and tribulations involving his sons, particularly Joseph (Yusef), his lineage became a great nation. Twelve sons didn't come from just one woman; that would have been an enormous burden on her.

As I ponder this, I think about my own family. I have 10 biological children—four daughters followed by six sons, not 12, although I do only have half the amount of wives Prophet Jacob had it makes me wonder if I married more wives, well, hmmm.! The desire to protect and provide for them is a powerful motivator for me, as it is for many men. It's not just about having multiple wives; it's about building a strong, enduring legacy.

The Challenge Seekers and The Biological Factor

While some men are driven by the desire for legacy, others are motivated by the challenge. These are the men who feel they've got it all together: high emotional intelligence, mental acuity, and strong leadership skills. They're high performers who are up for the challenge of managing multiple relationships. Their strong desire for women isn't a sign of dissatisfaction with their current spouse; rather, it's an expression of their authentic selves. They are, by nature, polygynous men.

The Myth Revisited

There's a persistent myth that if a man desires another wife, something must be wrong with the first one. This notion is not only unfair but also untrue. Sometimes, women may unintentionally encourage their men to act on their inherent inclination toward polygyny. This could be due to various factors, which we'll break down into three categories: physical, mental, and emotional.

The Physical Aspect

Let's dive right in. Men often feel physically unsatisfied, particularly in the sexual department. While I'm not a biologist, it's widely accepted that men generally have a stronger sex drive than women.

Studies back this up, see https://www.benchmarkpsychology.com.au/ its-a-fact-men-have-a-higher-sex-drive-than-women-are-all-relation-ships-doomed/

Biological Cycles: A Contrast

Men and women operate on different biological cycles. Women typically have a 28-day cycle, which aligns with the lunar calendar. This is the same calendar observed during pregnancy and is part of the Islamic Hijri calendar. Men, on the other hand, have a one-day cycle. Yes, you read that right—one day.

The One-Day Cycle

What do I mean by a one-day cycle? Well, men produce sperm continuously. Each ejaculation contains hundreds of millions, if not billions, of sperm cells. This "life fluid" is always ready to fertilize an egg. In contrast, a woman's menstrual cycle is a monthly event. If she doesn't become pregnant, her body prepares for the next opportunity.

Quick to Arouse

Men are often quickly aroused by sensory stimuli—a smell, a touch, a sight, or a sound can trigger arousal. This is another reason why men might be more inclined toward polygyny. They are biologically wired to desire sex more frequently and are ready for it much more quickly than women.

THE DYNAMICS OF DESIRE: EYES, EARS, AND EMOTIONAL FULFILLMENT

The Comedy of Reality

It's often said that men are seduced by what they see, while women are seduced by what they hear. This difference in arousal mechanisms is so universally acknowledged that it's become fodder for comedians. Dave Chappelle, a Muslim comedian, humorously tackled this subject in a sketch on his show. The skit highlighted the disparity between men's and women's sexual desire, a topic that's often joked about but seldom discussed seriously.

Weaponizing Intimacy

In societies that practice forced monogamy, sex can be weaponized. There are debates, influenced by religious texts like the Bible and even within Muslim circles, about whether a husband can sexually coerce his wife. This weaponization of sex impacts men not just physically but emotionally, affecting the connection they seek with their wives.

The Frequency Factor

When it comes to physical fulfillment, many men feel they're not getting enough. I've asked men what they consider to be an ideal frequency for intimacy. The answers vary, but most men in their twenties to early forties say they'd prefer intimacy once a day, health, work, and time permitting. This is in stark contrast to women, whose desires don't seem to match this frequency.

Sexual Transmutation: Channeling Energy is a Man's Superpower

So, what can men do with this pent-up energy? One concept I've come across is "sexual transmutation," discussed in Napoleon Hill's book, "Think and Grow Rich." This idea suggests that men can channel their sexual energy into productive endeavors. Much of what men strive for—be it cars, houses, or other status symbols—is driven by this intense energy and the desire to attract women. Women, in turn, are attracted to men who can provide security and strength.

The Attraction of Security

It's not just about physical or material things; it's about the ability to provide and protect. Men, understanding that this is what women desire, often channel their intense energy into achieving these markers of security and strength to promote attraction, and the cycle continues.

The Physical Equation: Fulfillment, Self-Care, and the Polygynous Impulse

Leveling Up: The Attraction Factor

Some argue that women are naturally prone to hypergamy seeking partners who can offer more. While I won't dive into that debate, I do advise men to "level up" in various areas. This not only makes them more attractive to their current spouse but also to potential additional wives.

The Eye of the Beholder: Physical Changes

Let's be real—men are visual creatures. Studies indicate that a man's marriage satisfaction can drop to around 30% after the birth of the first child. This period also sees a spike in divorces. Now, if a woman "lets herself go," especially as the child grows older, this can contribute to a man's sense of physical unfulfillment.

Beyond the Exterior: Inner Self-Care

It's not just about maintaining an attractive exterior; it's also about internal self-care. Here's where exercises like Kegels come into play. Both men and women can benefit from them, but for women, they're especially useful for reproductive and sexual health. Consistent Kegel exercises can significantly enhance marital intimacy.

The Unspoken Truth: Physical Unfulfillment

Men are often hesitant to voice their physical needs explicitly, especially when it comes to suggesting improvements. However, there are various treatments and exercises becoming increasingly popular for women's self-care. If you're a woman reading this, consider these options to avoid inadvertently contributing to your husband's physical unfulfillment, which could steer him toward his natural inclination for polygyny.

So, to sum it up, one of the leading reasons men lean toward polygyny is physical unfulfillment. It's not the only reason, but it's a significant one. And it's something that can be addressed with mutual understanding, open communication, and a commitment to self-care from both partners.

THE MENTAL EQUATION: EMOTIONAL BEINGS, DIFFERENT WAVELENGTHS, AND THE QUEST FOR CONNECTION

Emotional Beings: It's All About Perception

First off, let's acknowledge that we're all emotional beings. Men may feel mentally or emotionally unfulfilled, and it's not about whether they actually are—it's about how they feel. We can't fully grasp someone else's reality; we can only go by what they express and feel.

The Chemistry Conundrum: When Wavelengths Don't Align

So, what does it mean to be mentally unfulfilled? Essentially, it's a disconnect, a lack of chemistry between a husband and wife. I've coached young men who married early and later realized they weren't compatible with their spouses. They want to honor their marital duties but find that they're not connecting mentally.

The Personal Development Divergence: Growing Apart

This disconnect often occurs when one partner is committed to personal growth while the other isn't. Maybe the husband is diving into books, attending workshops, and expanding his horizons, but his wife isn't on the same journey. When one person grows and the other remains stagnant, they're not just standing still—they're growing apart.

The Wavelength Gap: When Chemistry Fizzles Out

Being on different mental wavelengths can be a significant issue. Maybe the chemistry was there initially but has since fizzled out. Or perhaps it was never there to begin with. Either way, when you can't engage in meaningful discussions or connect on a deeper level, you're essentially growing apart.

The Mental Unfulfillment Factor: A Path to Polygyny?

So, mental unfulfillment is another significant reason men may consider polygyny. It's not just about physical attraction or sexual satisfaction; it's also about mental and emotional compatibility. When any of these factors is missing, it creates a void that some men may seek to fill through additional marital relationships.

THE EMOTIONAL PUZZLE: PEACE, RESPECT, AND THE QUEST FOR FULFILLMENT

The Emotional Quagmire: When Giving Up Seems Easier

The third dimension of unfulfillment is emotional, and it's a complex one. Often, a husband feels emotionally unfulfilled because he's on the brink of giving up on resolving marital issues. Now, you might think, "Why not just divorce?" But life isn't that black and white, especially when kids are involved.

The Peace Paradox: A Sanctuary Amidst Chaos

Men highly value peace. In a world filled with friction, challenges, and thankless tasks, a man wants his home to be a sanctuary. If he's dealing with turmoil outside, he wants to come home to a peaceful environment. That means a supportive spouse who listens, cares, and appreciates his efforts.

The Support Gap: Where Men Can Turn

Support circles for men are few and far between. Sure, there's the manosphere and the Red Pill movement, but these often have their own agendas and can be reactionary spaces. What men really need is genuine support and peace, not just another battleground.

The Language of Love: Speaking the Same Emotional Tongue

Gary Chapman's book, "The Five Love Languages," is an excellent resource for understanding how to communicate love and appreciation effectively. When there's a lack of peace—marked by constant bickering, defensiveness, or competition—it erodes the emotional foundation of a relationship.

The Respect Factor: The Core Value That Trumps All

Above all, men value respect. It's often their top priority, and my core value assessments confirm this across the board. Whether it's shown through physical gestures, like having his favorite drink ready, or emotional ones, like listening without judgment, respect is the cornerstone of emotional fulfillment for men.

So, emotional unfulfillment is yet another reason men may consider polygyny. It's not just about filling a void; it's about finding a space where they are respected, appreciated, and at peace.

Reflection Points:

- Two things I learned from this chapter were...
- The one thing I should keep in mind regarding polygyny is...
- I commit to learn more about polygyny by...

Chapter 3

MY JOURNEY TO MONOGAMY
WITH COACH FATIMAH

I WAS NERVOUS BECAUSE IT WAS THE FIRST DAY OF SCHOOL AND I WAS A freshman. Only about 3 or 4 of my friends from my 8th grade graduation class would be joining me and I didn't know if we would have the same homeroom or classes.

I started playing football a few weeks earlier so I knew the bus route and made my way in my new 'first day of school' clothes and shoes. I was looking good.

It was a predominately white private Lutheran Christian high school and I prefer black girls so I knew I wouldn't have many options when it came to finding a girlfriend. I was an introvert after all, and kept to myself unless I was with close acquaintances. My self-confidence was non-existent.

On that August morning as I walked toward the entry doors, I was feeling nervous and wondered about the new adventure upon which I was about to embark. School and city buses lined up on the street right in front of the main entrance and I saw cars letting students out as I continued walking among a wave of my peers.

As I got closer to the entrance, I saw a black Ford Probe stop at the curb and its passenger door was open. Out stepped this gorgeous girl. Her caramel complexion made me forget all of the people who were around me and I almost forgot where I was headed. I was thinking she must be dropping someone off because she put the seat forward to let someone out to go to school. Not until I noticed she was grabbing her backpack off the back seat did I realize that she was the student!

I wasn't into fashion that much other than the typical brands. I liked solid colors and wore the trending fashions like Nike, Guess, Nautica, Girbaud, Kross Kolors, and Karl Kani.

I can still remember that she was wearing some type of reddish-maroon shorts suit that had 6 or 8 gold buttons on the front of the top, and she had on black stockings and black shoes with a buckle on them. Her hair was flowing in long curls with some gold matching beret thingy, and she was the most beautiful thing I had ever seen..

After school I had practice and realized that we didn't share any classes together, so I figured she wasn't a freshman. I asked around about her and it just so happened that the only black girl in my homeroom said that they were friends and went to the same Christian grade school. My hopes had been revived.

Revived until I was at football practice after school and saw her walking with another football player who was very cocky and chased every girl he could. My heart dropped.

I hadn't spoken to her yet, and had no idea if she'd even noticed me or knew who I was. I was hopeful that her friend may have mentioned me to her so I could get a vibe.

Back then there were no cell phones. Unlike today where it takes nothing to slide in a DM, you needed more courage to walk up to and address anyone of the opposite sex.

I learned she was a freshman and she wasn't interested in the cocky football player or another guy that was trying to get her attention. I didn't know if she had any interest in me, but I was going to muster up enough courage to see what was up with her for myself.

I decided I would approach her after class before lunch, and even though we had two lunch hours, she wasn't in mine. So, the slowest class ever was winding down to the bell and I knew her route by then, so I waited by the stairs until I saw her...

I introduced myself and asked if I could have her number. As I stood there she was holding her books to go to class, and she said something along the lines of, "I have to get to class right now!"

All I heard in my mind was, "What did you say? Who? You? Hell, NO!" And this is why it took courage to walk up and approach someone you were interested in during my high school years. I was crushed but held all my emotions together in front of her. I went to class and decided that she must not be the one for me.

I know you're wondering what happened because we eventually got married, and I'm glad you asked! I like to think that she had time to think about what happened and she saw the error of her ways. I say that because, at the final bell of the day, as I headed to the locker room for football practice, I saw her and she got my attention with a come-hitherto motion, so I complied.

She put a piece of paper in my hand that contained some of the most beautiful handwriting I had ever seen, or maybe it was that it contained what I felt were the keys to the vault. She had written her name, phone number, and address on it, and I was on a natural high. I still joke and tell my children that she quickly corrected herself and, later that day, returned to me with her phone number, address, social security number, birthdate, blood type, and all of her information so that I knew she was interested!

I couldn't focus during football practice and didn't know how to cope given I was all of 14 years old with no real experience with women.

That was during the second week of September, my freshman year of high school a few decades ago. She became my girlfriend and I told my father she was going to be my future wife. To his credit, he never dissuaded me.

I remember some parent-teacher conference or an evening event for freshmen that we had to attend. I was there with my father and she was with her mean old grandmother. My father saw my girlfriend for the first time and told her grandmother that I had told him I was going to marry her, and she responded to my father by saying, "over my dead body!" My father looked at her as only a cool, green-eyed, fawned after grown man could and said, "well, that's what he said" before walking away. He was confident in his son, even if his son wasn't confident in himself. Five years later, we were married.

It wasn't a straight line to marriage, as we were both teenagers. We were together for a large chunk of the time, however, we also had break-ups and went on with our lives without each other. Even when we weren't together, I held a place for her in my heart, so when I heard she was looking for me and wanted to communicate, I was happy and responded almost immediately.

I was beginning to study Islam after an extensive search of religion and spirituality, and Islam was the one thing I wasn't interested in studying, but I held myself to a high standard of objectivity.

Fast forward a bit, and I introduced her to Islam while I was still seeking and considering myself a Muslim, although I didn't have a regular practice or much of an understanding other than the basics. I was still studying and dabbling in the streets when she ended up accepting Islam officially before I did.

We were both dealing with the consequences of our life's choices and struggling to choose a righteous path. After learning that legitimate relationships between men and women in Islam are only through the honorable institution of marriage, I knew that I had to make some decisions.

After evaluating my life and recognizing that she was the only woman I truly loved for the most part, I felt that I should do the righteous thing and propose so we could marry. I was 19 years old and saw from the marriages of my father, uncles, and grandfathers that I didn't want what they had in marriage, so I planned to follow Islam to have something better.

That's how we met and married in a snapshot. I had no idea of polygyny nor did I know anyone who practiced it. I simply wanted to be righteous by staying away from fornication.

She didn't marry me for money because I had none. I did work as a school bus driver for Lakeside, appliance mover for Sears, grinder, and even as a CNC machine operator.

We had four beautiful baby girls first and I was a happy "Girl Dad." Then, after 10 years of marriage, we had our first son followed by our second son about 16 months later.

I worked several different jobs, grew a successful home-based business, but, most importantly, discovered the world of personal development. I began to learn timeless business principles on leadership, teamwork, sales, marketing, active listening, and how to grow professionally.

I practiced monogamy for almost 15 years with my incredible wife, who you know as Coach Fatimah.

Did Coach Fatimah and I ever discuss polygyny? Yes, we did. I can remember three or four occasions where the topic came up. However, we didn't directly have an open and honest conversation about it.

The first time it was mentioned, I was a brand-new Muslim and we both knew an older sister who was not married and looking. We both considered her righteous, and she even taught us some basics and led us in the right direction, when we were not part of a community that followed the last and final Messenger and Prophet, Muhammad ibn Abdullah ibn Abdul-Mutallib.

We were freshly married, perhaps not even one year, and I said to my newlywed wife that if I had the money I'd consider marrying her. That was not the right thing to say or even think out loud. I received a death stare and heat that entire day and was careful about the topic ever since that time.

The second time I recall mentioning polygyny was in some music I wrote. I noted how, under an Islamic government, I would love to have four righteous wives and provide for them with justice. Needless to say, that wasn't her favorite song on the album, nor do I ever recall her singing that lyric when she listened to it.

The third time the topic was addressed was when she had seen it in one of my business journals. I was studying how to make money and learning the importance of goal setting and writing down dreams as the first step to manifesting them while taking continual action.

I wrote that one of my goals was to have four beautiful and righteous wives. The story of how she saw that is still unclear. I think I left my journal on her dresser by mistake when I took a phone call. She probably saw it open and read what was there because she supported me in attaining my goals. Needless to say, she didn't support that goal at all! I ended up scratching that one out and don't remember if dinner was a hot meal or a sandwich that night.

I bought a book by Bilal Phillips and Jameelah Jones and on the original cover, there was an outlined silhouette of four women and one man. She didn't say much about it, as I was focused on learning as much as I could about our new way of life, but she simply rolled her eyes as she saw it among a stack of books I purchased from a bookstore on Devon Avenue in Chicago.

That being said, after almost 15 years in a successful and happy marriage and raising six incredible children, I chose to marry again.

I asked a brother for his advice about polygyny. I shared with him that he inspired me to look more into polygyny when I saw his situation and the number of children he had. I told him that there was no deficiency in my wife but I liked the idea that I could expand my family and practice a little practiced sunnah.

He told me then that I should tell my wife that being married to her was so good that I wanted to do it again by practicing polygyny. That advice may sound funny, but it was better than what I opted to do. More on that later.

Chapter 4

My Polygyny Journey Begins
With Coach Nyla

Monogamy provides you with what you need as a man. Despite its shortcomings, it provides companionship, intimacy, an honorable relationship, and many more blessings. On the outside looking in, it would appear that I had everything except variety.

Coach Fatimah and I had known Coach Nyla before her name was even Nyla because we were in a network marketing business together and sometimes those can be like family reunions, depending on the culture of the organization.

She wasn't directly part of my business organization, however, she was part of the larger team and we would cross paths regularly because, as I climbed the ranks in leadership, I was given more responsibility and was responsible for training 1,000s of entrepreneurs in the Wisconsin and Illinois markets, and the Midwest in general.

Other than a woman who was a single mother to a son who was doing business as part of a larger organization, we had no relationship other than a Midwest leader who was responsible for training the company's associates.

My wife, Coach Fatimah, told me that lots of women were crushing on me. I brushed it off but she informed me that some of these women saw me on large stages like MGM Grand in Las Vegas, and weekly in front of the room on stages wearing nice Super 150 Italian suits. They saw me demonstrating good leadership, and not looking too bad, so I should be aware.

She was right, and I later learned in private leadership meetings that, once you reach a certain level of success, there are groupies who treat you like celebrities or athletes, and are willing to risk it all.

Unfortunately, I had far too many women approach me on that level, but I never took the bait. Coach Nyla was growing her business and investing in personal development. She asked me for information about Islam and started her own spiritual quest. I later came to learn she went to numerous religious organizations seeking to understand why they believed what they believed.

I had no interest, or at least knew that I couldn't afford polygyny at the time, and carried on with my life. She eventually accepted Islam. Soon after this, she married a Muslim man and they had a baby girl. She wasn't actively involved in her business anymore so I didn't see her or any of her teammates.

A few years later I learned that her marriage hadn't worked out and she had returned to running her home-based business once more.

It was at this time that polygyny entered my mind. I recalled the book I had read about it because I saw an ambitious woman with two young children whose fathers were not much involved in their lives. She was someone who could possibly be supportive about what I was trying to build.

It was a fleeting thought because I wasn't where I wanted to be financially, and I had never known anyone who practiced polygyny. This was unlike other areas of the US, specifically the East Coast, where people openly practice polygyny all the time.

There were a few business events in the Milwaukee area and she was rising through the ranks and conducting small presentations that were doing well. Apparently she was open to polygyny and had even discussed it with an associate on my team after her divorce. It was brought to my attention because the associate wasn't Muslim but was intrigued with the subject of polygyny in general, as most men tend to be.

I informed him about the little I read about it and how it works and he suggested I marry Nyla. I laughed it off and he said he was serious because she had mentioned being open to it. I didn't pay it any mind, again because I felt that I needed to have a "bookoo," (plenty of) money and my business wasn't where it needed to be at that point.

Fast forward a bit and I received a phone call from a Muslim brother representing a national Islamic organization. He asked my name and we discussed a sister being interested in marriage with me. He didn't note who it was, but asked if I was open to marriage. Intrigued by the nature of the call, I said yes.

Technically speaking, a Muslim man may be married but available if he has fewer than four wives.

We continued speaking and I was surprised and honored to receive such a phone call. Immediately, I began to search online to find out more about how something like this could work, but there were limited resources. The little information I found was from overly sexualized people who were using polygyny as a guise for threesomes.

I appreciated the conversation with the brother but couldn't really commit to much because my money game wasn't right, I didn't know how my current wife would respond, and I didn't know how the dynamic would work. Before that first call ended, he informed me he was asking and investigating on behalf of Coach Nyla.

Needless to say, things felt a bit awkward as I conducted trainings and led business presentations while she was in the audience or had guests that I would greet and welcome to the company. I remembered Coach Fatimah's words about women crushing on me and wondered if she had been trying to tell me that Coach Nyla liked me. Too late now, but I did wonder at the time.

After some time had passed, I received counsel from a brother who had two wives and, at one time, was married to three, I decided that with some concessions, I would go ahead and marry Coach Nyla and practice polygyny.

I spoke to her representative and we arranged a time to meet in person to perform the marriage ceremony. I didn't feel the need to have a courting period because my family and I had already known her for several years.

I was only 19 years old when I first married and didn't know much about Islam. But, there I was at the age of 34 with one wife and six children, only moments away from having two wives and two bonus children. To say I was nervous is an understatement.

On that cold wintery day, we met at a neutral masjid, one which neither of us had attended prior to that day. I focused on being present, knowing that when I left the masjid, I would be married to two beautiful women and I'd be the only person I knew with more than one wife. My soon-to-be wife was excited, and I was thrilled.

I knew the load would be heavy and I prayed to be able to handle it all. The smiles from the imam, wakeel, brothers, and sisters and the love from everyone was uplifting.

Coach Fatimah had already noted how beautiful Coach Nyla was at an event we attended in Las Vegas, when she pointed out that she thought Nyla liked me and I heard a hint of jealousy in her voice. I didn't pay it much mind because she said that so many women were swooning over me. It was a common sentiment and I knew, like any man, that no woman could kidnap you or make you like her.

As Coach Fatimah had known me since I was 14 years old, she knew what I liked in women and she also knew that Coach Nyla possessed some of these preferences along with others.

When we speak of best practices, we aren't speaking from theory, we're speaking from experience.

What you read above was how I chose to marry Coach Nyla. Although the way I did it wasn't wrong, it did violate several unwritten agreements that Coach Fatimah and I had. My rationale for not telling her prior to marriage was that I knew she'd be upset based on previous experiences on the topic. I decided I'd rather deal with her being upset once after the marriage than beforehand as things could have been sabotaged or super stressful. Not. A. Good. Move.

Admittedly, this was not strong leadership; this was a conflict avoidance maneuver, and a way for me to exert my will without thinking things through. I could blame it on the lack of resources, but, in reality, I simply didn't want to feel the heat at that moment and opted for telling her later. Again, this was not a good move on my part.

However, this is how my polygynous journey began and everyone's is different. Some marriages fail and some marriages succeed. The factors that determine those that succeed tend to be the acceptance and focus on personal growth in several areas of life. These areas are discussed in this book and, prayerfully, you'll be able to use our journey as a guide.

Thankfully, we managed to focus on personal growth and, at the time of writing this book, my family has grown from 6 children in monogamy to 10 biological children in polygyny. Coach Fatimah birthed 7 of my children, and Coach Nyla birthed 3 of my children, two of whom I delivered with no assistance and one with a midwife at home. Also, under the umbrella of my family are two bonus children, a son and a daughter from Coach Nyla's previous marriage and previous relationship.

Chapter 5

DEBUNKING MYTHS: A CLOSER LOOK AT POLYGYNY

Myth 1: Polygamy is Lust-Based

The first myth that often circulates is that polygamy, polygyny in particular, is solely based on sexual lust. This is a simplistic and unfair characterization. In any healthy marriage, there should be a level of lust or strong sexual desire; it's a natural part of human intimacy. Men should lust after their wives, and wives should lust after their husbands. This is the person you've committed to, after all.

In a society that offers countless avenues for lust without responsibility—like prostitution, escorts, sugar babies, and easy access to pornography—polygyny stands apart as a form of marriage that honors women and elevates them to the status of "wife." To label this as merely "lust-based" is to downplay the complexity of human relationships and is, frankly, immature.

Lust-based relationships often involve pornography, prostitution, cheating and, in sick cases, even rape. These are all manifestations of sexual and power lust, not the principles that guide a responsible polygynous relationship.

Myth 2: Husbands Don't Care About Their Initial Wives in Polygynous Relationships

The second myth is that husbands who want to practice polygyny don't care about their initial wives. This couldn't be further from the truth. As you'll discover throughout this book, most husbands care deeply about their wives. Men and women may express emotions differently, but that doesn't mean men are less emotional or uncaring.

Men and women are emotionally and biologically different, but we also differ in terms of abilities and desires. We complement each other; we're not in competition. Husbands care about what their wives think and feel, and they make adjustments based on that.

In fact, my wives and I encourage men interested in polygyny to "level up" and become more than twice the man they currently are. This is not just about being able to handle the complexities and responsibilities that come with polygyny, but also about becoming a stronger, more respectable man in general.

The reality is that women often benefit more in various ways, from emotional support to shared responsibilities.

One way to gauge how much men care is by examining why they might lie about their interest in polygyny. Often, men lie not because they're deceitful but because they want to protect their partner's feelings.

They've already assessed whether their current wife can handle the idea of polygyny and may choose to keep their desires hidden to avoid drama. If you're a wife who's open to the idea and you ask your husband if he'd consider another wife, chances are he'll say yes—if all other factors such as finances and relationship health are stable.

Myth 3: Only Men Benefit from Polygyny

This is a significant misconception. The idea that only men benefit from polygynous relationships is far from the truth. In reality, women often benefit more. In a society that offers countless ways for men to fulfill their lusts outside of marriage, polygyny provides a moral and honorable alternative. Women in polygynous marriages gain a provider, security, and a stable family structure. They also have a committed partner with whom they can fulfill their own sexual desires, without the stigma attached to being a 'side chick' or mistress.

To put it into perspective, consider the time spent on sexual activities. Even if a man spends 2.5 hours a day (about 10% of the day) on sexual activities with his multiple wives, that leaves the majority of his time available for responsibilities, such as providing for and protecting his family. These are the things that women value most.

So, in the grand scheme of things, women stand to gain a lot from polygynous relationships—often more than men do.

Myth 4: All Parties Engage in Group Sex

This myth suggests that polygynous relationships involve group sexual activities like threesomes or orgies. This is not the case. In polygyny, the husband has separate, individual sexual relationships with each of his wives. The intimacy is between the husband and one wife at a time.

To be fair, it is possible that people who are married monogamously or polygynously participate in these types of things, however, these behaviors aren't defined by their marriage type. So a monogamous couple may choose to be swingers but that doesn't mean that their marriage isn't a monogamous one, or that swingers consider themselves monogamous.

Myth 5: The Wife Must Have Fallen Short

Another misconception is that a man seeks additional wives because his current wife has failed in her duties. This is not necessarily true. Even if a wife is supportive and the husband has the means to support another wife, he may still be interested in polygyny. Men may hesitate to express this due to fear of backlash or misunderstanding, but the desire for multiple wives doesn't automatically mean the current wife has fallen short.

In some cases, wives may face challenges like infertility or mental health issues, but the husband still wants to fulfill his duties to her. Polygyny allows him to do so while also seeking what he needs from additional relationships.

The Reality of Forced Monogamy

We live in a society that enforces monogamy while turning a blind eye to irresponsible behavior. Take celebrities like Nick Cannon, who has multiple children with different women but isn't married to any of them. Or consider high-profile cases of infidelity, like Arnold Schwarzenegger and

Maria Shriver, or Jay-Z and Beyoncé. These men have all the resources to be responsible, yet they step out of their monogamous relationships.

Polygyny, on the other hand, holds men accountable for their actions and desires. It allows them to be responsible providers for multiple wives, if they choose, without the societal judgment that often accompanies non-monogamous arrangements.

In reality, polygyny is not about shortcomings or irresponsible behavior. It's a relationship structure that can be fulfilling for all parties involved when approached responsibly and respectfully.

Myth 6: You're Sexually Unclean

This myth suggests that polygynous relationships are somehow unclean or prone to sexually transmitted diseases. In reality, people in polygynous relationships are often more open and honest about their sexual health than those in monogamous relationships who cheat.

The idea that polygyny leads to bacterial vaginitis (BV) is misleading. BV is not an STD and is common among monogamous women as well. Trying to pin this on polygynous relationships is disingenuous. The notion of being "sexually unclean" is a misconception often associated with savagery or street behavior, not with the sanctity of a marital relationship.

Myth 7: It's a Broke Men's Playground

Some people call polygyny "Poorligamy," suggesting that it's a way for financially unstable men to exploit women. This is a distortion. In a genuine polygynous relationship, the man is a provider and protector. Men who can't fulfill these roles are not practicing polygyny; they're playing games.

Whether you're cheated on by a billionaire or someone making much less, the emotional toll tends to be the same, although the consequences may be different for the one cheating. Many single mothers are already "sharing" men, knowingly or not. And I won't get into the ones who are willfully ignorant of their situations.

A polygynous family structure requires both leadership and financial stability. It's not a playground for men who are not willing to take on these responsibilities.

Myth 8: It's a Cheater's Safe Haven

The idea that polygyny is legalized cheating is another misconception. Cheating involves deceit and betrayal, whereas polygyny is based on mutual consent and responsibility. In a polygynous marriage, the man is committed to each of his wives and any children they may have. This is a far cry from the irresponsibility associated with cheating.

In today's society, cheating has unfortunately become normalized. But polygyny offers a different path, one that requires men to be accountable for their actions. It's a relationship structure that, when approached with respect and responsibility, can be fulfilling for everyone involved.

Polygyny is not about exploiting women, avoiding responsibility, or engaging in risky behavior. It's about forming meaningful, committed relationships based on mutual respect and shared values. Far from being a form of "legalized cheating," polygyny involves a high level of commitment and responsibility.

Myth 9: Women Have Half a Husband If He Gets Married Again

The idea that a wife only gets a fraction of her husband's time if he takes another wife is a myth. In reality, no one has 100% of their spouse's time even in a monogamous relationship due to work, hobbies, and other commitments.

In a polygynous relationship, I am 100% a husband to each of my wives, even if I can't physically be with them every waking moment. The key is not the quantity of time but the quality and the fullness of responsibility I bring to each relationship.

If there are emergencies, appointments, or times I need to do something with the other wife, I do it. There is no leash around my neck for someone to yank. The quality of time and relationship with the husband is more important than the quantity. Current stats indicate that in monogamous relationships, couples spend less than two and a half hours per day together.

Myth 10: Polygyny Must Be Practiced for Altruistic Reasons

Some people believe that a man should only practice polygyny under specific conditions, such as if there are many widows, divorcees, barren women, or single mothers. This view limits polygyny to a form of charity and is usually advocated by someone with low self-esteem. Generally the woman saying it needs to feel superior because something is wrong with her, but it's her way of saying he "married me for me."

While altruistic reasons are noble, they're not the only valid reasons for a polygynous marriage. A man can marry for love, desire, or any other reason, as long as he does so honorably and can fulfill his responsibilities to all his wives.

Myth 11: The Children Will Be Harmed

Another common myth is that children in polygynous families suffer due to limited access to their father. In reality, the quality of parenting is not determined by the family structure but by the intentionality and effort put into it.

In many polygynous families, there's a higher level of intentionality in parenting. For example, in my family, my children are well-cultured, travel extensively, and some are even budding entrepreneurs.

The notion that children are harmed in polygynous families is not supported by evidence. Children can become more well-rounded individuals when raised by intentional parents in a polygynous family.

Myth 12: Women Do Not Want Polygyny

The idea that all women are against polygyny is another myth. Women are not a monolith; their preferences vary. In my own experience, three of my five daughters have expressed a preference for a polygynous marriage for themselves, I'm guessing this is because they see the benefits it can bring to our family while also allowing for a level of autonomy.

So, the myths surrounding polygyny are numerous and often based on misunderstandings, ignorance, or societal biases. It's crucial to look beyond these myths to understand the complexities and potential benefits of this form of marriage.

Myth 13: It's for Bisexual Women

Polygyny is often misunderstood as being for bisexual women, but that's not the case. Polygyny involves a man married to multiple women and is family-based. It's not about sexual orientation; it's about family structure and growth.

Unfortunately, the many images proclaiming polygyny online tend to be sexual and show bi-sexual women with one guy. We get it. Threesomes and multi-partner sex is the number one fantasy for people, but that's not polygyny.

Myth 14: Men Lack Self-Control

Contrary to the myth, men who practice polygyny responsibly demonstrate a high level of self-control and discipline. They're not looking for flings; they're committed to building a family and taking on the responsibilities that come with it.

Generally speaking, those who want to win in polygyny and work to make themselves more attractive focus on their leadership, mental, and emotional intelligence which by itself demonstrates self-discipline and control. Lacking self-control points to addictions such as pornography, alcohol, drugs, and other vices. Practicing polygyny responsibly requires a higher level of self-control and discipline.

Myth 15: It's for Men to Collect Harems

The term "harem" is often misused in this context. In reality, harems were spaces where women in Muslim societies were protected from prying eyes. Since westerners weren't allowed to see the women of the royal families, they used their imaginations to paint a picture of what a harem is. Polygyny is not about collecting women for a "sex pool"; it's about building a family.

Myth 16: Women Must Have Low Self-Esteem

The idea that women in polygynous relationships have low self-esteem is unfounded. For example, Samia Suluhu Hassan, at the time of writing, is the current president of Tanzania, and she is the third wife to her husband. Clearly, being in a polygynous relationship doesn't equate to low self-esteem for her nor many other successful women.

To be fair, there are millions of women who are being medicated and suffer from low self-esteem regarding body issues in America. Low self-esteem is not dictated by the type of marriage in which a woman is involved. However, we notice that women who focus on their personal growth, in polygyny and otherwise, tend to be more confident and secure in themselves than those who choose not to grow.

Myth 17: Any Incoming Wife Must Serve the First Wife

This myth suggests a hierarchy among wives, which is not the case. Some cultures and traditions put the power in the hands of wives to choose a new wife and make her into a servant and some even feel that a new wife must be used as a utility for the wife or wives who were already present.

This is simply oppression as each wife is her own being and has her own individuality. Islam considers all wives as equals from day 1. Each wife has her own relationship with her husband and is not subordinate to any other wife.

Myth 18: Polygyny is Simply Pimping

Equating polygyny with pimping is misleading and outright disrespectful. Pimping is unlawful and degrading, while polygyny is a form of marriage. Each of these myths stem from misunderstandings or societal biases. It's crucial to separate fact from fiction to truly understand what polygyny is and what it isn't.

Far from being akin to pimping, a man in a polygynous relationship is more like a king who takes on significant responsibilities.

Myth 19: They Must Live Together

The living arrangements in a polygynous family are flexible and can vary based on the family's preferences. While some may choose to live together, others may opt for separate homes. The key is to find what works best for your family structure. In Islam, the women have a right to their own private and personal space which usually means separate homes.

I personally believe that this option is best because each wife has her own personality, decorating style, and deserves her privacy. It's beneficial to be in one home in some situations, such as when people are older or for health reasons, but it's up to you to figure out what works best for your family and you must be honest, no matter how difficult.

Myth 20: The Wife Must Be Old

The age of the wife is not a determining factor for entering a polygynous relationship. Some people may assume that a man would only seek additional wives if his current wife were older or unable to have children, but that's not necessarily the case. Polygyny can be practiced for various reasons, not just as a solution to an age "problem."

Myth 21: The Man Must Be Rich

While financial stability is important, a man should also be rich in emotional intelligence, leadership skills, and other areas to successfully practice polygyny.

So this point has truthful elements, but not necessarily in the way that it's interpreted in the traditional sense. He definitely should not be poor when embarking on this journey. He should get his weight up with proper preparation, then make moves with confidence that provide security for the people for whom he is responsible.

Final Thoughts

Polygyny is a complex and often misunderstood practice. It's essential to debunk these myths to gain a clearer understanding of what polygyny truly entails. The practice can be fulfilling and enriching when done responsibly and thoughtfully. It's not about fitting into a specific mold but about finding what works best for you and your family.

Chapter 6

FORCED MONOGAMY

ON A CRISP AUTUMN AFTERNOON, MY DAD CALLED OUT, "GRAB YOUR COAT, we're heading out!" I was five and thrilled to ride shotgun in his blue T-Top TransAm, a muscle car adorned with a majestic thunderbird on the hood. To me, that car was the epitome of cool.

My dad loved showing off his firstborn. High-fives were our thing, and every ride felt like a soaring adventure. But that particular afternoon took a different turn. My dad picked up a woman—a stranger to me and definitely not my mom. I watched their smiles and laughter from the back seat, my young mind resolute: "I'm telling Mama."

We eventually got home, and I bolted up the back stairs, bursting into the kitchen where my mom was by the sink. "Mama, Daddy had a woman in the car!" I blurted out before my dad could even close the door. I shrugged off my coat, making a dramatic exit, feeling my dad's eyes drilling into the back of my head.

Yes, I snitched. Even at five, I knew that woman had no business being in the car with my dad. Now, let me paint you a picture of my father at 21: a picked-out Afro, hazel eyes that shifted to green, and an air of confidence that made him irresistibly cool. He was a man of his era, rocking bell-bottom jeans and a Black Power fist. Women were naturally drawn to him, and he reveled in the attention.

His TransAm only added to his allure. In an age when muscle cars graced TV shows like "Starsky and Hutch" and "Knight Rider," my dad was a neighborhood celebrity. But let's be clear: being cool doesn't give you a free pass to cheat. I'm just laying out the context, so you get the full picture.

We exist in a culture that predominantly champions monogamy as the sole marital option, effectively creating a monopoly on the institution of marriage itself. While there are emerging movements like Ethical Non-Monogamy (ENM) that aim to broaden our understanding of relationships, they often don't extend into the realm of matrimony. In this discussion, we're zeroing in on monogamy and its alternative—specifically, polygyny.

Some might argue that calling monogamy "forced" is an overstatement. However, when the narrative omits polygyny as a viable choice, it's hard to deny that monogamy holds an unchallenged monopoly on how we define and engage in marital relationships.

The Paradox of Monogamy: A Star-Studded Exploration

When it comes to the topic of polygyny, the irony is both palpable and paradoxical. While society often frowns upon the practice, it simultaneously turns a blind eye to infidelity among its most celebrated figures across various sectors like politics, religion, entertainment, sports, and social media.

Interestingly, many of these iconic individuals seemingly have the financial means to support multiple wives. Yet, they opt for a different path, perhaps because they were only aware of monogamy, or found it more socially acceptable to practice monogamy while cheating, rather than taking on the responsibility of having multiple wives in a committed relationship.

The Political Arena

- President Bill Clinton: His affair almost led to impeachment
- John F. Kennedy Jr.: Known for his charisma, but not for fidelity
- Donald Trump: Multiple marriages and allegations
- John Edwards: A promising career overshadowed by a scandal
- Rudy Giuliani: His personal life has made headlines

- Elliot Spitzer: Resigned due to a scandal
- Anthony Wiener: A political career undone by indiscretions

The Pulpit and Beyond

- Pastor John Gray: A man of God, yet not without sin
- Pastor Carl Lentz: Led a megachurch but faced moral downfall
- Pastor Jimmy Swaggart: A televangelist caught in the act
- Reverend Jesse Jackson: A civil rights leader with a complicated personal life
- Tariq Ramadan: A scholar embroiled in controversy
- Elijah Muhammad: A leader with a complex legacy
- Dr. Martin Luther King Jr.: A hero with human flaws

Hollywood and the Music Industry

- Denzel Washington: A beloved actor with rumors swirling
- Jay-Z: His infidelity became a cultural talking point
- Kevin Hart: A comedian who laughed off his own scandal
- Arnold Schwarzenegger: His affair was a blockbuster of its own
- Adam Levine, Ashton Kutcher, John Legend: Heartthrobs with questionable hearts
- Ben Affleck: On the list for good reason
- Jude Law, Offset, Brad Pitt: Leading men leading double lives
- Bill Cosby: A fallen icon

The Athletic Elite

- Lamar Odom: A basketball star with off-court troubles
- Allen Iverson: A legend known for more than just his game
- Tiger Woods: His fall from grace was a hole-in-one for tabloids
- Steve McNair: A tragic end to a storied career
- Magic Johnson, Michael Jordan, Kobe Bryant: MVPs in the game, but not in marriage

Social Media's Double Standards

- Derrick Jaxn: A relationship guru who couldn't follow his own advice
- Kevin Samuels (Late): Advocated for fidelity but not for polygyny

The irony is as glaring as it is pervasive. Across various sectors—politics, entertainment, sports, and even social media—men of considerable means and influence often opt for infidelity over embracing polygyny. These men, many of whom boast eight or nine-figure incomes, could financially support multiple wives. So why don't they? Is it to maintain the status quo? Or is it because society has conditioned us to view polygyny with skepticism, while turning a blind eye to the children born from these extramarital affairs—children often left without the protection or presence of their fathers?

Let's be clear: I'm not labeling these children as "bastards," but it's noteworthy that society has coined a term for kids born from what are considered illegitimate relationships. These women and children are often seen as expendable, a byproduct of a culture that enforces monogamy at the expense of family stability.

Polygyny, on the other hand, demands responsibility. It calls for men to step up, to provide and protect, to be accountable to their wives and children. It's not a refuge for the weak or immoral; in fact, those who oppose polygyny are often the loudest critics.

Polygyny is for men of substance—those who invest in their leadership skills, emotional intelligence, and financial acumen. These are the men who attract quality partners, and thus have a broader selection of potential wives.

The irony deepens when you consider figures like Derrick Jackson, who publicly denounced polygyny while engaging in multiple affairs. Yet, he still commands a following for his relationship advice. This is more than a mere paradox; it's a societal blind spot.

In the U.S., even if every eligible man married every eligible woman, millions of women would still be left without viable marital options. This doesn't account for men who aren't interested in women, are incarcerated, or are otherwise unavailable.

The implications are far-reaching. From the "Me Too" movement to the economic toll of broken families on various systems, the lack of a viable alternative to monogamy has consequences. Polygyny, if considered a moral and viable option, could elevate the caliber of men in society—men who are not just father figures but committed husbands and fathers.

So, what does this say about a society that limits its understanding of marriage, thereby affecting its women and children? It's a question worth pondering as we consider the broader impact on various societal systems, from the prison-industrial complex to public education and mental health services.

Reflection Points:

- The most important thing to remember about monogamy is...
- My thoughts on forcing any form of marriage are...

Chapter 7

UNDERSTANDING POLYGYNY
THROUGH A VISUAL LENS

VISUAL AIDS CAN SIMPLIFY COMPLEX RELATIONSHIP DYNAMICS. IMAGINE each person as a unique sphere, capturing their individual likes, dislikes, and emotions.

MONOGAMY VS. POLYGYNY: A DIAGRAMMATIC VIEW

In a monogamous setup, two spheres represent the husband and wife. These spheres overlap to form a shared space, symbolizing their collective marital identity—a concept society has long recognized.

Polygyny, however, adds layers to this dynamic. Note the above blue central sphere for the husband, flanked by additional spheres for each wife. The central sphere represents the husband's role as a partner to multiple wives, while each wife's sphere captures her individuality and marital role.

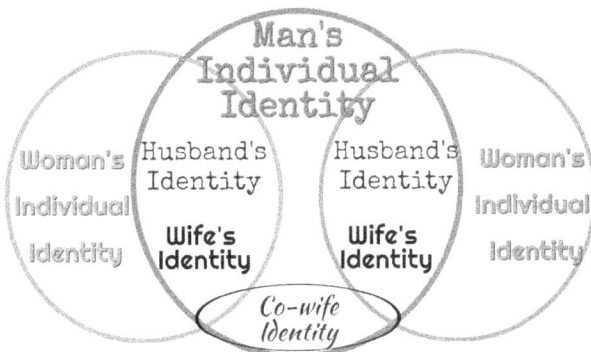

Man's Individual Identity

Woman's Individual Identity — Husband's Identity — Wife's Identity

Husband's Identity — Wife's Identity — Woman's Individual Identity

Co-wife Identity

SHARED MARITAL IDENTITY

Beneath these, look at the small black oval labeled 'co-wife.' This isn't all about the wives' relationship with each other or their shared husband; it highlights their parallel roles. The challenge is to maintain individual identities while sharing a husband.

Emotional Complexities

As Nadine Burke-Harris discusses in "The Deepest Well," unresolved issues can add emotional layers, such as jealousy or betrayal. Within the 'co-wife' sphere, the wives have choices:

- Maintain no contact with each other
- Develop a friendship
- Keep interactions cordial
- View each other as adversaries

The Expanding Sphere of Male Responsibility

In polygyny, a man's responsibilities grow exponentially. Take Michael, for example. He knew that polygyny wasn't just about adding a wife; it was a transformative journey. Michael invested in personal growth, focusing on leadership, financial acumen, and emotional intelligence. He saw his role as a guiding light for a harmonious household, laying a strong foundation for his polygynous marriage.

The Female Perspective: A Case Study

Sarah, a confident woman, faced a rollercoaster of emotions when her husband took a second wife. She realized the importance of maintaining her unique identity amid the evolving marital dynamics. By investing in personal growth, Sarah found a balance between her individual needs and her role as a wife, understanding that her family's success was also her own.

Adapting the Diagram

The diagram evolves with the addition of more wives, but the roles, responsibilities, and choices remain consistent.

The Importance of Cordiality and Respect Among Co-Wives

Maintaining at least a cordial relationship among co-wives is crucial for the overall harmony and stability of a polygynous family. While each wife has her own unique relationship with her husband, the interconnected nature of their lives means that they are part of a larger family unit. In times of emergency or tragedy, this interconnectedness becomes especially evident.

When crisis strikes, a united front is not just desirable—it's often necessary. Whether it's a medical emergency, a sudden financial setback, or an unexpected loss, these are moments that test the strength and resilience of any family. In such times, the last thing anyone needs is internal discord.

Being cordial with each other allows co-wives to handle these challenging situations more effectively. It ensures smoother communication, quicker decision-making, and a more supportive environment for everyone involved, including children who may be affected by the crisis.

Moreover, a husband would find peace of mind knowing that, in his absence or incapacity, the women he loves are capable of coming together for the greater good of the family. This level of maturity and unity can be a source of strength for the husband and the family as a whole, making it easier to navigate through tough times.

In summary, while each co-wife maintains her individuality, a baseline of cordiality can serve as a safety net for the entire family when faced with life's inevitable challenges.

Reflection Points:

- How will I work on my sphere?
- What steps can I take to foster understanding?
- List three ways to cultivate peace and strengthen relationships.

Chapter 8

MEN'S RESPONSIBILITY IN POLYGYNY

The Basics

Let's dive right in.

This chapter sheds light on the core responsibilities of men when practicing polygyny. We'll cover the best practices, what succeeds, what doesn't, and all the nuances in between.

Broadly, there are two domains to consider: the "Measurables" and the "Intangibles". We will explore both in this chapter.

The Measurables

Money. It's a simple word, but its implications are vast. It represents security. Historically, men have been the protectors and providers, a role that remains relevant today.

Historically, and by the very design of human nature, women often find themselves vulnerable, especially during phases like pregnancy. Their physical limitations during such times make the need for security even more paramount.

When the sanctity of marriage is bypassed, the consequences are evident, with women often bearing the more significant aftermath, especially from intimacy, such as pregnancy. The challenges of advanced pregnancy stages, from breathing difficulties to physical discomfort, underscore the importance of robust security, especially during these times and post-birth.

In essence, finances, or money, epitomize this security. Financial stability translates to choices – be it in food, housing, transportation, or safety. For men, fulfilling this role of provider not only magnifies their appeal but meets the inherent need women have for security.

Women often have aspirations that, to many men, may seem endless and occasionally, baffling.

There's a misconception that polygyny is solely for the mega-rich. Yet even many of these affluent individuals opt for monogamy. The financial expectations in a monogamous relationship aren't strictly defined. Many couples navigate financial challenges together over time. While many men aim to elevate their earning capacity, it's often driven by desire rather than a stringent obligation.

Monogamous marriages present their own set of challenges. Young couples, especially those in their twenties, are typically still charting their paths. The man may be launching his career, and financial stability may yet be a distant goal. During these times, the woman often becomes the bedrock of support. It's a shared journey of love, challenge, and growth.

However, when a couple has weathered early financial storms together and later attains stability, introducing the idea of polygyny can stir feelings of betrayal in the wife. She may recall the struggles they faced jointly and feel sidelined now that the situation is brighter. Remember, she's often been the silent anchor, whether caring for the family or supporting her husband during tough times. These sacrifices resonate deeply.

Emotionally intelligent men recognize this. If considering polygyny, it's vital to approach with empathy, acknowledging her steadfastness throughout your shared journey.

Having a wife with genuine friends is a plus for both partners. Sadly, true friends are rare. Coach Fatimah shared how one of her close friends advised her to value the unique moments we spent together in monogamy. This friend wisely noted that any additional wife wouldn't have the shared past that we did. She encouraged Coach Fatimah to stay strong, emphasizing that a new wife would inherently split her time, entering as a subsequent partner.

Financial Foundations for Polygyny

Diving right in, financial literacy is crucial for those considering polygyny.

Ever come across the Cashflow Quadrant by Robert Kiyosaki of "Rich Dad, Poor Dad"? Here's a quick breakdown:

- E - Employee: Steady paycheck territory.
- S - Self-Employed: The solo entrepreneurs or professionals.
- B - Big Business Owners: Those with self-sustaining systems.
- I - Investor: Your money working for you in various avenues.

If unfamiliar, "Rich Dad, Poor Dad" is a must-read. Available on Amazon, YouTube, or Audible, this book dominated personal finance lists for over a decade for good reasons.

So, how much do you need financially for polygyny? It varies by location due to diverse living costs. However, a good rule of thumb is to ensure you have an income supporting two households and a savings cushion of at least six months' expenses.

With changing financial landscapes, like the U.S. dollar's volatility, staying informed is key. For those keen on currency insights, Mike Maloney's "Guide to Investing in Gold and Silver" is a gem.

Any suggested avenues? Yes, digital assets and knowledge commerce. Sharing expertise can yield significant returns.

The Power of Digital Knowledge

The educational knowledge commerce industry is booming. From advanced topics like AI to basic skills like crocheting, there's a demand for knowledge. The skills you possess are digital goldmines. Traditional schooling is too slow and most graduates don't work in the field in which they obtained a degree.

Many critique the current education model. John Taylor Gatto, a celebrated educator who won the "Teacher of the Year Award" 5 times, offers enlightening insights in "Weapons of Mass Instruction." Echoing Mark Twain: "Never let schooling interfere with your education."

In this golden age of digital assets, creating value-laden content is invaluable. For example, our offerings include educational products that serve people on a high level: like the Polygamy Masterclass and Polygamy Bootcamp. The principle? Create once, reap endless rewards. Aim to empower. Interested in exploring this space? Check out where I teach people at MakeItMonetizeItMarketIt.com

Now, exploring beyond digital assets, here are more ways to enhance your income:

Expanding Your Earnings: Deep Dive into Marketing and Real Estate

Marketing for Businesses

In the U.S., a staggering figure shows that out of 36 million businesses, only a small fraction, less than 10%, manage to achieve earnings of over $100,000 annually. This gap is not due to a lack of potential, but a lack of efficient marketing.

Let's talk digital marketing. Mastering platforms like Facebook or YouTube can change the trajectory of a business. Digital marketing isn't just about visibility; it's about targeted visibility. Guiding the right audience to a product or service using efficient funnels can magnify their revenue and make you invaluable at the same time.

Remember the SYSTEM – "Save Yourself Significant Time, Energy, and Money." If you can guide businesses to expand their customer base through effective marketing, you're invaluable to them. For example, by charging $2,000 a month per client, if you can provide a 3 x or higher return, it's a win-win. 10 clients in and you're near the top 1% of income earners in the nation.

And here's a secret: Professionals, from lawyers to chiropractors, might be stellar in their respective fields but often lack marketing acumen. Therein lies your golden opportunity.

The Evergreen Real Estate

Real estate, age-old it might be, remains an investment powerhouse. Its tangible nature and historical appreciation make it a favorite.

Ponder on this: In many metropolitan areas, due to unpaid property taxes, local authorities become unintentional homeowners. Such scenarios offer a unique investment proposition. By leveraging mechanisms like the 501(c)3 nonprofit organization status, you can acquire properties at a fraction of the market rate. And the returns? A duplex, for instance, could be split and rented out for dual income.

Robert Kiyosaki, a maestro in the financial world, has long championed the virtues of real estate. His teachings not only highlight the importance of real estate but also underline the significance of passive income streams.

In a polygynous setup, where time is as crucial as money, such passive income routes are not just advisable; they're quintessential.

Now, an important realization: Many individuals work harder because their money isn't. Let's illustrate this.

A. Bob earns $25,000 annually, it'll take him 40 years to earn $1 million. Is he a millionaire? NO, he isn't. Why? Because it took too long!

B. Naser find ways to earn $25,000 monthly, he will hit $1 million in just over 3 years which is 10 x faster! Is he a millionaire? Not yet; still not fast enough.

C. Michael earns $25,000 weekly, over 40 x faster than Bob. He's a millionaire. Wealth is measured in time. The essence is clear: time efficiency in earning is as crucial as the amount itself.

So the problem isn't necessarily that individuals don't make enough money, I posit that they simply don't make the money quickly enough.

Closing with a reflection:

How deep have you dived into literature on finance, marketing, or real estate lately? Amassing wealth is as much about knowledge as it is about action. If you haven't yet delved into at least 10 books in these domains, there's your immediate roadmap. As the adage goes, leaders are indeed readers. Also ask yourself what courses, seminars, conferences, or events about financial education have you invested in? Follow that up with, how's that working out for you?

Time in Polygyny: Balancing and Boundaries

Grasping the Measure of Time:

Time is an asset. It's finite, calculable, and thus, a "measurable." We can chart out hours, segment them, and create a structured path. It's not an ambiguous concept; it's definitive and tangible.

Let's pivot to how time plays out within polygyny. The culture I've been nurtured in champions balance and equitable division of time. Although you could determine time allocations solo, sourcing input from your wives can create a harmonious balance, ensuring every voice is heard.

Remember, as the CEO of your family, you are in the driver's seat. My own schedule revolves around a 24-hour rotation, granting me the blessing of seeing each family member daily. Proximity might modify this decision, but fairness is non-negotiable. It's not about micromanaging every second; it's about assuring each relationship receives its due.

An essential insight: duration with your first wife doesn't predicate a hierarchy in polygyny. Every relationship stands on its own merit. Each bond is singular, and equitability is pivotal.

Your daily commitments matter. Should your day revolve around work commitments, consider avenues to cultivate passive income. As a rule of thumb, evenings are moments of connection, reserved for strengthening marital bonds.

Embrace flexibility but understand the core. Time divisions cater to the wives, not children. The children's presence doesn't dictate the division; the rhythm is steered by the wives. Sidestep potential pitfalls like manipulation or game-playing, especially regarding children. And remember, a house with kids doesn't necessitate additional time. Adaptability, mutual respect, and clear communication build the path forward.

A candid piece of advice: adulthood isn't an extension of high school. Since leaving my family home, no one's dictated my phone habits. Similarly, stand firm against micromanagement. Avoid pettiness, embrace maturity, and always respect boundaries. If it's crucial, communicate. If it's trivial, it can wait.

Jealousy, though natural, requires careful navigation. When choosing life wives, prioritize maturity and understanding over impulsiveness. As my great-grandmother told me when I was a boy, "common sense ain't all that common."

In the realm of polygyny, boundaries are imperative. Side-step those late-night interruptions unless critical. Being a husband is a 24/7 commitment, a continuous dance between challenges and joys that polygyny brings.

Open channels of communication, mutual respect, and a commitment to fairness will steer the ship through potential storms. As the family's CEO, your role is decisive: to ensure equity, fairness, and balance, come what may.

Reflection Points:

- To augment my earnings, one skill or strategy I need to learn or implement is…
- An innovative idea to bolster my income is…
- My preferred approach to balance time between wives is…
- To uphold harmony and reduce potential manipulative games, the boundaries and expectations I can institute are…

The Intangibles

The tangibles, by nature, are easy to define and measure. But here's an insight that's worth its weight in gold: more often than not, women are more drawn to the intangibles in a man than the easily quantifiable attributes. It's these intangibles that often distinguish mature men from the rest. As time unfolds, these intangibles either serve to elevate a man or reveal his inadequacies.

To borrow a wise saying of Abraham Lincoln, "I will study and get ready, and someday my chance will come." But let me offer you a modern twist: Coach Nazir says, "Stay primed ready so when the time comes, you don't have to get ready!"

Let's unravel these intangibles. Being elusive by nature, they're challenging to pin down or visualize. They represent the inner work a man does, evident only through his actions or, sometimes, the lack thereof.

Central to cultivating all admirable qualities is nurturing a growth mindset. Muhammad Ali's wisdom resonates here: "The man who views the world at 50 the same as he did at 20 has wasted 30 years of his life." Embracing a mindset of growth is pivotal to succeeding in any realm – be it sports, entrepreneurship, or relationships.

Let's dive deeper into the foundational intangibles vital for a man aspiring to practice polygyny at its zenith.

Confidence: Topping this list is confidence. A prevailing issue many men grapple with is low confidence, which is tantamount to reduced self-esteem. Instead of waiting for the "right feeling" to surge, take initiative.

Remember, genuine confidence isn't just about mastering a specific skill; it's about an intrinsic belief in your capacity to navigate and figure things out, regardless of your current knowledge base. When Tony Robbins said, "It's not about your resources but your resourcefulness," he was touching on this very essence of confidence.

Consider this thought: Picking up this book is a testament to your proactive approach to understanding polygyny's intricate dynamics. By seeking knowledge, you're already on a path toward fortified confidence.

The confidence-competence loop is worth noting here. As you refine a skill, your confidence in that area grows. It's a cycle we all undergo – from the rudimentary stages of learning, like tying shoes, to the complexities of leading a family or managing a business. The initial phases are riddled with challenges, but as we persist and hone our abilities, we become more competent, bolstering our confidence in the process.

In essence, confidence is about one's adeptness at handling challenges. And, in the realm of polygyny, it's pivotal to note women are typically more drawn to a man who exudes genuine confidence.

A quality woman, a prospective wife, desires a man who can lead, exude strength, and showcase leadership and capability. Such attributes are inherently attractive and rooted in confidence. Conversely, low self-esteem isn't appealing; it often attracts predators or narcissists who exploit vulnerabilities.

As we delve into the topic of mental health, it's crucial to understand that the pillars I outline in this chapter, though presented sequentially, are equally vital. Each one can bolster your stature independently as a man. However, when combined, they elevate you, making you not just a man of value, but what I would consider a "king."

Mental Health: The Hidden Strengths

Mental health is more than a buzzword; it's a vital component of our well-being, intricately entwined with our emotional health. While the term might sound all-encompassing, I'd like to narrow it down and focus on some crucial aspects.

In the context of marriage and polygyny, mental health pertains to the quality of our thinking – the clarity with which we perceive, process, and act. It encompasses our ability to think rationally, objectively, and discern between superficial and profound insights. Moreover, acknowledging any diagnosed or potential mental health issues, both in yourself and a prospective spouse, is paramount.

A pressing concern is that many of us might be grappling with undiagnosed issues. If you feel imprisoned by past traumas or find recurring triggers affecting your daily life, it's imperative to seek help.

"The Deepest Well" by Nadine Burke Harris, a book I highly recommend, delves deep into how Adverse Childhood Experiences (ACEs) can leave lasting imprints on our lives. Seeking help, be it from therapists, counselors, or coaches, shouldn't be stigmatized. It's time we dismantle the barriers around mental health, recognizing that, just like physical issues, our mental challenges deserve attention, even if they aren't always visible.

Reflect on your mental state: Are you charting a positive trajectory? Are you fostering a growth mindset? Or do you find yourself lost in the whirlpool of distractions, negative thinking, or feeling entitled due to factors beyond your control?

I am urging you to think deeply about the following questions:

- Where will your journey of personal growth lead you?
- How are you arming yourself with knowledge and growth?

Reading is a transformative tool, a compass pointing you towards a richer reality. What's currently on your reading list? Can you pinpoint the next five titles you aim to explore? Your selection can offer a window into your growth trajectory. Reflect on your last five reads. How did they mold your thoughts? If you don't have something to pull from, other than religious texts, then that can be problematic.

I would advocate for the works of John C. Maxwell, celebrated for his expertise on leadership and effective communication. Some of the titles I highly recommend include:

- 'Today Matters'
- 'Winning with People'
- 'Everyone Communicates but Few Connect'

Dive into these treasure of personal growth. Challenge yourself with this question: How am I consciously bolstering my mental prowess and well-being?

Every time you can answer this question positively, you are becoming more and that also means more attractive to women.

Emotional Health: The Pillar of Strength

Society often paints a picture where men are the pillars, the unwavering guards who stand strong against external adversities. Phrases like "men don't cry" echo from boyhood into adulthood, implying that to display emotion is to show weakness.

However, this portrayal is a double-edged sword. While certain situations demand stoicism – like a soldier in the heat of battle or a poker player holding a game-winning hand – it's critical to distinguish between managing emotions and suppressing them. Emotional health isn't about hiding feelings; it's about understanding, recognizing, and navigating them effectively.

Picture this: A heated conversation with your wife escalates. With emotional intelligence, you're equipped to decipher whether her words stem from love or momentary frustration. In this drama, your reaction is composed and stoic, avoiding extreme emotional outbursts.

Some misguided men believe that physically asserting dominance defines masculinity. In truth, genuine strength lies in being level-headed, providing stability, and ensuring that emotional reactions don't become the norm. The Prophet Muhammad (may peace and blessings be upon him) stated, "**The strongest are not the best wrestlers. Verily, the strongest are those who control themselves when angry.**"

Ask yourself, how are you nurturing your emotional intelligence? Reading remains a timeless tool for growth. Some highly recommended reads include:
- Winning with People by John C Maxwell
- "Multiple Intelligences" by Howard Gardner
- "Mindset" by Carol Dweck

Whether you're an old-school reader or an audiobook enthusiast, immerse yourself in these literary treasures. The act of reading, championed by the very first word revealed in Islam, "Iqraa" (meaning "read" or "recite"), underscores the essence of emotional health.

Your emotional health compass doesn't just guide interactions with your spouse; it also plays a pivotal role in understanding the emotions of children or parents, especially as they journey through life's various phases. Reflect on Tony Robbins' observation about adults having the emotional maturity of a five-year-old. Tantrums unfortunately aren't exclusive to childhood.

Our brain's decision-making hub, the prefrontal cortex, attains its full maturity around age 25. This maturity gifts us the ability to reflect, analyze, and act thoughtfully.

Men, especially those navigating polygyny's complexities, must cultivate this. And remember, refining emotional awareness isn't only beneficial for polygynous unions; it fortifies monogamous relationships and equips the yet-to-marry with an unparalleled advantage.

Leadership

First and foremost, leadership begins with guiding oneself. This requires discipline and self-awareness, particularly in navigating personal desires. Your role as a leader extends to your first wife, any subsequent wives, and the entire family unit.

By default, you are the family's guiding force, tasked with more than just protection and provision. Your vision steers the family's direction. While advice from your wives, children, and extended family is invaluable, the final decisions rest with you – likened to the CEO of a family.

For those looking to enhance their leadership skills, John C. Maxwell offers a plethora of insightful books, including:

- The 21 Irrefutable Laws of Leadership
- The 17 Indisputable Laws of Teamwork
- Developing the Leader Within You

- Developing the Leaders Around You
- Five Levels of Leadership
- 360 Degree Leader

Historical leaders offer lessons on influence and leadership. A notable read is "The 100 Most Influential People of All Time" by Michael Hart. While I won't delve too deeply into it, Hart lists Prophet Muhammad (peace be upon him) as the most influential figure, with Omar Ibn Al-Khattab also mentioned at number 52.

Hart's rankings are based on various metrics and stories, underscoring the significant influence leaders wield. The key is ensuring your leadership is constructive, leading to positive, meaningful outcomes rather than destructive paths.

Throughout history, we've seen a spectrum of leaders, from Adolf Hitler to Malcolm X, Marcus Garvey to figures like George Bush, Barack Obama, Donald Trump, Joe Biden, Nelson Mandela, Patrice Lumumba, Sisi, and Morsi, among others. The direction and underlying principles of each leader not only determine the effectiveness of their leadership but also its inherent quality.

It's vital to first master self-leadership before guiding others. Demonstrating this mastery over time enhances your appeal and opens more opportunities by increasing your attractiveness.

Make sure that time promotes you versus exposing you.

Physical Vitality

Physical fitness plays a paramount role in our lives, and while it might seem obvious, it's crucial to emphasize its importance. Being fit doesn't necessarily mean having a 10% body fat. Instead, it's about maintaining strength and agility, ensuring you can handle challenges or even emergencies.

Polygyny demands a robust constitution, and those who engage in it should exhibit this vitality. Being physically fit translates to being an asset to your family. If one's health is compromised, whether through obesity or other health issues, it can pose a liability, potentially disrupting the family's structure and leadership dynamics. Physical wellness is a facet of leadership, ensuring that you can efficiently carry out your responsibilities.

For those seeking resources on health, Tony Robbins'"Life Force" and Dave Asprey's "Superhuman" are excellent reads. If you aren't already exercising regularly, foundational exercises like air squats, planks, and wall-assisted pushups can be incredibly beneficial. Studies indicate that mobility is a key factor not just in the quality of life but its longevity.

While I believe the span of our lives is predetermined, the quality of those years is up to us. Proper care for one's body, through stretching and exercise, can mean the difference between aging gracefully, with agility and strength, or facing challenges due to neglect. Investing in physical well-being ensures you're active and engaged throughout your life.

Four foundational exercises for overall body strength are squats, lunges, planks, and pushups. These exercises not only enhance your core strength but also boost your attractiveness. Research highlights the benefits of weight training.

For instance, women who perform squats with weights increase their bone density. This not only strengthens them but also enhances mobility and certain aesthetic aspects of their physique. So, a gentle nudge for women: integrate weights into your workout routines.

A captivating study I encountered revealed that individuals who engage in weight training are healthier than their non-weightlifting counterparts, even if the former group smokes. In simpler terms, a smoker who lifts weights might be healthier than a non-smoker of appropriate weight who doesn't. This doesn't advocate for smoking but underscores the importance of weight training.

Regardless of whether you're lifting traditional weights, household items like water gallons or a sofa, or simply using body weight for resistance, it's crucial to integrate strength training into your routine. This physical robustness complements other areas of strength: mental, emotional, and leadership capacities.

Maintaining physical vitality is essential not just for overall health but also for specific functions. Engaging in regular exercise promotes proper blood circulation throughout the body. Adequate blood flow, especially to the penis, is crucial for male sexual function.

When aroused, the penis relies on increased blood flow to achieve and maintain an erection. Hence, a healthy circulatory system, free from blockages, can enhance intimate experiences and contribute to overall physical vitality.

Fiscally Fit

Financial intelligence is essential, especially when you're responsible for multiple family members. Being fiscally fit means not just increasing your income but also managing your finances wisely. To enhance your understanding, I'd recommend books like "Rich Dad, Poor Dad" and "Cashflow Quadrant" by Robert Kiyosaki.

If you're aiming for passive income or creating a digital asset, consider courses or tools that help in this domain. Whether it's from me or another source, having a digital asset that continually earns for you is invaluable. Furthermore, mastering marketing skills is invaluable for businesses everywhere; it's a skill that's always in demand. Another avenue I personally vouch for to grow and preserve wealth is real estate.

Ultimately, how are you making money work for you, as opposed to chasing after it? Money is a challenging master but an excellent servant. So, what strategies have you employed to ensure it serves you?

While mental, emotional, and physical vitality are key intangibles, there's one overarching element: Noble Core Values. I firmly believe we're spiritual beings experiencing a physical journey. Your core values not only reflect what's important to you but also shape your family's vision, security, and overall direction.

Noble Core Values

Noble core values are the bedrock of any fulfilling relationship. While some might approach polygyny with less noble intentions, often focusing on the physical aspect, it rarely results in lasting satisfaction. In my experience with thousands, such motives seldom lead to fulfillment.

True noble core values encompass love, trust, respect, honor, empathy, and kindness. However, it's essential to strike a balance – not becoming so kind that you're easily exploited. These values are about approaching life with love and responsibility, appreciating the good and detesting the wrong. Polarity always exists.

To build a successful marriage, you need to understand your core values. I urge you to complete the exercise and download the sheet provided to determine your core values within a marital context.

While you can apply this understanding to various areas of life, for this chapter, focus on marriage. By recognizing your core values and those of your spouse, you can navigate the intricacies of your relationship with more empathy and understanding. This knowledge helps avoid triggering sensitive points for each other.

For a deeper insight into your core values, access the exercise at outstandingpersonalrelationships.com/tools.

Recognize the spirit within you and elevate your life experience.

Reflection Points:

- Commit to reading or listening to a set number of books per month. List the next five books with a start date.
- Pledge to attend a specific workshop or course within a designated timeframe.
- Identify the people who will benefit from your personal growth and newfound confidence.

Chapter 9

SHOULD I MARRY MULTIPLE WOMEN? EVALUATING WITH THE POLYGYNY REPORT CARD

As we jump into this chapter, men wondering whether or not I think they should practice polygyny comes up. Here's the thing, it doesn't matter what I think. What matters is what you can do!

As men, we weigh and take risks all the time, and it's our responsibility to be wise while doing so. I won't tell you to go one way or another, but I will advise you evaluate all of your options objectively, especially if you're moving toward exercising your natural disposition.

What I call the 'Polygyny Report Card' is you looking at yourself honestly and objectively, not pumping up your own ego, but really looking in the mirror, writing down what you see, and making an open, honest analysis of self.

You may not have done this before, as it may not have been required by anyone. But when it comes to polygyny, this is a good place to start. So, let's talk about this report card and what you're going to do.

The very first thing you must ask yourself is *what is your risk threshold?* Many people are naturally risk averse, which is okay because people know their situations intimately. Risk threshold is a common term when it comes to investing. Investors know that the general rule is to only invest money that you're willing to lose, whether we're talking about crypto, stocks, or real estate deals.

When that rule isn't heeded, it can be akin to gambling. You might be in a monogamous marriage with children, further expanding your familial unit. So, it's paramount to define your risk threshold.

Start with your polygyny inclination. On a DESIRE scale of 1–10, where 10 implies an absolute need and 1 indicates a mere, fleeting thought, rate your DESIRE. Naturally, you must consider your current commitment — your wife and family. You've already stepped into the realm of monogamy, understanding the stakes at hand. When met with a spouse who does not favor polygyny, the challenge intensifies.

This is the issue many of my students grapple with — should they proceed if their wife opposes? The pivotal factor here is your risk threshold. This leads us to the resentment scale.

If you lean towards polygyny, but your wife doesn't align with this vision, and you capitulate because of her, a seed of resentment may be planted. Over time, this resentment can grow, stemming from a perceived suppression of your masculine essence. There's a potential feeling of being manipulated into a decision counter to your innate desires or biological inclinations.

In essence, you have to decide which is the bigger risk vs the potential rewards or consequences.

ASSESSING YOUR PREPAREDNESS FOR POLYGYNY:

A SELF-REFLECTION EXERCISE

As the head of the household, a man is tasked with the vision, strategy, and execution of plans for his family's welfare. However, obstacles may arise that challenge this vision. Such challenges can plant seeds of resentment. Consider this: "How would I feel towards my wife five years from now if I didn't practice polygyny?" Your feelings may range from indifference to deep-rooted resentment.

Now think about your feelings on the scale of RESENTMENT 1–10. 10 meaning you know that you'll be highly pissed, upset, and emotionally unsettled, which may interfere with your everyday interactions with your wife. 1 on the scale means that it's merely an annoyance, and not really a big deal.

Now compare the ratings of these scales. Which weighs heavier for you, DESIRE or RESENTMENT?

It's not always about math, like taking a hypothetical desire of 9 and subtracting a resentment of 5 to get 4. In reality, life's complexities don't fit into neat equations like this.

The real question: will potential resentment overshadow your desire? It's worth noting that unforeseen dynamics may emerge even if your wife approves of polygyny. The landscape of relationships, especially with multiple partners, can be unpredictable.

The common stereotype is that women are more emotional. In reality, both genders are equally emotional; the difference lies in expression. The human psyche is more intricate than a simple assessment. Yet, self-evaluation is a starting point.

Ask yourself, "Am I the man who embodies the qualities attractive to multiple women? Can I protect, provide, and exert personal power for the betterment of my family?" Alternatively, "Am I pinning hopes on an ideal scenario, like finding a wealthy woman who doesn't expect much in terms of tangible or intangible contributions?"

Be candid in this self-evaluation. Below is an exercise to help you evaluate:

Rate yourself from 1–10 on the following qualities:

- Leadership history
- Mental Strength
- Emotional Intelligence

- Financial Acumen
- Physical Health

Now, add all your scores and then double the total:

A: 90 – 100

B: 80 – 89

C: 70 – 79

D: 60 – 69

F: 59 or below

Do you excel? Are you marginally making it? Or are you lacking?

PLANNING FOR POLYGYNY: ADDRESSING THE CHALLENGES

Prepare for Potential Challenges

In this section, we'll delve into possible challenges when considering polygyny. It's vital to assess all you've built in your marital relationship, from trust, emotional investment, to tangible and intangible assets. Reflect on homes, vehicles, stocks, crypto, investments, businesses, and even intangibles like emotional bonds. And, crucially, if children are involved, their well-being should be a paramount consideration.

Legal Implications

Contemplate the legal aspects of your marriage. Is it recognized by your state, province, or country? Does the jurisdiction have provisions for polygyny, or is it simply not legalized like in the US? Understand the potential consequences: can your wife initiate a divorce? If so, is it common for 50/50 asset split?

The Risk for Fathers in Legal Disputes

Unfortunately, many men grapple with a court system that is usually in favor of women, often to the detriment of the children, particularly in the West.

Despite data showing that children often fare better in two-parent households, or even with single fathers, the courts frequently award custody and placement to mothers.

Children of divorced, single-mother households statistically show higher risks for incarceration, academic struggles, health issues, substance abuse, promiscuity, criminality, and becoming victims of crimes. Yet, the bias often persists, with mothers being the preferred guardians.

Understandably, real life court drama can be a primary concern. Some women might use the threat of taking the children away, leveraging the legal biases, although things aren't as black and white as they sometimes think.

Now, take a moment. List down the potential worst-case scenarios and ponder whether you're willing to face them in pursuit of polygyny. Reflect on your earlier self-assessment – did you rate yourself as a competent, loving, and capable man, fulfilling your 3 P's: Protect, Provide, and exert Personal Power?

Consider whether your aspirations come from a genuine place or if you're pumping up your ego or pride. As a man who desires to expand his family with polygyny, your decisions should be based on rational and objective evaluations. Remember, just because you may not be ready now doesn't mean you won't be in the future.

Revisit this chapter periodically, comparing your progress and growth over time. Ultimately, determine your boundaries and your willingness to accept potential challenges. The decision is yours – make it wisely.

Considering Polygyny: Delving into Complex Emotions

Ladies, if you're engrossed in this section, it's crucial to recognize that just because men might not always articulate their feelings, it doesn't mean they're driven by sexual lust when contemplating polygyny.

Anticipating Potential Issues

One of the severe outcomes to ponder on is divorce. It's an unavoidable consideration. Most marriages, regardless of type, face challenges that could lead to dissolution. Polygyny isn't particularly the cause. It's essential to ask: Can you cope with the possibility of divorce?

Some men, in their moments of reflection, may feel they have made sacrifices, believing that if their spouse left to find something better, she might end up disappointed. Many times people think the grass is greener on the other side, but they don't realize this is simply because it's been fertilized more. In other words, there is a whole lot more bovine excrement to deal with!

There's no denying some women might resort to manipulation. Yet, as the family's leader, it's essential not to let these tactics plant seeds of resentment. Miscommunication and misunderstanding can stem from past traumas and experiences that emerge when polygyny is considered. However, it can also expose a person for who they really are on the inside which may not be an easy realization.

I can't emphasize enough the value of the book, "The Deepest Well" by Nadine Burke Harris. It focuses on ACEs (adverse childhood experiences). This understanding is crucial as past traumas, such as abandonment or exposure to abuse, can trigger an array of emotions when polygyny is introduced. Equipping yourself with this knowledge can elevate your role as a spouse and parent.

Starting the Conversation

Initiating a conversation about polygyny is no small feat. But, before addressing this with your partner, you need to communicate honestly with yourself. Reflect on your motives and feelings. You might think your spouse is your closest confidante, but certain topics, like polygyny, can challenge that notion.

The best friendships and relationships should harbor an environment of openness and trust. If considering polygyny causes unease, it's essential to address this early, ideally during marriage discussions. Educate your family about different marriage types to encourage open dialogue without heightened emotions. This begins with our children and youth.

Here's one of the ways I let men know they can use to address the topic. I suggest they use a 3rd party to break the ice. What do you mean 3rd party, Coach Nazir? I'm glad you asked. Sometimes an indirect approach is better than a direct approach because being too direct may cause apprehension, and a woman may put up her guard quickly.

Instead of saying, "hey let's talk about polygyny", perhaps saying something more common like, "have you seen this video or channel" or "I saw this video and was wondering what you'd think about it." We live in a world where videos and memes get shared all the time, from the weird to the funny, so this has proven to be a lighter way to approach the topic.

Khalid was married for 7 years when he inquired about polygyny. He owns several apartment buildings and a barbershop. He wanted to practice polygyny but he knew his wife would "have a fit" as he called it. I suggested he share one of our YouTube videos with her. He knew her personality and, instead, he watched our channel while she was around, which prompted her curiosity and led her to ask what he was watching.

He told her he was intrigued. She began watching with him while frowning her face up and sucking on her teeth when she heard some of the things my wives were saying. He ignored her antics and kept watching because he considered it a win. He then went to a different video and they discussed our viewpoints.

She later told him that she binge-watched our channel in a week and was more open to polygyny. He hasn't married again at the time of writing, but he has been in talks with his wife's knowledge and support.

If your husband has used 3rd party with you, firstly I want to congratulate him, and secondly, let you know that you can blame me. I'll shoulder that responsibility, sister.

Understanding the Dynamics between Men and Women

You are the man and must understand the sexes are different, in that healthy men generally have 10 times more testosterone than women and healthy women have 10 x the estrogen levels than men. Men generally have more muscle mass than women. That's simply how men are designed.

However, women have this other thing that tends to be a lot more refined and sharp, called the tongue. From this may come many manipulation games. Beware of her tongue and your actions by being aware of your emotions and the games that are played when the tongue is used as a weapon.

Navigating Emotional and Psychological Challenges

It's not uncommon for men to experience guilt or a sense of duty, particularly in the context of polygyny. The term "Death by a Thousand Concessions" is analogous to the ancient Chinese torture method called "lingchi." It's where a person would be cut up to a thousand times and, although each specific cut was not fatal, the cumulative effect of so many of these cuts would cause one to bleed to death.

In a relationship, making too many concessions can feel like numerous small wounds to one's masculinity. Being excessively accommodating, especially to avoid confrontation, might lead you to compromise your values or aspirations.

In polygynous settings, you might feel a need to reassure or appease your first wife, especially if she shows signs of unease or opposition. This is where it becomes crucial to strike a balance.

When it comes to polygyny, you may have that feeling that you want to go ahead and reassure her that you'll be there for her and that you understand it's quite a change. This is noble and good, however, when nobility shifts to you making more concessions that you wouldn't normally make, it's no longer good and starts to become a slippery slope.

She is likely absolutely aware of this and may choose to wield this against you as part of the manipulation game. Indeed, she will find herself on top of every podium of the Manipulation Games just as Simone Biles dominates the Olympic games.

The aim isn't to suppress or deny women their feelings or fears. It's about recognizing manipulation and responding appropriately. You might find yourself making grand gestures, like expensive trips or gifts, to ease tensions. These acts, while noble, should be equitable across all your relationships.

Establishing Boundaries and Setting Precedents

In all relationships, there's a component of "training." How we allow others to treat us sets a precedent for future interactions. Rewarding negative behavior or reacting impulsively can set unhealthy patterns. Instead, acknowledge good behavior, create an atmosphere of trust, and be prepared to address bad behavior immediately.

Modern society presents numerous temptations, from casual dating apps to more explicit content online. Some might argue that these alternatives are less challenging than a polygynous commitment. As men striving for honor, remember your intent is to build a noble and loving family, not to capitulate to fleeting desires or societal pressures.

When these games rear their ugly heads, be aware of them. They come in many forms, and all you have to do as a man is slow down. Let your prefrontal cortex do its job by evaluating the entire situation and asking yourself, is this a manipulation game? Or is this something that's genuine? And what's the best way to get clarity and respond?

Reflection Points:

- 3 areas of my life that need work are…
- I really need to have a difficult conversation about…
- I am or I am not willing to risk…

.

Chapter 10

TRUST IS PARAMOUNT

TRUST IS THE LINCHPIN OF POLYGYNY. IN THIS CHAPTER, I'LL HIGHLIGHT trust's significance by discussing its best practices and showcasing how trust can be breached. But first, let me share a personal story.

I vividly remember Christmas when I was five years old. The anticipation was palpable, with gifts under the tree and the thrill of being the eldest of two siblings. That Christmas Eve, I was abruptly awoken by my father's excited voice. "Santa just left," he shouted, lifting me up and rushing to our top porch door. I felt the sharp winter chill as we stepped onto the top porch. My father pointed to the starry night sky, asking if I could see Santa's sleigh. The wonder of that moment was accentuated when I saw a shiny new tricycle waiting for me indoors.

Yet, not long after, my belief in Santa was shattered. A classmate declared, "Santa isn't real. Parents just play the part." Eager to disprove her, I sought confirmation from my mother. Her hesitant nod was all the answer I needed. The realization was a visceral blow. My parents, the most trusted figures in my life, had upheld a cultural fiction, and the pain of that betrayal lingered.

You might wonder, how does this connect to trust in polygyny? My parents, driven by societal norms, chose to perpetuate a widely accepted narrative. Their decision, well-intentioned as it might've been, became a breach of my trust. The ramifications extended beyond just Santa – I soon questioned the existence of the Easter Bunny and even the Tooth Fairy who left a fifty-cent piece under my pillow when I lost my tooth!

In relationships, especially in the new dynamics of polygyny, trust is paramount. While monogamy might have its own set of expectations—chiefly fidelity—it's crucial not to assume loyalty is a given.

ARE WE BEST FRIENDS?

In monogamous relationships, there's often an implicit assumption that spouses are best friends. Typically, best friends can openly discuss anything without fear of judgment. However, if introducing the topic of polygyny leads to tension, it's a sign that the foundation of friendship in the marriage may not be strong as perceived.

Trust doesn't equate to sharing every detail. People might have deeply held secrets, but withholding information that could harm rather than protect the family is problematic. A true test of partnership is the ability to engage in open, civil discussions, even on challenging topics.

From personal beliefs to physical preferences, there shouldn't be taboos between spouses. If such subjects are off-limits, it's a red flag indicating potential "trouble in paradise."

Unspoken expectations can pave the way for misunderstandings, miscommunications, or worse, no communication at all.

When considering polygyny, best practice dictates discussing it before commitment. Young men, particularly, might not consider polygyny initially, focusing solely on their first marriage. However, as they evolve, their desires might change.

It might be about expanding legacy, having more children, or other reasons. Keep in mind that choosing polygyny doesn't necessitate some altruistic reasoning. Addressing this before marriage is ideal. Yet, it's equally essential for both partners to remember they can revisit such topics as the relationship matures, ensuring both are in tune with each other's evolving desires.

FEELINGS AND THEIR INTERPRETATIONS

As a child, I recall the mixed feelings of anxiety, surprise, and joy when my father woke me on a winter's night to show me a new tricycle. Later, discovering the untruth of Santa Claus left me feeling betrayed. I wondered, "What else did my parents lie about? Can I trust them?" With time, I realized they were merely perpetuating a widely accepted custom, one many know isn't rooted in truth.

Imagine how many other things we accept simply because they are custom, like monogamy as being natural despite it only being the norm over the last couple of centuries.

In marriage, honesty is paramount. The weight we attach to our emotions is significant. Many women express feelings of betrayal when their husbands remarry without prior communication.

Speaking from experience, I believe discussing such decisions beforehand is ideal. Yet, I admit I didn't inform my wife, Coach Fatimah, before marrying Coach Nyla.

When I chose to tell my wife, Coach Fatimah, about my marriage to Coach Nyla after the fact, it was against a backdrop of unspoken expectation. Despite the longevity of our relationship, this decision felt like a breach, and she experienced feelings of betrayal. Understanding my value for loyalty, she recognized the weight of this decision.

My reasoning at the time was rooted in trying to avoid immediate conflict, given our prior discussions about polygyny. Though I now see the importance of transparency, back then, I rationalized that if an argument was inevitable, it might as well be postponed to after the fact.

Sometimes, husbands might withhold such information to prevent any disruption to the upcoming marriage, fearing objections, potential drama, or stress. This is classic conflict avoidance and is far from the best way to handle things.

Yet, the primary issue emerges when dishonesty and deceit come into play, especially if immoral actions were involved prior, such as intimate encounters.

In the West, polygyny is often perceived as cheating. The feelings and interpretations we assign to events shape our mood and long-term temperament.

THE SIGNIFICANCE OF TRUST IN RELATIONSHIPS

Both husbands and wives can contribute to trust issues, but how they do so varies, especially in polygyny. A husband's lack of communication on crucial matters like polygyny can strain trust. Keep in mind that it is our belief that anyone can bring up the polygyny conversation. Wives don't need to wait for their husbands to initiate the conversation so they can get clarity. Women have all the power in the world to initiate the discussion and a wise woman does it in a healthy way.

Conversely, a wife's threat to separate the family, especially using children as leverage, deeply wounds the trust foundation. Actions like these are seen by many, including me, as more than just hurtful — they are shameful and, perhaps, evil. The reason for such threats, whether due to pain or anger, doesn't excuse the responsibility and accountability everyone holds.

Similarly, a man can't use his emotions as a justification for beating a woman. Both scenarios equate to betrayal. It's commonly believed, particularly among Muslims, that a key aim of shaytan (Satan) is to fracture families. Yet, many people (Muslims included) actively participate in, or prevent the formation of, strong family units, especially through polygyny.

Trust, though laborious to establish, can be shattered instantaneously. Regaining it can be an extensive and long process, making it pivotal for both parties to communicate openly.

For a man, it involves demonstrating courage, responsibility, and understanding. For a woman, it means being a supportive, understanding partner.

Building and maintaining trust requires comprehension, not assumptions or external societal pressures. Entering into polygyny doesn't diminish a wife's value; it's essential not to let insecurities or societal judgments dictate feelings or reactions. The key is to address and understand these new dynamics with clarity.

WHY YOU DON'T TRUST YOURSELF?

Many individuals struggle with self-trust because they're the only person who has heard every lie they've ever told. This distrust can lead some to justify questionable actions or develop terms like "secret marriages."

While there might be private wedding ceremonies, especially in Islam, there's no such thing as a "secret marriage." Wedding or nikah ceremonies require other participants. At least two witnesses of good character, a representative for the bride, and person officiating is the bare minimum.

It may be private, or the wedding may have been kept secret from some people, however, that doesn't make it a secret marriage; it makes it a private wedding. The marriage is a social contract and means these people are now lawful for each other as husband-and-wife versus all other public relationships.

To avoid miscommunication and unmet expectations, couples should openly discuss their core values and expectations. Engaging in the exercises from this book can help deepen connections.

AN OLD STORY ABOUT BLIND MEN AND AN ELEPHANT

In a village in India, six blind men were curious about elephants, having only heard tales about them. Each had a different perception based on the stories. One thought elephants were powerful giants, another believed they were like magical beings, and yet another denied their existence entirely. To settle the matter, the villagers took them to the palace to touch an actual elephant.

On reaching the elephant, each man touched a different part. One felt the solid side and thought it was a wall. Another touched the trunk and believed it to be a giant snake. The third felt the sharp tusk, likening it to a spear, while the fourth thought the leg meant the elephant was a huge cow. The fifth believed the ear was a magical flying carpet, and the sixth, after feeling the tail, insisted it was merely a rope.

Their arguments grew loud until the Rajah intervened. He explained that the elephant was vast, and each man had only felt a small part. He suggested combining their experiences to understand the whole creature. The Rajah's wisdom made them realize the need to gather all perspectives to see the full picture.

This story illustrates the importance of holistic understanding. Instead of making assumptions, we should communicate openly and honestly, sharing our feelings and experiences.

Only through open dialogue can we build lasting trust and deep connections.

Reflection Points:

- To trust myself more, I'll focus on these three areas:

    1. _____

    2. _____

    3. _____

- I will confidently communicate with these individuals and deepen the trust and connection with them…

Chapter 11

UNMASKING PAIN'S RICH LESSONS

Happiness: A Fickle Friend?

Let's get real. Today's mantra? "Chase happiness, avoid all pain." The world tells you to cut out the noise, and eliminate anything and anyone not making you smile from ear to ear. Cancel anyone who disagrees with you. But to keep it a buck, life is far more complicated than a "Don't Worry, Be Happy" song. If Dad's being a pessimist or your boss is just being... well, a boss, do you just ghost them? In the game of life, it's not that simple.

Life will hand you its share of lemons. But instead of making lemonade, why not try a lemon pie, or a lemon tart? See, the truth is that pain's got different flavors. Remember those old tunes? "No Pain, No Gain"? That wasn't just a catchy phrase; it was a lesson.

My mother used to play the song when she would clean the house on the weekends. We'd wake up to the smell of Lysol and Murray's household cleaners while that song played on my mother's record player.

From The Mouth of Giants

Ever heard of Jim Rohn? He was a grandmaster in the personal development game. He mentored Tony Robbins for example. He had this golden nugget: there are two kinds of pain – discipline and regret. Discipline weighs ounces, regret weighs tons."

We know that daily decisions impact us over time and health is an easy example. It isn't the cigarette you smoke today that causes cancer and kills you, but over time, the dozens of carcinogens contained inside each cigarette add up and it's no surprise except to the smoker that they have developed lung cancer.

Now, think about your food choices. That double cheeseburger might feel like hitting a jackpot today, but what about tomorrow's health bills? That's like buying a shiny new widget on credit, only to be buried in interest later. Or, you could play it smart. Invest in your health today, reap the rewards tomorrow. I'm writing this while on a treadmill (speaking it into a microphone), and trust me, this isn't just burning calories; it's banking health.

The Discipline Payoff

At its core, discipline is the ultimate asset. It's like a prized property that appreciates over time. You need to manage your emotional funds, balancing the credits and debits. The key? Regular check-ins, self-audits, and the occasional market study. As you play the game, remember it's about strategy, not shortcuts.

Let's think of life as a complex relationship puzzle. Now, to complete this puzzle, you need to slot in several pieces, each representing a challenge or pain point. You might aim for that perfect body or dream of being a top-notch doctor. Each ambition has its unique set of pieces to slot in.

Take the path to becoming a doctor. It's not just about attending classes; it's about commitment to years of study, internships, and sacrifices. Skip a class, miss an assignment, and suddenly, you're missing a puzzle piece. Can you still complete the puzzle? Probably not.

In relationships, think of those early stages of courting. The chase, the uncertainties, the "does she or doesn't she?" moments - these are all puzzle pieces, sometimes challenging to slot in but crucial to see the bigger picture.

Whether it's physical, emotional, or mental, the pain in the world of polygynous relationships can echo these stages. It's intense, it's raw, and yes, at times, it feels like you've lost a puzzle piece. But the severity and outcome of this pain often rests in your hands.

Ever thought about getting in shape? It starts with a choice. The term "decide" comes from the Latin root meaning "to cut off." It's like choosing one path in a relationship and committing to it, come what may. Think of fitness as a romantic relationship with your body. You know the drill — move more, eat better. But the magic lies in the discipline, much like staying committed in a relationship even during tough times.

Imagine waking up early for a workout. It's cold outside, your bed's warm, and the last thing you want to do is lift weights. But, much like a committed lover, you show up, again and again, pushing past the pain, because the end result? Worth it. It's the same when you decide to lift emotional weights in a relationship, especially in polygyny. At first, it's uncomfortable, even painful. But as you adjust, grow, and learn, the rewards are beyond measure.

At first, you're actually going to feel worse and you'll feel worse because, as you're lifting weights with these muscles, you're putting tension there. It's going to cause little micro tears in your muscles. Any micro tears will heal in this period of soreness. They become better and stronger and become firmer in order to support your skeletal and nervous system.

As you are consistent to the commitment you've made, results tend to come. You feel better, you have more energy. You can think clearly. You have BDNF (brain derived neurotropic factor) that allows you to think more clearly and accelerate learning.

All this is the result of the little pain you chose to accept as your choice of discipline. Whereas, in the TV Show "My 600 Pound Life", you don't get to 600 pounds because you exercised discipline. You get to 600 pounds because you exercised your will to shove things in your mouth that are destructive to your body.

I could list 10 reasons why you don't want to be obese, morbidly obese, or overweight. Yet, I'm in a country where two out of three adults are obese, despite having more information at their fingertips than ever before in human history.

We intellectually get that this lack of discipline can lead to an early demise, a horrible quality of life, the inability to be mobile, damage to the joints, and the ability to play and be present with your loved ones. There are many detriments, and we know this.

Do we have fear and anxiety about doing the work? Are we giving ourselves an easy way out? If a person is experiencing physical pain in a relationship where there's intimate partner violence, whether that be men beating on women or women beating on men, (less discussed, but it still happens and there are far too few resources for men out there) this type of abuse can lead to all kinds of challenges and issues and help should be sought out immediately, especially when facing physical danger.

When diving into the world of polygyny, it's a profound journey of self-awareness and emotional discovery for both men and women. Some women have confided about a deep physical pain, describing it as an aching heart or a feeling of emptiness that sometimes leads to changes in their appearance. Neglecting oneself, skipping meals, or experiencing restless nights — all these can manifest as signs of internal turmoil. Sleep deprivation can have severe repercussions, from hallucinations to cognitive disarray.

On the flip side, men also face their own set of challenges. The exhaustion, the emotional weight leading to sleepless nights, or even the unease in intimate settings are physical echoes of inner battles. Now, understand this: Our emotional, mental, and physical beings are interwoven. We don't operate in silos. Our bodies and souls aren't separate entities, but are deeply interconnected. Think about it — while losing a finger doesn't take away a fragment of our soul, every aspect of our being impacts the other.

Diving deeper into the emotional arena, let's talk about jealousy. It's a natural emotion. And in the context of family, spouses, children, even how we see ourselves, a protective form of jealousy can emerge. It's a caring, guarding kind of emotion, not the destructive, possessive kind. However, it's essential to differentiate between these two.

Now, there's another aspect I find intriguing. Assumptions. They're these tricky little thoughts that often lead us astray, especially among wives who might speculate about the goings-on in their husband's other house.

Here's a curious thing: sometimes, women envision their husbands in a light brighter than reality. Picture this: A husband, in a decade-long marriage, decides to venture into polygyny. Now, the wife who has been with him, shared countless memories, and weathered storms with him, suddenly imagines him being an even more extraordinary partner to his other wife.

It's a natural human tendency to assume. But she isn't truly aware, nor should she be, of the dynamics of the other household. After all, the sanctity of private matters in households is paramount.

Rumors, Assumptions, and the Struggle of Comparison

There's a toxic trap some men fall into, immaturely sharing or even boasting about one wife's strengths or attributes to another, causing unnecessary hurt and chaos. Let's be candid here: using gossip as a weapon between one's wives is not just immature, but deeply harmful. That does nothing but showcase your weakness as a man.

Beyond this childish behavior, the traditional source of wives' emotional pain often emerges from assumptions and unchecked speculations.

Comparisons. They've been rightly called the "Thief of Joy." Here's some food for thought: When navigating a polygynous marriage, would it not be wiser to cherish the uniqueness of each relationship rather than constantly comparing? These comparisons are often based on mere assumptions.

Take, for instance, the never-ending competition for a husband's heart. Is there truly a scale that can measure love? Can one really quantify emotions on a scale from 1 to 10? Love, in its purest form, expands; it doesn't confine. When wives start comparing and making assumptions, they might venture down a self-damaging path, questioning their self-worth.

Understanding men isn't rocket science. Despite the societal narrative that paints them as straightforward beings, they too have complexities.

Historically, men were often counseled to protect, provide, and exert their personal power with compassion. On the other side, the modern portrayal of women has been influenced by various waves of feminism, emphasizing independence to the extent of sidelining men. This led men to begin asserting their independence of that type of thinking, sometimes to the detriment of women's value whether red pill or MGTOW counter-movements.

Here's the reality: Men and women, in their core essence, are pieces of a puzzle meant to complete and complement each other. Let's shift from a space of division to one of mutual respect and understanding.

Tackling Mental Pain and The Dynamics of Polygyny

Polygyny, by its very nature, carries unique challenges that standard relationships might not face. And this is where mental strain seeps in. When you're walking uncharted territories, without a map or a guide, doubt and uncertainty are your constant companions. This lack of clarity was what inspired us to create Outstanding Personal Relationships.

After learning, adapting, and reverse-engineering our experiences, we finally started seeing the light. However, the absence of support systems for men, like support groups or circles where they can discuss the intricacies of polygyny, can be deeply isolating. On the flip side, women's support circles tend to be filled with negative, spiteful, angry women who have no intention to find solutions to making polygyny work, but instead seek to destroy any semblance of light.

Here's a light-hearted example to illustrate the small, everyday challenges: When maintaining two households, managing belongings becomes a funny challenge. Let's talk about clothes. Say you have a favorite shirt. If you're rotating between homes like I do, that shirt might be in one house while you're in another.

Sounds trivial, right? But imagine this scenario before an important meeting or event and you're thinking it's in the closet! The real-life logistics of polygyny can sometimes be comically challenging!

Another example may be that your wives have similar tastes and want to see a certain movie or visit a certain restaurant. Well, now you become an actor with those on the screen because you may have already seen the movie and you want to be present with the wife you're with. Yes, you can go all together if you're mature enough to do so, but in my experience, it's better to go with one at a time so they have their special time without anyone else.

But the challenges aren't always light. As a man, you quickly realize you can't please everyone. You might find that while your initial wife is lovingly embraced by your family, your subsequent wife might face resistance or cold shoulders from the same relatives. This can lead to feelings of exclusion and emotional pain.

Navigating Societal Judgments and Self-Reflection in Polygyny

In any relationship framework, especially polygyny, the whisper of societal judgments is loud and omnipresent. Suddenly, you might find that family functions have an underlying tension, and you might even find fewer invites landing on your doorstep. Isn't it ironic? Society might be more accepting of cheating, secretive relationships than an open, honorable commitment like polygyny. But here's the real question: Why do we allow society's judgments to weigh on our personal choices?

Many navigate this path with questions echoing in their minds, like, "What would others think?" or statements like "I must have lost my value." But, honestly, who are 'they' to make such judgments? Isn't it wild how some might be quick to label, saying things like, "Find your own man," as if there's a hidden treasure trove of eligible single men just waiting? If so, I'd like to know where because, at the time of writing, I am looking for quality sons-in-law.

This societal pressure, combined with self-doubt, culminates in a sort of mental pain. It's not just about how others see you, but how you perceive yourself. The question that many miss asking is: "How do I feel about my own decisions?" Remember, in this journey of life and relationships, you're your primary companion.

Being a husband in a polygynous relationship comes with its own set of reflections. Am I giving my best? Despite possible lack of community or familial support, am I stepping up as the leader, provider, and partner I envisioned myself to be?

The road to mastery requires commitment. If you're actively striving, showing ambition, and leading with intention, respect will naturally follow. However, if complacency takes over, expect to face the consequences. It's simple to understand you reap what you sow.

Transforming Pain into Purpose

Everyone, in some form or another, faces pain – be it physical, emotional, or mental. But, isn't it fascinating how society often equates the experience of pain with low self-worth? As many leaders in personal development will tell you, enduring pain and emerging triumphant on the other side is a testament to your strength and wisdom.

Let me take a moment to share a story of a young girl, subjected to unfathomable atrocities. She was raped and physically abused for years by her cousin starting at the age of 9. She was betrayed by those who should have protected her, and thrust into a life of poverty and silence. She gave birth to a stillborn child at 14 years old that she named Cannan. He was a result of rape.

Yet, her story isn't defined by her past, but by her choices. Instead of succumbing to her trauma, she carved her own destiny. She weathered societal racism, built her brand, and now pretty much "owns" the letter O. Yes, I'm talking about Oprah Winfrey. Her story is an emblem of resilience, demonstrating that we aren't mere products of our circumstances, but architects of our destiny.

Inspiring change doesn't always need a global stage. Movements like Mothers Against Drunk Driving or America's Most Wanted were birthed from personal pain. The key differentiator? Choice. The power lies in how you act on, or react to your experiences.

But, it's equally essential to acknowledge the weight of overwhelming pain. Some feel it so deeply that they contemplate ending it all. And if you've ever felt that despair, please know there are resources to help and people who genuinely care. Call 988 if you are in the US or please search for your local hotline or website where you can speak with someone who cares.

Isn't neuroscience fascinating? It reveals our brain's capacity to rewrite its narrative. Just like a record player, our brains have grooves and patterns. With effort and intention, we can scratch out the old, harmful tunes and instill empowering, uplifting ones. Our life, our reality, can be designed to be not just good, but outstanding!

Viktor Frankl, an inspiration to many, showcased this very idea. Locked in a Nazi death camp, amid horrifying conditions, he exercised control over his mind and found purpose. His writings serve as a timeless reminder: We have the power to find meaning in the direst of circumstances.

Reflection Points:

- I will challenge all negative thoughts by...

- I will practice active listening by...

- I will stop assuming by asking myself _____ when a whisper or thought arises.

- I will list five things I am grateful for in the morning

- I will practice deep breathing or Wim Hof breathing X times per day

Chapter 12

LET'S TALK ABOUT SEX

BUSTING THE "ALL-IN-ONE WIFE" MYTH

Myth: Wife says, "I can be all 4 wives for you!"

The reality, however, is not so black and white. While women indeed possess an incredible versatility, can one woman, even with all her dynamic transformations, truly quench a man's desire for polygyny?

Take Safiyah, for instance – a woman who believed she could emulate the roles of multiple women, thinking it would be the secret to keep her husband from considering polygyny. But what she didn't anticipate was the emotional journey this experiment would take her on. Here's a closer look.

Week 1 – The Gentle Muse:

Safiyah stepped into the soft and nurturing persona with enthusiasm. Adorning herself in light pastel outfits, experimenting with her hair, and switching up her fragrance every day, she aimed to be the epitome of femininity.

As she anticipated her husband's needs, whether it was in cooking, cleaning, or just being present, she felt a sense of accomplishment. Yet, each night, as she reflected, a nagging thought arose: Was this sustainable? Her husband, meanwhile, seemed to thoroughly enjoy this gentle version of Safiyah.

Week 2 – The Professional Partner:

The second week saw Safiyah shift gears dramatically. She became the strong, assertive backbone of her husband's professional life. Sleek, dark-toned attires replaced pastels, and her entire demeanor echoed efficiency.

While she felt empowered taking charge and supporting her husband's work, there were moments of vulnerability. Was she losing her essence? But then, the sensual surprises she had for him when he got home gave her a sense of control. The blend of professionalism and sensuality had her husband intrigued and appreciative.

Week 3 – The Bold Adventuress:

The third week saw Safiyah embrace her inner wild side, a persona she herself never knew existed. Clad in leather and latex that molded to her figure, she was definitely for his eyes only. The sharp clack of her high heels echoed through the home, and with each step, she felt a mix of empowerment and vulnerability. But it wasn't just about her appearance.

She introduced playful toys and unexpected costumes, creating an atmosphere of thrilling unpredictability. Her makeup palette evolved to brighter, more provocative hues, and her demeanor shifted to a perfect blend of boldness and submission. Her husband, initially taken aback, soon found himself captivated by this edgy version of Safiyah.

Week 4 – The Carefree Laidback Chick:

As the final week began, Safiyah opted for a refreshing change of pace. Gone were the seductive attires and the bold makeup. Instead, she stepped into the comfortable world of workout gear, accompanied by just a hint of lip gloss and mascara. As she stretched and worked out, she felt free and invigorated.

But what truly warmed her heart was seeing her husband's appreciative glances as he admired her commitment to her health. Her culinary skills shone as she whipped up healthy, yet delightful meals. This week, Safiyah's approach was simple - be herself but with an added touch of sporty zest. Her husband loved every moment. It reminded him of the early days of their relationship.

Safiyah's Emotional Rollercoaster:

Throughout this experiment, Safiyah encountered a whirlwind of emotions. Each persona she stepped into made her question her identity. Was she doing this for her husband, or was she trying to prove something to herself?

There were moments of empowerment, but also moments of self-doubt. The emotional toll was becoming palpable. Would her husband notice? More importantly, would he appreciate the lengths she was going to? And, as the weeks progressed, Safiyah had to grapple with an essential question: Who was she beneath all these personas?

THE POWER OF ADAPTABILITY:

Safiyah's journey over these four weeks has been nothing short of chameleon-like. By stepping into these distinct personas, she navigated the intricate balance between self-expression and the desire to reignite passion in her relationship. Such dynamism is no small feat, and the intricacy of the endeavor can't be denied.

Yet, as you read, I'm sure many of you felt a rush of questions and even skepticism. "Isn't this a bit much?" you might wonder. Some might argue, "Isn't love about accepting one's authentic self?" And, let's be real, in the midst of all this, what about the children? Balancing household chores, responsibilities, and then this experiment might feel overwhelming to many.

And yet, as dynamic as Safiyah's actions were, there lies an inevitable factor – biology. Over a month, there will naturally be times when intimacy is off the cards due to her menstrual cycle. This isn't something that can be changed or adapted to, unlike her personas. It's a natural part of life that couples navigate. This poses a challenge on what one wife can do on a simple biological level.

Men & Periods

Many believe that men don't have a cycle or period. At first glance, it might seem like a far-fetched idea. However, I propose that men indeed have a cycle, and even a period, though not in the same way women do due to biological differences. Stay with me here.

A man's cycle isn't monthly; it's daily. You might wonder, "Coach Nazir, what are you talking about?!" Consider this: Men produce sperm every day, with their entire sperm supply replenished every 64 days. So, in a way, men experience a daily cycle.

Additionally, a man's "period" is referred to as the "refractory period," which occurs post-orgasm. This period often induces fatigue and can range from mere minutes to an entire day. This duration is influenced by the man's health, underlining the importance of maintaining physical well-being.

If we entertain the idea that a woman could be available for physical intimacy every day, studies suggest that only 7% of women express a preference for daily intimacy, while 51% of men lean that way. Women's bodies aren't the same as men's and their bodies may need recovery time where that isn't really an issue for men.

Moreover, happiness levels in marriages tend to peak with intimacy a few times a week. Some women, depending on their age bracket, even find once a week satisfying. (*https://www.benchmarkpsychology.com.au/its-a-fact-men-have-a-higher-sex-drive-than-women-are-all-relationships-doomed/*)

Before concluding this chapter, I want to emphasize that polygyny goes beyond merely introducing an additional wife or wives. Even if women could adapt their personas as described earlier, they might soon realize that polygyny offers more than just the inclusion of another partner.

It's not just about variety in intimacy. It's about a husband's capacity to manage multiple situations, encountering distinct challenges, needs, and dynamics in each setting. It's truly about a man's journey of growth and expanding his life's dimensions.

Reflection Points:

- I will work on being better at these 3 things in my relationships;
    1. _____

    2. _____

    3. _____

- I will express my love and appreciation by doing these 3 things;

    1. _____

    2. _____

    3. _____

- Three things I value that I learned in this chapter are;

    1. _____

    2. _____

    3. _____

Chapter 13

LEGAL OR LAWFUL? UNDERSTANDING THE DISTINCTION

SEAN CARTER, BETTER KNOWN AS JAY-Z, ONCE LYRICALLY PAINTED A potent image, saying, "I'm not a businessman, I'm a business, man." This statement resonates deeply, especially when I'm frequently asked about the legality of polygamy where I reside. My response usually centers on the belief that polygamy is inherently lawful, though its legal status might differ.

What Proper Planning Looks like

Abdullah had always been fascinated by the concept of polygyny and the potential it held for creating a strong, loving family. He was also keenly aware of the legal complexities surrounding the practice. Inspired by one of his coaching sessions, Abdullah decided to take a proactive approach.

First, he delved into understanding the difference between "legal" and "lawful," as outlined in Black's Law Dictionary. He realized that while polygyny might not be "legalized," it wasn't explicitly illegal either. This distinction was his first step toward practicing polygyny wisely.

Abdullah then focused on asset protection and legacy building. He consulted professionals to set up irrevocable trusts, following the "Rockefeller Method." He also established an S-Corp, thoughtfully allocating shares to his two wives and children. This ensured that his family's interests would be protected in any unforeseen circumstances.

He didn't stop there. Abdullah also set up contracts and agreements, covering everything from power of attorney to child-rearing arrangements. He even opted for private insurance to avoid any governmental strings attached to his family's well-being.

Years later, Abdullah's family not only thrived emotionally but also financially. His children went on to prestigious universities, and his wives started their own successful businesses. Abdullah's proactive approach, guided by the strategies noted above, had set them on a path of lasting success.

What Planning to Fail Looks Like

Jaweed, unlike Abdullah, was more cavalier in his approach to polygyny. He had heard of some of the principles but chose to ignore the intricacies, especially those related to legal standing and asset protection.

Jaweed assumed that love and good intentions would be enough. He didn't bother to consult professionals or set up any trusts or corporations. He also ignored the importance of contracts and agreements, believing that verbal commitments were sufficient.

When Jaweed unexpectedly passed away, chaos ensued. With no will or legal structures in place, his assets were frozen. His wives were left in a precarious financial situation, and the children had to drop out of school. To make matters worse, family disputes over assets escalated, leading to a complete breakdown of relationships.

Jaweed's failure to plan had indeed been a case of planning to fail. His family was left to pick up the pieces, their lives irrevocably damaged due to his lack of foresight and preparation.

By contrasting Abdullah and Jaweed, it becomes evident how crucial it is to be informed, prepared, and proactive when practicing polygyny. I may offer a roadmap to success, but it's up to each individual to take the journey.

LEGAL VS LAWFUL

To gain clarity, let's refer to Black's Law Dictionary since it has been used in western law since 1891. It says Law constraineth every act to be lawful when it standeth indifferent whether it should be lawful or not. Wing. Max. p. 722, max. 194; Finch, Law, b. 1, c. 3, n. 76.

The word 'legal' refers to something that has been established by law or 'color of law'. This distinction is pivotal, especially if you're practicing, or intending to practice, polygyny with wisdom and care.

Remember the age-old wisdom: "If you fail to plan, then you plan to fail." As a man, and as a leader, the onus is on you. Whether you're single, in monogamy, or polygyny, the task of creating and executing a vision rests upon your shoulders. It's a relentless journey, but it's your responsibility to steer it right.

In my current residence, polygyny isn't "legalized." However, it's crucial to note that it isn't explicitly illegal either. What many might deem as "illegal polygamy" is, in legal parlance, bigamy. It pertains to possessing two active marriage licenses simultaneously. It's this specific action, being state-sanctioned married to more than one person at the same time, that's prohibited.

Legal Standing, Asset Protection, and Legacy Building

As of the writing of this book, the case of West 49th Street, LLC vs. O'Neill is still making its way through the legal channels. New York

Civil Court Judge, Carrie Maybach Dion, took a progressive stance by ruling in its favor, especially regarding legal protections and leasing nuances. For those keen on delving deeper, we might provide a link in our resources section. But in the grand scheme, the specifics of this case aren't my focal point. I've always been wary of excessive governmental involvement in personal affairs.

But there's something I've always found fascinating. As I grew up, I'd often hear stories of individuals bequeathing their fortunes to their pets, maids, or non-relatives. It made me wonder: How does one ensure such a legacy?

As I delved deeper into the world of wealth maintenance and asset protection, I stumbled upon the stark differences between legacies like the

Rockefellers and the Vanderbilts. The Rockefellers, for instance, utilized irrevocable trusts and life insurance wisely to preserve their wealth, a strategy that's now emblematically termed the "Rockefeller Method". Another noteworthy approach they employed is the "waterfall method", which incorporates insurance, trusts, and other mechanisms to ensure wealth longevity. Research Infinite Banking.

As the patriarch of your family, I encourage you to think forward and embrace this visionary mindset. This isn't legal advice, but a thought prompter. Consider the intelligent founder of a company. They structure their company's shares meticulously, ensuring equitable distribution among stakeholders.

Similarly, in a polygynous setting, a man could ensure fairness by thoughtfully allocating shares of corporations to his wives, children, or other key figures. After all, a corporation, viewed as a legal entity, could perpetually sustain, paving the way for a lasting legacy. This ensures that in any unforeseen circumstances, your family's interests remain protected and continue to thrive.

THE NEXUS OF LAW AND POLYGYNY: ENSURING RIGHTS AND RESPONSIBILITIES

Ensuring everything's in order, from dotted 'i's to crossed 't's, is of paramount importance, especially in the world of polygyny. And while this information provides an overview, it's essential to consult with a professional to tailor your decisions to your unique situation.

Trusts, both revocable and irrevocable, offer a protective layer for your assets, ensuring you have the right trustees and beneficiaries in place. Contracts and agreements, from power of attorney to child-rearing arrangements, are critical.

Interestingly, in the US, I've never been asked to present a marriage license or certificate, be it at hospitals or elsewhere. But, the international scene might require more documentation, sometimes even just proof of a religious ceremony.

Remember, these contracts and agreements represent the mutual understanding and commitments between parties, and they stand strong. However, a crucial point is government intervention. If you're benefiting from governmental welfare programs, there may be a claim on how they can be used and if you may be responsible for paying back any welfare received. For instance, if you birth a child in the hospital and don't have private insurance and the government pays for it, they have a right to be paid back. Opting for home births or private insurance might free you from these strings.

Consider the benefits of setting up a company. Not only can you provide employment, but you can also extend fringe benefits, including health insurance. Even employing minors and providing them with compensation falls within this domain, all subject to local regulations and periodic updates, of course. Always ensure you're in compliance with the prevailing laws, both in business practices and tax matters.

It's imperative to recognize that the institution of marriage predates any state or governmental structure. It's a bond rooted deeply in human history and society, and understanding its legal nuances is key to practicing it seamlessly in today's world.

Before the emergence of nation-states and their arbitrary borders, marriage existed. It was, and still is, a powerful social construct. There are traditions, like 'jumping the broom', which still persist today, hearkening back to the times when our ancestors had to discreetly express their commitment because marriage was viewed as such an esteemed institution.

But here's the pivotal point for you: there are tools and strategies available to ensure the security of your assets, family, and legacy. Courses and professionals stand ready to guide you through the maze of corporate structures, from S-Corps and C-Corps to LLCs (Limited Liability Companies). Then there's the realm of trusts – revocable, irrevocable, even offshore trusts. Understanding the distinction between a 'person' and a 'natural person' can be invaluable when forging contracts and agreements. These instruments, constructed with diligence, can be your safeguard, enforceable in a court of law if disputes arise.

Further, let's touch upon insurance and the benefits of entrepreneurship. Having your business, whether a small home-based venture or a large-scale operation, offers a slew of advantages. From group health, dental, and vision insurance benefits to cultivating a sense of ownership and direction in your life. Now, some may argue: "Why not simply add them to an employer's insurance?" As of this writing, typically only one 'partner' can be added, limiting your options.

In our ever-evolving societal structures, one has to remain alert to shifts and nuances. Consider the insurance policy structures: previously, it was limited to a husband or a wife, inclusive of their immediate offspring. Now, with the advent of same-sex marriage rights, the dynamics are shifting. But depending solely on an employer's policy, resigning your power and placing your fate in their hands, is it truly the best approach?

See, no matter how harmonious your family appears, you cannot predict the complexities that arise in stressful situations. Especially in times of grief or loss, emotions run high and often, the most unexpected disputes emerge.

From my life experience, I've seen the aftermath of unexpected deaths, the chaos of misplaced wills, and the disintegration of family bonds as greed and insensitivity reign. It's essential to be proactive in preserving the unity and legacy of your family.

One effective approach I recommend is through irrevocable trusts. Research the 'waterfall method' or delve into 'infinite banking.' While I won't endorse any particular expert, Marvin Mitchell is a known and respected figure in the US for those wanting a starting point.

There's a misconception, especially among newer Muslims, suggesting that one must strictly follow the law of the land, sometimes using this as an argument against practices like polygyny.

Whether you're looking to shield assets from greedy ambulance chasers, ensure future generational wealth, or just trying to tread the waters of legalities and traditions, remember this: Take proactive control. Protect your family's legacy and be informed, prepared, and proactive.

Reflection Points:

- One strategy I need to learn more about protecting my family with is…

- My understanding of legal and lawful is…

- I'm committed to learn more about _____ strategy and will start by…

Chapter 14

BUYER BEWARE: SPOTTING THE RED FLAGS

THE LANDSCAPE OF RELATIONSHIPS IS VARIED, AND WHILE LOVE AND harmony are common aspirations, it's crucial to acknowledge that not all intentions are noble. In this chapter, we will shine a light on potential hazards you might encounter on your journey. While we won't focus on clinical terms like "narcissism," we'll address specific traits that signal trouble, especially in the realm of polygyny.

Given the unconventional nature of polygyny in many societies, it's a territory ripe for exploitation by those with harmful intentions. The practice's taboo status might even deter victims from seeking help or sympathy, leaving them even more vulnerable.

This is one of the reasons we implore people to study the subject matter deeply, especially if you are following a spiritual path and are choosing polygyny on that path. So whether you are a new Muslim, or you are learning a religion, or you're venturing into a spiritual walk that endorses polygyny, make sure you thoroughly familiarize yourself with the rules, the rights, and regulations before considering any polygynous union or entertaining the discussion.

This is particularly important if you don't have the guidance of a guardian, representative, wali, or wakeel who would have your best interests at heart. There are praying men and there are preying men who prey on new converts or those who might feel they have limited options.

I've heard sentiments like, "I feel I have no other option but to settle for polygyny." However, it's crucial to understand that polygyny is a viable and robust choice for anyone, but must be approached wisely.

Let's delve into the five essential traits that should be on your radar.

I've labeled these the "Five Ps."

1. **Predatory**: While both genders can exhibit this behavior, it's more commonly associated with men. Here, the term "predatory" refers to individuals who actively seek out others to exploit or oppress the prey.

    Their aggressive approach in personal or business matters is aimed at domination or causing harm. Sadly, in the world of polygyny, such individuals may specifically target women open to polygamous relationships.

    They might perceive single mothers, divorcees, or widows as "easy targets," assuming these women are more vulnerable due to their circumstances. Much like a predator in the wild singles out the young or the weak, these individuals look for those they deem naive or struggling.

2. **Pernicious**: Often subtle and gradually harmful, pernicious behavior works its way through sweet words and whispered promises. Women are often said to be seduced by their ears, making them vulnerable to men who use honeyed words as their main weapon, weaving a web of trust only to abuse it later. Some of these traits do overlap because they are all ill-intentioned.

3. **Parasitic**: You don't have to look far to witness parasitic behavior, where one individual feeds off another. In the realm of polygyny, some men shirk their roles as providers and protectors, instead opting to live off their wife or wives. Whether it's a woman's personal income or assistance from the government, these men, rather than elevating their families, bring them down. This dynamic might remind some of the notorious pimps from yesteryears, where men exploited women for financial gain, an act far removed from the honorable practice of polygyny. This lends to the insulting word po'ligamy.

4. **Pompous**: Ego can be a double-edged sword. While confidence is essential, a pompous attitude characterized by arrogance and a need for constant validation is a warning sign. A man who constantly boasts about his multiple marriages, treating them as trophies rather than a responsibility, is missing the point. It's not about the numbers; it's about the bonds built, the love shared, and the families nurtured. Puffed up chests are simply chests filled with hot air.

5. **Patronizing**: Patronization is another trait to be wary of. It's a mask of kindness worn by those who feel superior, often reminding the other of the favors done or the aid provided. It's as if their kindness comes with a constant reminder of the 'debt' owed. In polygyny, a man might remind a woman continuously of how he 'rescued' her from her circumstances, holding it over her head and undermining her self-worth, which is a sign of a very weak man.

Remember, awareness is your first line of defense. Recognizing these signs early can save you from a world of hurt.

Watch out for the 5 Ps: Predatory, Pernicious, Parasitic, Pompous, and Patronizing behaviors. Being forewarned is being forearmed.

BEWARE AND BE AWARE

Tabitha had always believed in the values of love, understanding, and mutual respect in relationships. As she grew up, she'd often heard tales of polygynous unions that were filled with love, respect, and a sense of community. This was rare because most stories she heard were negative. As she stepped into the world of dating and relationships, she felt drawn to the idea of polygyny, believing it to be a path where love could be multiplied.

However, as she navigated the waters of relationships, she encountered Omar. At first glance, Omar seemed like a dream come true. He was charming, eloquent, and seemed genuinely interested in polygyny. Yet, as the days turned into weeks, Tabitha began noticing unsettling patterns.

Omar exhibited a predatory behavior. He seemed to have an uncanny ability to sense vulnerabilities, zeroing in on them like a hawk spots its prey. He made it a point to remind Tabitha continuously of her past struggles, subtly hinting how she would have been lost without him.

As their relationship progressed, Omar's words took on a pernicious tone. Sweet nothings whispered in the night turned into veiled threats by day. His assurances of love and care began to sound hollow, feeling more like a trap designed to ensnare rather than a bond to cherish.

Tabitha soon realized that Omar was parasitic in nature. While she worked long hours, he seemed content doing little, living off her earnings. He often cited past instances where men were the primary providers, but his current actions didn't align with those tales. It reminded Tabitha of stories she'd heard of men exploiting women, leeching off their resources by not wanting to work for the man and she should be his Khadijah. His behavior echoed the term 'po'ligamy' that she'd heard in hushed whispers.

Then there was his pompous attitude. Every gathering they attended, Omar would boast about their polygynous relationship, treating Tabitha and his other wives as trophies. His stories were less about the love they shared and more about how he, Omar, was man enough to handle multiple wives. It wasn't an expression of love; it was a show of power.

But what hurt Tabitha the most was Omar's patronizing behavior. He often "reminded" her of where she'd be without him, of how he'd "rescued" her from her previous life. It felt as if every kind gesture he made came with a price tag attached.

It was a chance meeting with an old friend, Nzinga, that became Tabitha's turning point. Nzinga, sensing Tabitha's distress, gently guided her through recognizing the signs she'd been missing. She was careful not to be condescending because she didn't want Tabitha to get defensive. They talked about the five Ps: Predatory, Pernicious, Parasitic, Pompous, and Patronizing. As they dissected Omar's behavior, Tabitha felt a cold realization dawning upon her.

Armed with her newfound knowledge and Nzinga's unwavering support, Tabitha mustered the strength to break free from Omar's toxic grasp. She realized the importance of being aware of understanding that not everyone who steps into the world of polygyny does so with pure intentions. It was a lesson learned the hard way, but Tabitha was determined that others should recognize the signs before they too got ensnared in a web of deceit.

To every woman out there, Tabitha's story is a beacon, a reminder that, while love is beautiful, it's crucial to recognize the shadows that sometimes lurk in its corners. Be aware, be strong, and always remember: Being forewarned is being forearmed. This is also one of the many reasons women should use their wali/wakeel (representative/guardian) in talks with any man.

NAVIGATING THE FIVE DS: RECOGNIZING RED FLAGS IN WOMEN

While polygyny has its beauty and essence, understanding potential challenges and keeping an eye out for certain behaviors can safeguard one from unnecessary heartaches. When observing women in polygynous relationships, some negative patterns can emerge. We label these patterns as the "Five Ds."

1. **Deceptive Behavior:** Deception is the art of showing one thing while hiding another. It can appear in many forms—broken promises, altering previously agreed terms, or the acting out of ulterior motives. Whether it's the first wife, feeling threatened by the new union and resorting to manipulative tactics, or the potential second or additional wife attempting to undermine the first, deception can emerge from any corner. A man must arm himself with knowledge and emotional intelligence to discern genuine intent from manipulation.

2. **Disingenuous Nature:** Being insincere or feigning ignorance is a classic strategy. Just as Robert Greene's "The 48 Laws of Power"

highlights "never outshine the master," a disingenuous individual might suppress their intentions or abilities. They might see a relationship merely as a means to an end, be it material or emotional, rather than a true bond. Their use of words with double meanings or feigning ignorance is a very common tactic.

3. **Duplicitous Actions:** While similar to deception, duplicity focuses on inconsistency. Speaking one way to one person and differently to another, particularly about the same subject, is a clear sign. This two-faced approach, especially when it involves playing the victim, can ensnare families in webs of misunderstanding and distrust, pulling in extended family, friends, or even children.

4. **Domineering Attitude:** While confidence can be empowering, an overbearing, domineering nature can suffocate a relationship. The social landscape has shifted over the years, sometimes unfairly tipping the scales. In certain situations, some women might weaponize societal biases for personal gains, be it through false accusations or emotional manipulation. Beware the individual who demands royal treatment but offers less than regal behavior in return.

5. **Demeaning Disposition:** One of the harshest blows to a person's self-worth is to be demeaned, especially by someone they care for and support. Ungratefulness and a sense of undeserved privilege can corrode the foundation of any relationship. Both the first and the potential wife can manifest this behavior, highlighting the importance of vigilance.

Awareness and preparedness are your best allies. Recognizing these patterns early can navigate the complexities of polygynous relationships, ensuring a healthier and more harmonious union for all involved. Whether you're just considering polygyny or are deep in its embrace, remember to watch out for the Five Ds: Deceptive, Disingenuous, Duplicitous, Domineering, and Demeaning.

So make sure you are aware of these red flags before or when you are in a courting phase for polygyny.

If any of these things come up, they should weigh heavily on your scale as a warning to steer clear of anyone displaying these characteristics, whether it is the five P's for men or the five D's for women.

Prayerfully, you'll heed that advice and not see any red flags while pursuing polygyny.

MARCUS'S DIFFICULT JOURNEY WITH TASHA: A UNION TESTED

Marcus had always been a man of deep faith, rooted in morals that emphasized the sanctity of marriage. When he envisioned his future, it was of love, trust, and commitment. With the blessings of both families, Marcus and Tasha's union was celebrated as they embarked on their journey together, intent on eventually forging a bond under the canopy of polygyny.

The early days of their marital life were filled with shared prayers, dreams of raising children, and expanding their family through polygyny, honoring its noble traditions. However, as the days turned into months, Marcus began to sense that beneath Tasha's loving exterior lay a complex web of deceit.

The first inkling of Tasha's deception came when she shared that she had left her job to dedicate herself to their new family. It was only through an unexpected conversation with her former colleague that Marcus learned she had been dismissed due to consistent negligence and repeated absences.

When confronted, Tasha's disingenuous nature came to the forefront. She twisted her narrative, claiming she concealed the truth to shield Marcus from unnecessary worries. She invoked their shared faith, positioning herself as selflessly bearing burdens for the sake of their marital harmony.

Marcus's heart grew heavy as he recognized more of Tasha's duplicitous actions. She portrayed him as overbearing and jealous to her circle, all the while playing the devoted wife at home, using their vows as a shield against any criticism.

Her domineering side grew pronounced over time. She fervently insisted Marcus limit his interactions with certain friends, citing marital propriety and morals. Yet, she frequently spent evenings online chatting with men who previously expressed interest in marriage before her wedding, and dismissing Marcus's concerns by distorting the very teachings she previously cited.

As the days grew longer, the strain between Marcus and Tasha became palpable. Both had entered their union with dreams of expanding their family through polygyny, a shared vision that had once bound them together. However, with the revelation of Tasha's various indiscretions and the steady erosion of trust, Marcus felt compelled to revisit their original intent.

One evening, after a heartfelt prayer, Marcus approached Tasha about the prospect of practicing polygyny, hoping it might bridge the growing chasm between them. But, to his surprise, Tasha vehemently opposed the idea. She cited a myriad of reasons, ranging from societal perceptions to the potential emotional toll on their future children. Her arguments, however, seemed at odds with the principles they had both cherished.

Marcus found himself at a crossroads. The woman he had married, with dreams of a shared life built on mutual respect and faith, seemed to have diverged from the path they had set. After much introspection, Marcus came to a painful decision. Their union, he realized, could not continue in its current state of discord and deceit.

The subsequent divorce was a time of reflection for Marcus. He revisited his faith, seeking solace and guidance. It was during this period of healing that he crossed paths with the wali of Aaliyah, a woman whose values resonated with his own. Their bond grew, nurtured by shared aspirations and mutual respect. With Aaliyah, the vision of practicing polygyny, built on trust and shared goals, seemed not just achievable but destined.

Together, Marcus and Aaliyah married and embarked on a journey of love, understanding, and faith, proving that with patience and perseverance, the path to fulfillment, even when laden with obstacles, can lead to newfound joy and purpose.

Reflection Points:

- I will be more conscious of predatory behavior by…
- I will not allow my emotions to get the best of me by…
- I will continually review my intentions by…

Chapter 15

WHO IS THE PRIZE?

IN TODAY'S FAST-PACED, PICTURE-PERFECT WORLD, THERE'S A PERSISTENT illusion of perfection that sweeps many off their feet. The allure of seemingly flawless relationships can often distort our expectations, leading us to lose sight of the foundational truths of genuine connections.

When considering unique relationship choices like polygyny, understanding and embracing realism and accountability becomes paramount.

The 'Prize' is an Illusion

Society often places women on a pedestal, portraying them as the coveted "prize." While it's essential to honor and appreciate women, it's equally critical to understand that a genuine relationship isn't about conquests or entitlement.

Both partners, in a monogamous or polygamous union, bring invaluable essence and spirit to the union. Treating one as merely a "prize" diminishes their role, potential, and contribution. The reality these days is that men have far more options to choose from and, unfortunately, due to the current climate, they're simply choosing not to marry.

The continuous debate about equal contribution or the importance of one's past in relationships often detracts from the main essence of companionship. It's foolish to witness women feeling their past exploits don't influence a man's perspective or modern women seeking traditional men while discarding the virtues that traditional men desire.

The numbers tell a story as well. US Census data from July 2021 reveals that there are around 3,130,000 more females than males. In a hypothetical world of perfect pairings, this still leaves over three million women without partners. The imposition of strict monogamy would, in essence, deprive these women of love, companionship, intimacy, and potentially children unless they venture into paths less virtuous. And in reality, factors like homosexuality, incarceration, education, health, and compatibility, simply compound this ratio far beyond the simple 3:1 in the US.

Jasmeen's Journey to Understanding Accountability

The city of Atlanta, ATL as it's so often referred to, was pulsating with life, and Jasmeen was right at its heart. With a prestigious job in marketing, a group of friends who'd cheer her every win, and a penthouse with a view many envied, she seemed to have it all. But every night, she'd stare at the city lights, feeling a chasm in her heart she couldn't bridge. Relationships had come and gone, and with each failed one, she fortified the walls around her heart, blaming everything but herself.

One crisp autumn afternoon, seeking solace, she visited her grandmother Lauretta's quaint home, hoping the familiar scent of old books and Lauretta's famed pecan pie might offer some comfort. Over cups of hot cocoa, she found herself unraveling, laying out her pains and frustrations about love and life.

Lauretta, with the soft wisdom that only years can bring, began recounting a tale from her younger days. It was about her dearest childhood friend, Nia. Nia, with her radiant smile and infectious laughter, was the heart of their little community. But her life took a sudden turn when her husband, Malik, approached her with a proposal that was not commonplace, even in their tight-knit community.

He had met Aaliyah, a young widow burdened with the weight of the world, raising two children amid heartbreak and financial strain. He wanted to bring her into their lives as his second wife.

Nia's world shattered. Her home, her love, everything she held dear, suddenly seemed on the brink of collapsing. Days turned into nights as she wrestled with feelings of jealousy, fear, and insecurity. But Nia, with her boundless strength, chose introspection over impulse.

She met with Aaliyah one summer evening, and as the two women talked, they realized their shared love for Malik and their mutual dreams for a family filled with warmth, trust, and love.

Embracing this connection, they jointly built a haven where their children grew up with double the love, laughter, and wisdom. Nia's courage in facing her insecurities and choosing accountability not only saved her family but fortified it.

As Lauretta concluded the story, Jasmeen's eyes were misty. The tale was more than just a narrative; it was a mirror. She realized that the walls around her heart were of her own making. The world hadn't failed her; she had failed to take responsibility for her choices and feelings.

With a renewed perspective, Jasmeen began her journey towards self-awareness and accountability. She recognized that the complexities of relationships, including polygyny, weren't just about societal norms but about personal introspection, understanding, love, and above all, the courage to hold oneself accountable.

In embracing this newfound wisdom, she felt a warmth she hadn't in years. The city lights no longer felt distant; they felt like a reflection of the hope and clarity glowing within her.

Accountability and Choosing Wisely: A Call to Action for Better Decisions

The rhythm of life presents its unique set of challenges, and for many women, making informed decisions about relationships and family is crucial. Among the myriad of choices, one stands out as often overlooked: considering polygyny as a viable relationship option.

Remember that scene from "Boyz 'N Da Hood"? Tre's mother, played by Angela Bassett, reaches a point where she recognizes the limitations of her circumstances. She decides to send Tre, portrayed by Cuba Gooding Jr., to live with his father, played by Laurence Fishburne. It's a poignant moment that emphasizes the significance of environment, influence, and the undeniable need for a strong male presence in the upbringing of a young man.

The Significance of Trust

Trust is not merely a word. It's a commitment, an emotional sanctuary we promise, especially to our young ones. Circumventing accountability can strain this bond. Children, with their astute senses, might internalize feelings of distrust or uncertainty when faced with inconsistent actions and words.

Life brings challenges. While adversities can be formative, it's essential not to get caught in the perpetual narrative of victimhood. Such an outlook might unintentionally convey to children that they're bound by external circumstances, diminishing their belief in their innate power to shape their futures.

The Domino Effect of Avoiding Responsibility

Children learn by observation. When they witness a pattern of evading responsibility, they might accept it as the norm, which can hinder their personal and interpersonal growth. Moreover, this avoidance can inadvertently cause them to internalize guilt or wonder if they're part of the problem, potentially leading to deeper emotional challenges as they mature.

Polygyny: A Considered Option

Becoming a single mother often isn't a conscious choice, but a result of circumstance. However, embracing polygyny can offer a structure and support system that benefits both the woman and her children. This choice can provide a balanced family environment and prevent the challenges associated with single-mother led households.

Towards a Future of Accountability

Accountability serves as a compass, directing us towards growth, trust, and a cohesive society. For women, especially those considering starting a family, it's essential to make decisions with foresight. By considering all relationship options, including polygyny, we can work towards creating a stable environment for our children, ensuring a legacy of responsibility, trust, and empowerment for generations to come.

PART 2

Let's Talk Polygamy with Coach Fatimah

Chapter 16

THE BEGINNING

I PONDERED THE MOST EFFECTIVE WAY TO START MY NARRATIVE, REPEATING it in my mind like a vintage 70s film. Personal questions swirled within me: *Who would be interested in hearing my unique story? How would it be received? How could I reveal parts of myself without feeling overly vulnerable?* I wrestled with these queries for days, searching for the optimal approach. Ultimately, I arrived at a simple truth—my truth.

The answer lay in starting from the beginning, embracing vulnerability, allowing emotions to flow, summoning the courage, and sharing my unfiltered self, just as I do in my everyday life. The undeniable reality is that my life is genuine, my feelings are authentic, and my journey— however arduous—is as real as anyone else's. Though the details may differ, we all confront life's trials. Life itself is a proving ground, and I've discovered it.

So, let's journey back to the winter of 1975, specifically February. Ten days after my father's birthday on February 4th, I entered this world to my 20-year-old mother and father. My parents never tied the knot, and I was, bluntly put, what society labels a "bastard." It's a sobering truth, but that's how it was. I came into existence out of wedlock, much to the chagrin of my paternal grandparents. They had envisioned a different path for their son, one without grandchildren from unmarried parents.

On the other hand, my mother had spent a significant portion of her life in foster care. She didn't share that same disappointment, having already given birth to my sister in 1973 to a different man. At that point, I wasn't a significant part of the picture. Two years later, I entered her life when she was just 20. During the brief period he was part of my sister's life, my father attempted to raise her as his own, a gesture he later extended to me.

Fast forward a few years, and my parents decided to part ways when I was only three years old. My father, fiercely possessive and protective, didn't want my mother's new partner to be a part of my life, and made no secret of it. Conversely, the new man in my mother's life didn't want me around, as I served as a constant reminder of the love my parents once shared. The situation grew increasingly volatile between my father and this new boyfriend. Caught in the middle, my sister and I witnessed the discord.

One day, my paternal grandmother stopped by to retrieve something my father had taken from her house—borrowing things being one of his habits. She heard my cries when she entered the home they rented to my parents. My grandmother asked my mother why I was so distressed, and my mother replied, "I just can't handle her anymore."

As I've been told, my grandmother called my grandfather, asking if she could bring me home with her. He agreed, with the only condition being that they wouldn't officially adopt me. My grandmother accepted this condition.

To my father's surprise, I began living with them as part of their family. Living with my grandparents, I felt loved and believed they were doing their best with the tools they'd inherited from family members who had practiced the same generational patterns. My strong-willed grandfather worked as a Brew master, crafting beer at a local brewery. My grandmother served as an anesthesia technician, assisting doctors as they administered anesthesia to patients. They led hectic lives.

Alongside their demanding jobs, they juggled the care of my mentally disabled uncles. In our family, they assumed the role of parenting my uncle, who had suffered a nervous breakdown by the age of 5 and never fully recovered from the trauma. Following him, my father was the middle child, and his younger brother was born prematurely and with severe mental disabilities.

Navigating Through Turmoil

I believe all the trauma played a role in my grandfather's struggles with alcoholism, among many other problems. Unfortunately, he was a functioning alcoholic. With an abundance of beer readily available, my father also embarked on a journey into alcoholism and, later in life, drug use. He, too, became a functioning alcoholic. However, his alcoholism took a dark turn following the tragic loss of my sister to childhood cancer. Amid all this, my grandmother remained resilient but became bitter toward men.

Her marriage had soured due to my grandfather's numerous affairs and his alcoholism, and she patiently plotted her escape. She aimed to have all her ducks in a row before pulling the trigger on her shattered marriage. As a teenager, I seemed to fade into the background of their dysfunctional nuclear family, unaware of how deeply their divorce in 1989 would shatter me.

Several months passed, and I was set to begin high school in August 1990. I was overcome with fear. Looking back, it feels like yesterday. I woke up that morning with the sensation that my life was starting anew and simultaneously shattering. My grandparents were locked in a mental battle with each other, and here I was, heading to a new school filled with intimidating high schoolers. I had no idea what to expect at home or school. I remember that day vividly—I had picked out my outfit the night before, my hair was just right, and my accessories were on point. But internally, I was a wreck.

I climbed into the car, riddled with anxiety, as my grandmother drove me to high school, where I would encounter new friends and old adversaries. Little did I know, my future husband waited just around the corner. I was oblivious to the fact that I already had a secret admirer, someone who had shared my first day of school experience, albeit from a distance. My future husband had disembarked from the bus as I exited my grandmother's car, watching me from afar.

Fast forward a short time into that school week. As I navigated the bustling halls of our colossal high school, I felt as though someone's eyes were fixed on me. And indeed they were. It was the young man who had admired me from the bus stop. At that time, I had no clue that these two were the same person. He seemed to be assessing me as I glanced back at him, yet showing no interest. Judging by his expression, he wasn't too keen on me. It's amusing in hindsight, because he did like me, but wasn't willing to make a spectacle of himself to express it. I can laugh about it now because he was as close to my childhood celebrity crushes (singer Prince, El DeBarge, and actor A.C. Slater from "Saved By The Bell") as I was ever going to get! I remember thinking, *if I ever get married, I want my husband to look like that guy!*

As a naive freshman, I failed to realize he was in the same grade as I was. He was not an upperclassman. I had assumed this because he exuded confidence, courage, and strength and I was drawn to him. He possessed qualities that the men who had raised me seemed to lack. While my grandfather and others had their strengths and weaknesses, I believed they allowed their weaknesses to dominate them. Even though my admirer was young, he already exhibited greater mental strength in my eyes.

A Fateful Encounter

As school began in the warm August embrace of fall, September rapidly approached, and there had been no meaningful interactions between the boy I admired and me. We'd cross paths in the hallways, see each other at morning school assemblies, and even share a high school religion class. Whenever he appeared in those places, I was cute but utterly nervous! Then, one September day, he decided to make a move in the hallway, and I felt like I might stop breathing. There he stood in all his splendor, with his curly hair and the intoxicating scent of men's cologne. It was akin to meeting a celebrity! My stomach didn't flutter; it felt more like giant dragonflies were fluttering inside.

I needed to play it cool. And then, it happened! He asked for my number, and like a complete fool, I replied, "I have to get to class." A quick side note: my grandmother was vehement about not being late for class and often said she'd "tear my behind up" if I received detention. I believed her. So, reluctantly, I brushed off my crush while dying inside because I worried he might lose interest in me for not entertaining his advances. Unfortunately, I was right. He seemed to lose interest, and I knew he must have felt utterly rejected. We've since shared a good laugh about it, and I'm sure a guy as good-looking as him had never experienced someone saying, "I don't have time for you." He had no idea how much I truly liked him until I made it my mission to get his attention.

I needed a strategy to win him back. That night, I realized I had messed up and hatched a plan. I committed to writing down my number and my address. This way, I could avoid awkward moments and have my contact information ready to place into his hands. I was stealthy about my movements, getting to school early and positioning myself in places where I'd seen him before. It may sound amusing, but I was on a mission!

There he was, and I mustered every ounce of courage my little body could muster to stop him and offer up my "digits." To my delight, he accepted them! I was over the moon and determined not to let him slip away. He still teases me about it to this day, but that's alright because it worked, and I'm still laughing out loud.

That's how our relationship started. I accepted him as my boyfriend, protector, partner in crime, and, most importantly, my rock when my world seemed to crumble around me. Of course, our relationship faced its fair share of challenges as we were both so young. We navigated through divorces, jealousy, the politics of teenage social circles, upset parents, irritated teachers, and our adolescent hormones. I wouldn't say I liked the attention other girls gave him, and he intensely disliked any boy who ventured within a ten-block radius of me.

As a young couple, we cherished each other in ways that couldn't be reached by anyone else. In doing so, we set high expectations for ourselves. I saw my future husband as my "hero" who would protect my mind, body, and soul for as long as we were together. Whenever I needed him, he came to my rescue, for the most part. In our family, he became known as my "bodyguard."

A Path to Islam and a New Beginning

A few years later, he was given some materials about Islam, and being an essential part of my life, he decided to share the information with me.

Interestingly enough, I vividly remember thinking that Muslims were eccentric, especially their women, who covered their hair because men required it. I told myself, I'd never cover up like that; those women must be quite peculiar! It's remarkable how everything falls into place when you look back. But, I digress. Surprisingly, after reading the materials, I grew intensely curious about Islam. I found clear answers to some of the questions I'd had for a long time.

My mind felt open and cleansed of all misconceptions, preconceived notions, and historical misunderstandings. A sense of tranquility settled into my heart as I realized that Islam held the answers I sought for my spiritual and personal life. It didn't feel like anyone was trying to persuade me; it just felt right. Independently, I delved deeper into my studies, becoming increasingly engrossed in the religion. Convinced that Islam was the path for me, I wholeheartedly embraced it by reciting the shahada (Islamic oath), and I officially became a Muslim!

Overjoyed and brimming with enthusiasm, we decided to move forward and create our own family. We decided to marry and embark on this new chapter as a married couple. My heart found a profound sense of peace in these choices. I had set my intentions on marriage and building a life free from the dysfunction that had plagued my upbringing.

Preparing for Marriage and Embracing Islam

I fondly remember being the flower girl at my father's first wedding, which wasn't to my mother. Vivid memories of that occasion danced in my head for years—exquisite flowers, lavish decorations, beautiful bridesmaids, and dashing groomsmen. I was captivated by the entire process, even though that marriage sadly ended in divorce. Not being a stranger to divorces happening within our family, I began to approach the idea of marriage with caution. In my mind, marriage seemed like something destined for failure. However, I had something in my life that was divorce-proof: Islamic Marriage. Everything about Islam brought beauty into my life, so why should I fear marriage, anymore?

Inspired by my self-assurance, the day came when I was to get married. Many questions swirled through my mind like old foes that I no longer wanted in my life. *What if this doesn't work out? What if I don't know how to be a good wife? What if he leaves like all the rest?* Deep in my heart, I knew these fears were unfounded, but doubt and negativity still sought a place on my special day.

I recall entering the mosque with everyone present except my mother, who had reconnected with me during high school. Before I got married, she requested a private conversation with me, and I agreed. We sat in a quiet room, and she apologized for past mistakes. It was a surprise, but I remained determined to focus on my marriage and nothing else. I respected her for apologizing but disagreed with the timing. After our brief conversation, I entered the formal mosque and embarked on my new journey as a wife.

We were married, and filled with hope and excitement for our future together. He was the man of my dreams, and I was the woman of his. Our little family meant the world to us, and our shared aspirations were deeply aligned with our religion. My life took an unexpected turn when my grandfather passed away in the spring of 1995, just two weeks after my wedding. It shattered my world, but at least I had the love and support of my husband, who stood by my side every step of the way. The grief was heavy, but I knew I had to move forward.

In the fall of 1995, I became a new mother to a strong and beautiful baby girl! She brought immense joy to our hearts, and I was ecstatic to see more of her father than me in her face. We showered her with love, hugs, kisses, and everything she needed. Our family and relatives supported us as we ventured into parenthood together. Being a parent has been one of the most rewarding experiences of my life.

Eager and inspired to be a wife filled with honor and trust, I worked tirelessly to create a loving and nurturing environment for my husband and our baby girl. I became fiercely protective of them, often likening myself to a lioness guarding her cubs. If anyone had anything negative to say about them, I was quick to defend them. My husband was equally committed to protecting us, mind, body, and soul. We were a team!

As time passed, we continued to add to our family and fell in love with it more and more with each new addition. We ultimately had seven children—four beautiful girls and three handsome boys! Meanwhile, I continued my studies and deepened my understanding of Islam.

My friends and I would take turns hosting study groups during those days.

We were eager to learn more and would choose different books for our sessions. During one of these meetings, the topic of polygyny came up. I had questions about polygyny and everything associated with it. Listening to our study group leader, I learned that men in Islam could have more than one wife. Most of my friends and I were practicing monogamy at the time. While polygyny was not as openly practiced in the 90s as it is now, I suspected some community members secretly engaged in this lifestyle.

Despite being familiar with the concept of one man and one wife, actively embracing polygyny was something in which I was 100% not interested. However, I was also aware that every father figure in my life had longed for more than one woman. In many cases, they had acted upon those desires by having a girlfriend on the side. I understood that polygyny was different, and it was challenging to hear.

Yet, deep down, I couldn't escape the possibility that my husband might desire it one day, just like the other men I'd known. It was a bitter pill to swallow, but in my private moments, I acknowledged this truth. As the years went by, we continued nurturing our marriage and children, and our journey into polygyny was about to begin.

Transitioning from Monogamy to Polygyny

I was a staunch advocate of monogamy, and I held onto that belief with unwavering commitment. I had never wanted that to change. The intrinsic value I placed on our marriage was immeasurable and remains so to this day. However, life had unexpected plans for us, and I found myself navigating uncharted territory.

For many years, I had wrapped myself in a comforting but fictitious security blanket, assuring myself that I would never be involved in polygyny. I felt I wasn't the type of woman who could handle or entertain the idea. I wasn't ignorant that polygyny was allowed in our culture, but I hoped it might never enter our lives. Little did I know that our marriage was about to undergo a series of critical tests, and the growth that would come from it would be profound.

The future unveiled itself in a way for which I wasn't prepared. In 2010, my husband entered into a polygynous marriage. There are many layers to this story that need to be uncovered. The marriage I had known and been a part of had been reconstructed, and I felt lost in it. I spiraled into full-blown anxiety and panic attacks.

These undesirable jitters and uncontrollable episodes of panic left me feeling vulnerable, a feeling I had never wished to embrace. For a long time, I had constructed a vision of "family" based on my childhood dreams. I hadn't taken the time to consider my husband's vision for his family. I was too consumed by the terror I felt regarding the subject of polygyny.

A barrage of questions flooded my mind, and I was hysterical. I asked myself: *What did I do wrong? How could this happen? What was he thinking? What will my children think? What will my relatives think? Can I restore things to how they used to be? What if he doesn't love me anymore?* I drove myself to the brink with these relentless inquiries. I held nothing back from myself, and it eventually led to one of many difficult conversations with my husband.

Remarkably, he reassured me repeatedly that I was not the issue in any way, shape, or form. I heard his words, but I still felt a nagging doubt—perhaps I was too old, or maybe he was just being kind, reluctant to express his true feelings for fear of hurting mine. In hindsight, I am confident that he meant every word he said and still stands by those heartfelt reassurances.

I had to silence my thoughts to escape the ambivalence, animosity, and heartache that engulfed me. My first task was to break the news to those closest to me. They were as bewildered as I was, and I couldn't answer their questions because I was grappling with my anguish. I first told my grandmother, who was incredibly upset but had a deeper understanding of men than I did then. She pointed out that my husband was still very young and that most men desire more than one wife. It was my worst nightmare, and I braced myself for the "I told you so" comments.

She remained furious but recognized that I didn't need her displeasure added to my own. Her anger would never exceed my own. I then told each of my parents, and their reactions were similar. They, too, were disappointed. Given their own experiences with divorce, I wasn't eager to seek advice from them. At that moment, I only needed to hear them say, "I love you."

Self-Care Amid Turmoil

My life turned upside down, and I was in mental distress. I grew increasingly despondent and withdrew from my usual everyday activities. I felt like a mere shadow of my former self, and the passionate joy I once exuded seemed to have suddenly vanished. I knew it was crucial to delve into self-reflection and reevaluate my marriage. Trapped in an emotional minefield, I recognized that I was going through the seven stages of grief.

The first stage I encountered was shock, characterized by the initial paralysis of receiving distressing news. My mind was paralyzed by the idea of polygyny becoming a part of my life as I had known it. I had to reassess my emotions and regroup, but until then, I grappled with many conflicting feelings.

Some of the most common symptoms of shock include:

- Anxiety attacks: sudden episodes of intense fear
- Brain fog/confusion: feeling bewildered or unclear
- Exhaustion: overwhelming tiredness and low energy
- Mental disorganization or feeling "all over the place."
- Temporary personality changes: alterations in appearance, actions, opinions, and emotions
- Negative thoughts: focusing on the negative and disregarding positivity
- "Fight or flight" response: cool, pale skin, trembling, and a rapid heartbeat

"Living with anxiety is like being followed by a voice. It knows all your insecurities and uses them against you. It gets to the point when it's the loudest voice in the room—the only one you can hear." Unknown

Moving on to the next stage of grief, I began to craft a narrative that there was no way this new marriage could be a reality.

Denial, the act of avoiding the inevitable, was the next emotion I had to confront. Unknowingly, I had immersed myself in a whirlpool of unfounded assumptions. The more I heard myself repeating, "He is married to someone else. He's married to someone else," the more I rejected the undeniable truth. Was this a healthy form of self-care? No. It was an incredibly challenging circumstance that I had never envisioned for myself. Day in and day out, I dragged myself through emotional highs and lows, thanks to my life's unexpected turn.

Navigating the Emotional Rollercoaster

Amid my turmoil, I created a symbolic toy I now refer to as my "Emo Yo-Yo," or the "emotional rollercoaster." Whenever I felt anguish or anger, I'd pull out this imaginary emotional yo-yo and play with my feelings like toys. One moment, I stood by my husband's side, and the next, I was ready to abandon my marriage. I couldn't make sense of the situation quickly enough. I longed to rediscover joy in life, but I wasn't allowing myself that opportunity or, should I say, the chance to change.

Before long, I found myself succumbing to uncontrollable outbursts of anger. When I perceived an action as unjust or heard even a whisper of the word "polygyny," I transformed into a version of myself I didn't like. I allowed myself to wallow in despair, resisting any challenges to my emotions. In hindsight, during my lowest moments, I saw growth, but reaching that point was arduous. I became my own greatest trial.

Grief is a delicate emotion that can evoke a range of reactions, including the "bargaining" stage—the "what if" phase of grief. It offers a temporary escape from pain. I remember asking numerous questions about schedules and striving for more family time to try and find a compromise. But there was no compromise to be had, as I respected our cultural norms. At the time, I couldn't fully grasp that I was deep into the bargaining stage.

Regrettably, I felt hopeless, bleak, and sorrowful without warning. I was undoubtedly in the grip of depression. I yearned to recapture the feeling of my life before polygyny, the safety blanket of monogamy. I had unwittingly altered my sense of self. Family and friends began to notice and talk to me about my depression, and I knew then that it was a stark reality. I mourned the marriage I once knew.

In hindsight, I sincerely appreciate the personal growth I have experienced. I had to understand that development wouldn't simply arrive in my life but would require a sincere effort on my part. Mourning the marriage of the past wasn't conducive to my mental well-being.

With cautious skepticism, I began cultivating a slightly improved sense of self, entering the next stage of grief: testing. I deemed it essential for my self-care to comprehend polygyny and its role in my life. Even though I had been a wife for 15 years before polygyny, I still was one. My most cherished role was that of a mother to six children at the time, and I needed to figure out where I fitted into this new equation.

Recognizing the impact of polygyny upon our children, I desperately sought solutions for what would be the best approach. My search yielded little, but it led me to a profound revelation—I was growing. Initially underestimating the depth of my inner strength, I realized that I was actively participating in the next stage of grief: acceptance.

Embracing Acceptance and Self-Care

Acceptance is the key to moving forward. Permitting myself to accept that my husband had transitioned from monogamy to practicing polygyny was a power I had always possessed. Recognizing that I had complete control over processing this information was crucial for our family's growth.

Acting as an individual was no longer serving us as a family. Considering my future was essential for becoming the best version of "Fatimah" I could be. I was prepared to redefine what family meant to me. Our marriage and family would no longer resemble my past; it was evolving into a diverse family unit.

I understood that mastering my mornings was essential to staying focused and centered during this period of change:

- Firstly, I allowed myself to wake up without feeling rushed, as rushing often led to anxiety. Taking things slow and savoring my mornings became a priority as I navigated my new life.

- I created my own "morning soundtrack," filling my mind with pleasant sounds like birds chirping, soft music, or customized noises from my smartphone, such as ocean waves or rainfall, while I engaged in creative activities.

- Planning my day in advance helped me establish control over my environment and reduce unnecessary stress.

- Incorporating stretches and exercise into my morning routine improved my energy levels and enhanced muscle circulation, especially for the most vital muscle, the heart.

- I consciously blocked out negativity, as it only hindered productivity and provided no benefits to anyone.

- Morning meditation became a daily ritual, allowing me to clear my mind of emotional clutter and start the day with vibrant clarity.

Additionally, I recognized the importance of changing my language. I ceased using absolute terms like "never" and "always." For example, while it was okay to say, "I will always love you," using phrases like "you never do anything right" was unproductive.

I embraced positive affirmations, understanding that hearing them could shape my mindset, enabling me to achieve my goals or make room for improvement.

Chapter 17

C.A.R.E. - Centered, Active, Reasonable, Elevation

Centered - Focus on Your Goals and Accomplishments

Why are you doing this? Why is it crucial to become the best version of yourself? These are questions I had to ask myself during a challenging relationship. I remember when my neighbor asked me, "Why now?" She had seen my husband and co-wife in a car a few days earlier. I replied confidently, "It's his time now." I wish I could go back and capture the look on her face, as it was a moment of personal triumph. I had permitted myself to continue fighting for my family and my marriage.

I created a detailed list of personal goals, including individual, marital, parenting, and career goals. Consistency became my guiding principle in ensuring productivity in each area.

Active - Take Immediate Action On Your Goals

Early in my marriage, I did not understand marital and personal goals. I witnessed traditional gender roles in my grandparents' 1950s-style marriage, where my headstrong grandfather worked while my independent grandmother managed the home. In my marriage, I intended to follow a similar path, but neglected to define specific personal goals for my future.

- What exactly did I want to achieve?
- What truly mattered to me?
- What were my strengths?
- What did I enjoy doing most?

- What results was I striving to achieve?
- What time frame did I set to achieve them?

After asking myself these questions, I scheduled time on my calendar to develop a clear vision for each goal. I discovered that consistency and dedication were my greatest allies in finding the fulfilling life I had been missing.

<u>Reasonable</u> - Be Realistic About Each Goal

Developing and refining each goal required me to be reasonable. As a wife and mother, my vision for myself needed to align with the vision of my family as a whole. For instance, if I needed some personal time and my work week was demanding, I couldn't simply go to my favorite place, Chicago, on a whim.

I had to communicate my needs to my family and ensure they understood my plans. Creating reasonable goals meant making decisions based on logic and critical thinking, regardless of my emotions.

I asked myself the following questions:

- What are my priorities?
- What resources do I have?
- How will I know when my goals are accomplished?
- Who do I trust to listen to my goals?
- What results do I wish to achieve with each plan?

Elevation - Strive for Growth in Personal Development

Identifying who I aspired to be was challenging. I wanted to reach my full potential but didn't know where to start. I needed self-evaluation to understand my mental state. Transitioning from monogamy to polygyny was uncharted territory, but I was determined to face the challenge head-on. With my goals set and clear in my mind, I embarked on a journey of personal development and self-awareness.

Self-awareness is the conscious knowledge of one's character, feelings, motives, and desires. As I went about my daily life, I realized that I wasn't practicing self-awareness, which hindered my healing. When we lack self-awareness, we suffer in many aspects of life.

Personality tests like the *Myers-Briggs Personality Type* assessment can provide valuable insights into dominant behavioral patterns associated with different personality types. Understanding your personality type can enhance self-awareness and improve your relationships with others.

When I decided to get married and start a family, I did not know how personality types could significantly benefit my marriage and relationships with others. My husband always came across as very reserved, a trait I noticed from our initial conversation as teenagers in high school. I sometimes wondered if something was wrong with him because I was pretty talkative. I used to believe something must be amiss if someone didn't converse much.

I remember my grandmother's words: "Still waters run deep." She would say this when she observed his quiet nature as a teenager. Her judgments gradually influenced my opinions about people who were introverted. Over the years, I realized how different my husband's personality was from mine. While we shared common family goals, our personalities had significant distinctions.

However, it wasn't until later that I learned the significance of my husband being an INTJ (*Introverted, Intuitive, Thinking, and Judging*) personality type, often referred to as "The Architect." This presented a challenge for me. I knew he valued respect and loyalty, but I didn't understand why these traits were vital to him.

As an ENFP (*Extraverted, Intuitive, Feeling, and Prospecting*) personality type, also known as "The Campaigner," I placed great importance on trust and empathy for myself and others. Recognizing the importance of personality types in relationships has been and continues to be significant to me.

Transitioning from monogamy to polygyny, I discovered that people with different personality types react in various ways to other emotional aspects, such as:

- Mistrust

- Betrayal

- Heartbreak

- Triumph

- Love

- Fear

Understanding these variations in personality and emotions has been invaluable in navigating the complexities of my evolving family dynamics.

Our journey as a married couple, characterized by actions and reactions, proved to be one of the most intricate experiences of my life. It necessitated a deeper understanding of myself and my assumptions about my husband. As a young Muslim wife, my knowledge of marriage was confined to a personal fantasy, an illusion that our world would remain unaltered. How wrong I was.

Unbeknown to us, we unwittingly placed an invisible marital noose around our necks, subjecting ourselves to a spectrum of emotions, including mistrust, betrayal, heartbreak, triumph, love, and fear. While these emotions were expected, the unique manner in which we processed and evaluated them became apparent. As an unsuspecting ENFP, I was perplexed by my husband's INTJ emotional landscape. I initially assumed that his way of experiencing emotions was somehow flawed compared to mine. However, I soon understood that his feelings were simply different, not inferior.

My natural inclination as a strong feeler was to openly express my emotions, whereas my INTJ husband felt emotions deeply, but was less inclined to display them outwardly. I realized that expecting him to react as I did was unrealistic. Instead, I needed to become a student of his personality type, not the teacher. This journey involved delving into our stories, life experiences, and upbringing.

Despite our marriage, we remained distinct individuals, each with our own autonomy. Balancing togetherness and individuality was crucial for the success of our relationship. Here are some guidelines for achieving this balance:

1. **Establish Personal Identity Boundaries**: Recognize that your love for each other should not overshadow your identities. You are two unique individuals with different likes and dislikes.

2. **Cultivate Friendships Outside of Marriage**: Maintain friendships independent of your partner. These relationships serve as reminders of your identity.

3. **Avoid Smothering**: Allow yourselves time apart to miss each other and recharge individually. The "honeymoon phase" is temporary, and personal space is essential for emotional well-being.

4. **Celebrate Your Uniqueness**: Embrace your individuality and recognize that you and your partner can be unified as a team, yet distinct.

5. **Communicate Expectations**: Have detailed conversations with your spouse about your identities. Similarities may exist, but you are not identical.

6. **Embrace Evolution**: Understand that you and your spouse will evolve. Encourage each other's growth and change.

7. **Pursue Personal Hobbies and Interests**: Maintain your passions outside of marriage. Identify what inspires you as an individual.

Maintaining a balance between what holds personal meaning and what matters to your partner is essential for the overall health of your identity and relationship.

As a wife and mother, I had lost sight of my identity. My fantasies about marriage and family did not align with reality. To gently navigate forward, I cultivated new personal habits, starting with focusing on self-care.

Self-care encompasses five areas: *spiritual, psychological, physical, emotional, and professional.* It involves being mindful of what you need for your overall health and well-being. Whether we actively engage in self-care or neglect, it can significantly impact our daily lives. Recognizing that self-care is a priority is a crucial step toward personal fulfillment.

The journey begins with self-awareness.

I needed to establish personal care goals in each of these five areas. While transitioning from monogamy to polygyny, I had lost my way and neglected these aspects of my life. I revisited old journals, photos, art, and poems to rekindle the practices that once brought me balance. I was astonished by how much I used to manage and decided to return to what had worked for me. My journey began with renewing my spiritual care.

Spiritual Care

Spirituality involves nurturing your sense of connection with Allah. As a Muslimah, I was acutely aware of the delicacy of this particular area in my life, and it continues to hold immense significance for me. My journey of self-evaluation began by examining who I was and who I aspired to become. I recognized that I was dealing with considerable confusion and merely existing rather than truly living to my full potential.

My existence consisted of going through the motions of life—praying, caring for my children, cooking, and cleaning. In this process, I came to a profound realization: I wasn't seeking the understanding and knowledge necessary to become the best version of myself. Longing for transformation and actively working towards it are two distinct endeavors.

Some of my daily practices for spiritual growth included:

- Offering my salat (prayers) and earnestly seeking understanding and knowledge
- Reading the Quran
- Finding a spiritual accountability partner

- Attending Friday Jummah services
- Journaling my day and providing an honest self-review
- Donating to my local masjid (mosque)
- Staying connected with spiritual women
- Listening to lectures and reading Islamic books

Engaging in my spiritual renewal became an integral part of my life that I had to unearth. While my Muslim identity remained intact, I needed to revive what had become buried. I aspired to become a better person, and this was impossible without a healthy, spiritual mindset.

An unhealthy spiritual mindset exhibits several red flags, such as:

- Compromising commitments by lacking consistency and follow-through with spiritual goals
- Focusing on external distractions rather than spiritual growth
- Neglecting to maximize the lessons inherent in life's trials and hardships
- Needing to discover a deeper purpose in life
- Succumbing to fatalistic or pessimistic thinking that hinders spiritual progress
- Not allocating time for spiritual self-care

On the other hand, healthy spirituality is characterized by:

- Committing to a healthy daily spiritual routine
- Setting spiritual boundaries
- Practicing gratitude
- Encouraging positive self-talk

Psychological Care

Psychological care encompasses activities that promote overall mental health, enhance mood, and reduce anxiety. It empowers us to focus on aspects within our control. For instance, in my own life, I had no control over whether my husband practiced polygyny. Still, I had control over whether I chose to react to it positively or negatively. The choice was mine.

Every decision we make carries a cause and effect, but it's essential to introduce a psychological pause and reflect. I began to pause, wait, quiet my thoughts, and reflect on what I could control versus what I couldn't. Psychological care involves creating a list of controllable aspects alongside self-awareness.

I asked myself pressing questions:

- How am I feeling mentally?

- Am I content with my life's current status?

- Am I effectively managing stress?

- Am I focusing on what I can control?

These specific psychological care questions should be answered to hold you mentally accountable for your goals and decisions. The most crucial step in psychological self-care is establishing a detailed set of psychological goals focusing on consistency. What should be on your psychological self-care checklist?

Psychological Self-Care Checklist:

- Begin a psychological self-care tracker. Document your day, events as they occur, and your progress. Grade yourself on a scale from 1–5, with one indicating that you're not at your best and five signifying a mentally positive day.

- Allocate time for mental relaxation. Dedicate time to engage in activities you're passionate about.

- Take breaks from smart devices like phones, laptops, tablets, or iPads.

- Implement a social media fast. Refrain from all social media platforms such as Instagram, Facebook, Twitter, and TikTok, among others.

- Write down positive affirmations or set daily notification reminders on your phone.

- Cultivate a circle of trusted friends with whom you can confide and who offer support.

- Begin a collection of personal development books. Recommended titles include "*Today Matters*" and "*Everyone Communicates, Few Connect*" by John C. Maxwell.

Physical Care

Physical care involves any activity that contributes to your physical well-being.

I cannot stress enough the importance of caring for your physical health. During some of my darkest moments, I vividly recall being consumed by emotional turmoil to the point where I utterly neglected my physical well-being.

I treated my body as an abandoned vessel without the nurturing elements required to sustain my life. Those around me often reminded me of the vibrant, healthy woman I used to be, full of laughter and zest for life. Recognizing your physical care needs is crucial. What does physical care encompass?

Physical Care Checklist:

- Establish detailed physical care goals
- Maintain balanced nutrition and hydration
- Ensure you get adequate rest without oversleeping
- Commit to regular exercise

One of my primary physical goals was to safeguard the health of my heart. Reflecting on 2011, after learning of my husband's second marriage, my heart began to exhibit electrical issues, a condition known as *tachycardia*.

In medical terms, tachycardia is characterized by a fast heart rate, which can occur due to various factors such as exercise, fear, anxiety, stress, anger, or even love. At times, I also experienced episodes of *bradycardia*, where the heart rate slows down.

Symptoms of tachycardia may include:

- Shortness of breath
- Lightheadedness
- Chest pain
- Fainting (syncope)
- Rapid pulse

- In medical terms, heart palpitations are characterized by a racing, uncomfortable, or irregular heartbeat or a sensation of "flopping" in the chest

Symptoms of bradycardia may include:

- Fatigue or weakness
- Dizziness or lightheadedness
- Near-fainting spells
- Exercise-related difficulties
- Confusion
- Cardiac arrest (in extreme cases)

I remember talking to a friend who was also transitioning from monogamy to polygyny. She shared that my story resonated with her because she, too, was experiencing heart issues. After updating her on my current health and physical care goals, she realized the importance of scheduling a cardiology appointment.

Physical activity, a healthy diet, and exercise can improve your health and reduce the risk of developing severe diseases. But what if you aren't particularly attuned to your body's signals? Many symptoms go unnoticed; we often fail to listen to what our bodies tell us. In my case, I had family members with heart disease, but the causes of their heart issues were apparent—diet, drug use, alcoholism, and smoking.

My story differed significantly. I never consumed alcohol, smoked cigarettes, used recreational drugs, and maintained a healthier diet. Ultimately, despite the doctor's appointments and medications, I took matters into my own hands. I made a conscious effort to prioritize my health. I gave myself a year to achieve personal physical health goals.

I started slowly, consistently, and at my own pace. Self-judgment was not an option, and I became my biggest cheerleader. It wasn't always that way, but I was no longer interested in being my worst critic.

Emotional Care — Actions you Take to Reduce Mental Tension or Strain

Enhance your ability to understand your own emotions. Be honest about your feelings, especially when addressing negative emotions rather than positive ones. Sometimes, experiencing negative emotions motivates us to make changes. It's intriguing how marriage often leads us to invest deeply in the emotional aspects of our union.

When I reflect on the early years of my marriage, I feel transported back to when I found security in monogamy. As a married woman who didn't originate from a marriage, I felt a sense of protection in monogamy. However, becoming overly emotionally attached to my wedding was a significant mistake. In doing so, I neglected my emotional self-care. Why is it unhealthy to form an excessive emotional attachment to someone else?

Some signs may indicate an unhealthy level of attachment:

- Losing your sense of self

- Preoccupation with the needs of others

- The need to rescue your loved ones

- Harboring selfish feelings & prerogatives

- High levels of anxiety and fear

I was constantly preoccupied with the well-being and happiness of my young husband and baby girl. I felt a fierce need to protect and love them unconditionally. A stable family was something for which I had yearned for so many years. I was determined to do whatever it took to safeguard them and my marriage. I was so afraid of being abandoned by them that I became overly emotionally attached to both of them.

I felt confronted by an inner voice I had grown accustomed to hearing over the years. That voice, so familiar to me, belonged to my grandmother. She offered a gentle yet firm caution in her distinct southern accent, saying, "You're becoming overly reliant on your husband and that child." She explained, "It's not healthy for a woman's entire world to revolve around men and babies." Grandma then shared a piece of her history, admitting that she had grappled with a similar pattern in her life.

She explained to me and confessed that she practiced the same thing in her own life. Placing my grandfather and sons first proved to be the chink in her armor. Repeating some of the same patterns as my grandmother proved to be my mistake.

After several years of expanding our family, I noticed I was falling back into some old habits.

Little did I know I would face one of my most significant tests: polygyny. I wasn't emotionally prepared because I had made the unhealthy decision to create a protective bubble around my family.

After 15 years of marriage, I didn't want to confront the reality of polygyny, but I knew I had to make a change sooner rather than later. Immediately, I felt hit by a tidal wave of emotions: confusion, depression, jealousy, anger, betrayal, mistrust, and rage all washed over me simultaneously. It was as if I felt everything and nothing at once, and eventually, I became numb to it all. I realized that numbness was another unhealthy emotion, rendering me powerless because I wasn't facing my feelings head-on.

One day, a close friend called and invited me over for a visit. I knew exactly why she was doing it — she wanted to break me out of my mental prison. I agreed to spend time with her, and we had a wonderful time, sharing jokes and laughter, as close friends often do. But our laughter gradually turned into a serious conversation between friends.

She asked me what I was doing to take care of my emotional well-being, a question that caught me off guard at the time.

She inquired about my emotional care goals and whether I had set any. The truth was, I had nothing of the sort on my agenda. That day, she gave me valuable advice. She encouraged me to write down what was important to me as an individual and why. I started documenting what held emotional significance for me as a woman, not just as a wife and mother.

My emotional care list included the following:

- Prioritize offering salat
- Practice daily gratitude
- Engage in activities that make me happy
- Practice active meditation
- Share only positive content on social media
- Use adult coloring as a stress-relief tool
- Explore mindfulness exercises
- Embrace positive affirmations (with a word for the day)
- Work on my trust issues
- Expand my understanding of emotions through education
- Confront my emotional fears
- Set new goals each week
- Maintain regular communication with my emotional accountability partner
- Utilize art as a form of therapy
- Dedicate 30 minutes a day to reading personal development books
- Listen to my body and rest when needed
- Journal daily, capturing the lessons from my lows and the inspiration from my highs

Initially, I wondered how this list would work for me. However, I recognized that having a plan was crucial. More was at stake if I committed to consistency and purpose. Emotional care plays a vital role in our overall health and wellness, especially when it comes to healing, whether mental or physical.

The choice is ultimately ours to make. My grandmother and a dear friend were willing to engage in the difficult conversations I needed to hear to engage in self-evaluation. Sometimes, we lack the clarity or experience required to identify potentially unhealthy aspects of ourselves.

Professional Care

Professional care involves setting specific, measurable, achievable, relevant, and time-bound goals in alignment with your life. Early on, I never saw myself as a professional in any way. I focused solely on balancing my domestic roles as a wife and mother. Part of becoming a professional is first identifying yourself as one. Since I hadn't acknowledged my professional identity, I couldn't recognize it within myself.

I could start setting professional goals once I embraced the roles of coach, thought leader, interior designer, and artist. Establishing professional goals is the first step in your journey toward professionalism.

To begin, I asked myself some crucial professional goal questions:

- What would I like to learn more about in my field of expertise?
- Do I plan to pursue additional education to enhance my knowledge?
- What am I willing to sacrifice to improve professionally?
- Do I have a professional accountability partner?
- What are my future career goals, and how do I plan to achieve them?
- What skills or knowledge would make me better in my current role?
- Will my family be negatively affected by my profession?

With each question, I consciously tried to be honest with myself. This allowed me to see the pros and cons with clarity. Despite my concerns about the unknown, I was an undefined professional who chose to move forward. I immersed myself in my work across various areas. Moving forward meant something other than appearing busy; it meant being productive and achieving results.

For many years, I had kept busy with my roles as a wife and mother, along with numerous hobbies. However, this time, I was a professional in multiple areas, and the pressure started to mount. Complete burnout loomed as I became exhausted from trying to be everything all at once. I struggled to ask for help from my loved ones because I didn't want to seem weak or burdensome. While my family never saw me that way, I wrongly assumed they would. As a professional, I neglected to consider my own well-being.

Just as I established different care routines in the other four areas of self-care, I neglected my professional self-care. So, what exactly is professional self-care?

A Professional Care routine is tailor-made to suit your schedule, ensuring you avoid burnout. It's about allocating enough time to refine your professional life while maintaining harmony between your personal and professional spheres.

Here are some essential components of a Professional Care routine:

- Engage in regular supervision or consulting with a more experienced mentor
- Form a peer-support group with other professionals in your field of expertise
- Establish clear boundaries between clients, your audience, and any staff members you may have
- Expand your knowledge by reading books written by authors specializing in your field, as more knowledge can reduce professional stress
- Attend professional development programs that focus on your area of expertise

Professional self-care is about maintaining your well-being and continuously enhancing your professional skills and knowledge.

Chapter 18

THE TRANSFORMATION

MAINTAINING THE PROPER PERSPECTIVE IS CRUCIAL IN ANY MARRIAGE, whether monogamous or polygynous. However, when transitioning from monogamy to polygyny, the questions I needed to ask myself were pretty different. I had to confront challenging inquiries, such as: *Do I truly want to remain with a man who practices polygyny? What will my life look like from now on? How can polygyny strengthen our marriage instead of weakening it? How do I navigate sharing a husband with someone else?*

To rediscover my authentic sense of self, I needed to redefine my self-esteem and reshape the dynamics within my marriage. My personality became both my internal and external armor. The modifications I needed to make to regain what I had lost became increasingly evident.

In parallel with the pain I sought to overcome, it became abundantly clear that I had to invest in my personal growth and recovery.

I began by creating a list of the things I missed about "me," the qualities that defined "Fatimah." What I *missed* about myself.

This list included:
- A strong relationship with The Creator
- Enjoying motherhood with fun and enthusiasm
- My inner beauty
- The ability to find humor in everyday life and share it with others
- A unique sense of style
- The capacity to empathize with others' pain without making it about

myself

- Rationality
- Independence
- A sense of security
- Confidence
- Authentic emotions
- Commitment to self-care
- An outgoing nature
- Fearlessness
- Courage to speak my truth no matter the circumstances
- The drive to learn new things
- A zest for life
- A love for art and design

Rebuilding myself and my life required a conscious effort to reclaim these qualities and values integral to my **identity**.

Learning that I could regain all those things was a revelation I never thought possible until I acknowledged my worth, which I had been denying. Recognizing the significance of what I meant to my life was crucial as I moved forward. My starting point was to strengthen my relationship with Allah, and from there, I had to rebuild a relationship with myself and reconnect with what I loved to do: art and design.

After several years of not indulging in this passion while raising my daughters, I resumed painting. During that time, I was deeply invested in their growth and development, which caused me to neglect my desires. While I did create a beautiful home and put my artistic touch into it, I also took on a few interior design projects.

However, I was rushing through my creative pursuits. I yearned to experience so much more but had denied myself that need in favor of prioritizing my children's upbringing. The reward for that sacrifice was my 22-year-old daughter expressing gratitude that her father and I raised her instead of leaving her in the care of a nanny or babysitter.

As she grew older, she heard stories from girls in her school about how their mothers didn't have time to raise them due to their demanding work schedules. While I felt indescribable joy upon hearing my daughter's appreciation, I was humbled by her words. I deeply admire the remarkable young woman she has become and pray for her future success.

My own adult daughter's words triggered vivid memories, particularly the powerful realization that my husband and I had been intentionally raising our children with purpose. Something incredible happened as I embarked on the journey into polygyny – I began to transform.

The word "TRANSFORM" became an acronym for my life. I unintentionally crafted a distinct path, fully committed to seeing my marriage through without divorce. Neither my husband nor I entered this marriage intending to divorce.

I took ownership of my actions and my positive intentions for my life. Uncovering what my transformation would look like was a possibility I had yet to consider. I was on the verge of undergoing a psychological, emotional, and mental marital metamorphosis.

The following acronym represents the roadmap I created from monogamy to polygyny.

T. R. A. N. S. F. O. R. M

T = TRUTHFUL

Truthfulness in a relationship is like the foundation of a solid and enduring structure. It doesn't mean you must reveal every detail of your life to your partner, but it does mean consistently sharing your genuine thoughts and feelings.

I mustered the courage to share even the most minor truths with my spouse daily. For instance, if I felt confused about something, I would simply admit it. Saying, "I am confused," was a straightforward yet effective way to communicate. When I was uncertain about our schedule for dividing our time, I would ask for clarification.

Why stay confused when seeking clarity could bring peace? I learned that trying to be petty or dishonest only led to trouble. My husband was willing to work together and find the best solutions when I approached things with honesty.

Benefits of Truthfulness:

- It uncovers the truth and addresses underlying issues in the relationship
- Truthfulness creates a safe space for both partners to get closer on personal, emotional, intimate, and spiritual levels
- It inspires trust and loyalty, eliminating doubts about where each partner's commitment and beliefs lie
- Honesty reflects self-awareness, and both partners must agree to work on it for transparency to thrive

Relationship Challenge:

- What are some things I desire to be truthful about but haven't found the time or courage to discuss?
- Why do I believe having transparent conversations in my relationship is essential?

R = RATIONAL

The first year of my polygynous journey is etched in my memory, and while there are moments I'd rather forget, they shaped my growth. I faced overwhelming emotions, heartbreak, anger, and raw terror daily. Rationality seemed elusive during those times. I had never considered myself irrational, but polygyny exposed me to a whirlwind of emotions, making it challenging to recognize irrational behaviors and triggers.

To address this, I embarked on a journey of self-improvement. I began praying more sincerely and educating myself, realizing I needed to identify and change my irrational behavior.

Common Symptoms of Irrational Behavior:

- Loneliness

- Paranoia

- Uncontrollable jealousy

- Possessiveness

- Anger

- Grief

- Disappointment

- Unjustifiable actions

- Making accusations

- Exaggeration

- Aggression

- Selfishness

- Practicing narcissism

- Diminishing accomplishments/achievements

- Maintaining unrealistic expectation

Suffering from these symptoms can be detrimental to any relationship, and I was fortunate to have a circle of friends and family who gently, but firmly, called out my behavior. My pain consumed me so much that I couldn't see beyond it. Through self-education and seeking advice from others, I began to understand what rational behavior entails.

I committed to learning the signs of rationality as part of my journey to self-improvement.

Signs of Rational Behavior:
- Not needing to control the other person
- Non-threatening communication

- Acceptance of different perspectives
- Never using guilt as a tool
- No snooping or requests for disclosure
- Respectful demeanor
- No desire to argue or belittle
- Celebrating your wins
- Supportive partnership
- Practicing emotional stability
- Willingness to hear others' points of view

Being rational means understanding the facts and not being driven solely by emotions. It involves asking essential questions rather than creating scenarios in your mind.

Mindful Marital Motivation Prompts:
1. I would ask myself two questions each morning to promote positive rational behavior, which would be…
2. Some new positive thoughts to include in my day would be…
3. To reinforce positive lucid moments throughout my day, I could add this to my daily routine…

A = Alignment

Alignment in a relationship signifies that you and your spouse are living and loving in the same direction, following shared boundaries and core values. On a personal level, as the initial wife, I found myself out of alignment with my relationship boundaries and core values. Loyalty, honesty, trust, healthy communication, balance, peace, and love had all been shaken, and I had lost control over my pre-conceived values.

Unintentionally deactivating compassion, empathy, mutual respect, peace, and understanding, I realized I had taken on more than I could handle. Interestingly, recognizing that I was "out of line" meant I had much work to do. Personal development had to become a constant practice in my life.

Side effects of being "out of line" in your relationship:

- Lack of healthy communication skills
- Quick judgments without collecting all the facts
- Avoiding your spouse
- Finding reasons to argue
- Overreacting to the most minor mistakes
- Being easily annoyed
- Lack of mutual respect

Unwillingness to be understanding, empathetic, or loyal Mindful Marital Motivation Prompts:

- Is my attitude in alignment with my core values?
- Am I playing the victim to seek attention or sympathy?
- Who would that ultimately serve?

N = Neutralize

Sometimes, when we face challenging times in relationships, we tend to respond by developing "ruminative thinking," which involves repeatedly dwelling on the same worrisome, sad, or dark thoughts. The habit of rumination can be detrimental to your mental health and well-being, intensifying or prolonging feelings of depression and hindering emotional processing.

Signs of Ruminative Thinking:

- Excessive thoughts
- Persistent negative thinking
- Self-defeating thoughts
- Thoughts about traumatic events
- Anxiety surrounding the same issues
- Repeating the same information repeatedly
- Disruption of your routine due to these thoughts
- Self-blame
- Obsession over consequences

- Feeling like you're stuck like a broken record
- Constant worry

I was undoubtedly guilty of most of these negative thought patterns. I often unconsciously circled back to thoughts about marriage, especially polygyny. Many people have asked me how I managed to stop dwelling on these negative thoughts.

Recognizing that I was engaging in reflective thinking was a crucial first step. After months of being trapped in reality, I decided to break free from these unhealthy, negative thought patterns.

How to Stop Ruminative Thinking:

- When you recognize that you are starting to ruminate, deliberately create a distraction to break the cycle of negative thoughts
- Develop an action plan to address your thoughts and feelings
- Reassess your life goals and adjust them as needed
- Identify your triggers, such as people, phrases, topics, places, or events that set off your rumination
- Question whether your thoughts are rational or if emotions drive them
- Work on improving your self-worth and self-esteem

Create a plan to manage your emotions, whether anger, jealousy, betrayal, depression, or fear. Feeling these emotions is okay, but not letting them control your actions is crucial. For instance, avoid destructive behaviors or physical violence if you feel angry. Instead, focus on personal growth and permit yourself to experience the emotion without becoming consumed.

Becoming consumed by your emotions won't benefit you or your relationship. You cannot change the past or control the choices of others, especially those you love and care for. I realized that I couldn't hold what wasn't my responsibility to manage. My role was to work on self-improvement, meet my husband where he was, and not let my emotions dictate my choices.

While acknowledging my feelings, I consciously tried not to become those emotions. Achieving personal growth and becoming the woman I wanted to be took time and effort.

Self-preparedness involved recognizing and addressing problematic emotions which were interfering with my daily life.

Steps for taking control over my emotions:

- Avoiding circumstances that could trigger negative emotions, such as distancing myself from toxic people, places, events, and feelings
- Safeguarding my focus and attention
- Evaluating situations that might be unhealthy, like interactions with hostile relatives or people in my religious community
- Learning to self-soothe when I felt frustrated
- Adjusting my response time when I felt upset, intentionally delaying reactions to avoid responding out of anger or impulse
- Deep breaths and quiet time were helpful tools. Reacting negatively typically leads to undesirable outcomes
- Practicing gratitude for the things going well rather than dwelling on what was going wrong
- Cultivating a grateful heart, even in the face of heartbreak, was essential for my personal growth and development
- Creating a peaceful space dedicated to art in my home allowed me to heal

Feeling emotions and experiences is a fundamental aspect of being human. We are designed to feel, think, and evolve. The first step is permitting ourselves to do so. I had to grant myself the freedom to heal and let go of what I couldn't change. I also allowed myself to change and transform into the best version of "Fatimah" I could be.

Adapting to my new way of life was achievable, but self-improvement was essential to facilitate that change. The ultimate goal wasn't just adaptation but finding happiness and fulfillment in my life.

S = SOLUTIONS

The transition from monogamy to polygyny wasn't as straightforward as possible because I tended to focus on problems rather than solutions. Polygyny wasn't the issue; the real challenge was my inability to step out of my way. I was the only one who could free myself from the mental stress I kept creating.

Solution-oriented individuals don't just solve problems, they also address the underlying reasons behind those issues. They challenge the status quo and offer the most rational solutions to handle problems. Problem solvers and peacemakers use various strategies to regain control of challenging situations and consistently maintain a positive mindset.

The process of becoming solution-oriented:

- Practice accountability. Solution-oriented people see solutions, while problem-oriented individuals see obstacles in everything.

- Take action. Identify potential positive outcomes.

- Maintain a positive mindset. Possess the right attitude and demeanor when tackling problems.

- Base decisions on facts, not assumptions. Ensure your actions are grounded in reality.

- Lead with solution-oriented questions. Ask questions that shift your focus from problems to solutions.

- Approach situations positively. Resist negative thinking that may lead to reactivity rather than thoughtful responses.

- Activate your courage. Face problems head-on, as ignoring them makes finding solutions difficult.

Mindful Marriage Motivation Prompts:

1. What are some situations you currently face where being solution-oriented is necessary?
2. Moving forward, what are you willing to practice more to adopt a solution-oriented mindset?
3. What new gratitude routine are you prepared to implement into your daily life?

4. What are three questions you can ask yourself each evening to cultivate positive energy for the next day?

F = FOCUS

The first step in my journey to improvement was to focus on myself. I realized I couldn't help my marriage if I wasn't committed to personal development. Emotional dependency would have kept me in a perpetual state of mental confinement if I hadn't taken steps to better myself. As I began this journey of self-improvement, I noticed a significant positive shift in my happiness and contentment.

Instead of dwelling on bitterness, it's essential to redirect your focus towards personal growth and self-improvement. Here are some ways to shift your focus:

Set personal growth goals: Define specific objectives for self-improvement.

Enhance your communication skills: Become a better communicator within and outside your marriage.

Pursue hobbies and interests: Invest time in activities you genuinely enjoy.

Spend quality time with your children: If you're a parent, prioritize bonding with your children.

Continue your education: Consider taking classes or courses to further your knowledge.

Establish a self-care routine: Schedule self-care appointments, such as spa days, grooming, and medical check-ups.

Nurture your social connections: Maintain connections with friends and family members.

Mindful Marital Motivation Prompts:

1. What can you add to your schedule to redirect your focus towards self-improvement rather than solely on your marriage?

2. What enjoyable activities do you find comfort in during your free time?

3. How can you introduce more moments of fun and enjoyment into your current routine?

O=OPTIMIZE

As my husband's schedule became increasingly busy due to practicing polygyny, I discovered I had more time for personal growth and development. Creating a schedule for myself was straightforward because I understood my routine. I realized I could allocate time for self-care, even if it meant dedicating just one or two days a week.

The need for alone time is normal and essential for recharging amid life's demands. Spending time apart from our spouses can strengthen our relationships by promoting appreciation and providing opportunities to miss each other. Taking breaks during the day is crucial for maintaining healthy relationships. Having time for yourself and reuniting later is refreshing, sharing updates and experiences.

To keep the love alive in your marriage after the initial honeymoon phase, consider incorporating some simple weekly practices:

- **Kindness:** Interact with your spouse compassionately, a key component of staying in love

- **Shared laughter:** Take advantage of good moments and share laughter

- **Support:** Be supportive when your spouse needs it most

- **Personal development:** Establish a routine and share what you've learned

- **Presence:** Be fully present when spending quality time together. Not every moment needs to be filled with conversation. Quiet, independent reading time together can also be enjoyable

- **Avoid touchy subjects:** Resist the urge to discuss sensitive topics that could disrupt the positive energy

- **Surprise date nights:** Plan surprises with your spouse, taking turns to schedule them. Coordinate with your spouse's schedule to ensure you both have free time for these special moments

Mindful Marital Prompts:

1. Where can you create a schedule for spending quality time with your spouse?
2. How would you and your spouse enjoy each other's company during these moments?

R = REDEFINE

Grant yourself the freedom to redefine your life without worrying about the opinions of others. Realize that you will draw attention, and that's perfectly acceptable.

- Establish new guidelines and boundaries as a couple
- Focus on becoming an expert in understanding yourself and fulfilling your own needs
- Lead by example, but refrain from expecting others to do the same. Giving without expecting something in return is a generous act
- In what ways can you set an example to enhance your relationship?

M = MASTERY

Living with purpose and mastering your life through personal development are both essential. Self-determination, or the ability to take charge of your life, is pivotal in shaping the person you aspire to be.

One thing I had been neglecting was my personal growth and development. I wasn't aware of this until I reached a point of disgust. This point of disgust prompted me to engage in self-reflection and open discussions with myself.

I discovered that practicing the following principles was new to me but necessary:

- Be transparent
- Be willing to put in the effort required to become the best version of yourself
- Set achievable goals for yourself
- Celebrate your small victories each day
- Acknowledge both the positive and negative moments in your life

- Don't allow others to steal your joy

- Monitor your progress and maintain a journal to track your journey

- Find a mentor or an accountability partner

- Reflect on your experiences each day

- Understand that making mistakes along the way is inevitable and essential for growth

- How can you incorporate these practices into your daily life to work on becoming the best version of yourself?

Manifesting the change I desired in my relationship was crucial. Still, I recognized that substantial personal work was required to bring my authentic self to the forefront. I decided to seize each day with determination and a sense of purpose. Letting go of my negative ego while amplifying my positive ego made a significant difference. Negative egos often disguise our insecurities. My primary focus needed to be self-improvement. Trying to control my husband's life was not my responsibility, nor did I desire such control over anyone else.

Self-evaluation as a wife was a challenging task I had to undertake. Transforming my attitude proved to be more demanding than I had initially anticipated, mainly because I needed to understand the influence of my ego. I realized that I had placed myself on a self-righteous pedestal without even realizing it. My negative ego clouded my judgment, and I mistakenly believed that if my husband embraced polygyny, he needed to compensate for what I felt I had lost. I was profoundly mistaken.

Even if, for the briefest moment, I thought I could assign blame elsewhere, the truth was that the responsibility ultimately lay with me. The ego is incredibly fragile, and it can easily lead one astray. Overindulging my ego left me feeling exhausted and burnt out. I decided to remove that toxic ego from my life because it was detrimental to my well-being. My bad ego consistently fueled defensiveness and fear in me, pushing me towards a mindset of scarcity and apprehension.

Adopting a beginner's mindset became my greatest asset. I had to start anew, essentially beginning from scratch, with a clean slate. This is not to imply that I was instantly perfect or had everything figured out, as I certainly didn't. How can you transform your ego and adopt a healthier mindset in your life and relationships?

Recognizing that my tendency to isolate myself and avoid communication was a significant issue, I realized that my ego was a major obstacle to my personal growth. Blaming others and harboring negative thoughts about being wronged had not benefited me or my marriage. Through introspection, I discovered that my enormous ego was at the root of many problems.

While I couldn't control all the issues I was facing, I could control my ego. For years, I had been unwilling to bend or change in any way, and this transformation was taking a toll on both myself and my family. I was becoming unrecognizable, even to myself.

Acknowledging that I was representing myself in a negative light motivated me to change. I began educating myself about my destructive habits and worked on dropping my ego. Here are some positive habits that I started incorporating into my daily life to help overcome my ego:

Best practices for taming your ego:

1. **Focus on your positive efforts:** Shift your thinking towards positivity. Stop dwelling on negative thoughts that rob you of your peace and joy. Practicing positive thoughts, words, and actions will help restore happiness.

2. **Manage your intentions and attitude:** Align your positive intentions to stay on track with your personal development goals.

3. **Let go of your pride:** Sometimes, when we feel insecure, we mask it with arrogance. We identify flaws in others before facing our own. Pride can be detrimental and signifies superiority. Aim for dignity by showing composure and self-respect.

4. **Avoid creating a false "grand narrative":** Refrain from crafting a master narrative in your imagination that isn't based on the facts of any given event. Becoming too arrogant or believing in your negative self-image can lead to problems.

5. **Stop protecting your ego:** A know-it-all attitude can be unattractive in a romantic relationship. Be willing to let go of self-absorption and the need for control to nurture humility.

6. **Don't pressure yourself to have all the answers:** Understand that it's okay not to have all the answers in life. Growth occurs when you step out of your comfort zone, so don't hold back.

7. **Eliminate the voice that demands all the answers:** Release the need to know everything and accept uncertainty as a part of life.

8. **Maintain optimism about your responsibilities:** Embrace a positive outlook regarding your obligations and responsibilities.

9. **Accept that you're on a self-improvement journey:** Recognize that personal growth is a process, and it's okay to be a work in progress.

10. **Don't let others rush your growth:** Understand that your self-improvement journey is on your own time, and you shouldn't let others pressure you into rushing it.

By implementing these practices, I could address my ego and work on becoming a better version of myself which, in turn, positively impacted my marriage and personal life.

Fighting Insecurities in Polygyny

Confronting insecurities is a challenging endeavor that demands the courage to face inner issues we may prefer to avoid. This is especially true when entering or actively practicing polygyny. Dealing with your insecurities doesn't have to be overwhelming; you can start small. Dedicate some time without distractions to focus on the areas where you struggle, not just as someone in a marriage but as an individual. It's vital to remember that marriage involves two people who have chosen to be together, not just one.

For instance, if you're struggling with weight-related issues, focus on finding the best weight-loss plan that suits your overall health and well-being. Let go of past judgments about yourself, whether from someone you love or another source.

In my marriage, I often felt judged by my grandmother. Her critical gaze seemed to anticipate my marriage's failure, perhaps because hers hadn't worked out. I carried this insecurity with me for many years, feeling like she was waiting to say, "See, marriage never works."

I understood that my grandmother's disapproval was rooted in her disagreement with Islam and my decision to marry at a young age. Unfortunately, she made her disapproval evident through snarky remarks and a pessimistic outlook. I knew she meant well, as she didn't want me to experience the same struggles she had as a young married woman.

I got married at 20, fully committed to my husband and child. To my grandparents, I was too young to make such commitments. However, as a Muslim, I felt the timing was spiritually, logically, emotionally, socially, and morally correct. Over the years, everyone's opinions remained unchanged.

I continued practicing Islam, and my grandmother judged me for it. It wasn't until I entered into polygyny that she softened her judgments. As time passed, my insecurities became more apparent. Increasingly self-aware, I developed the ability to recognize and address these insecurities. I was willing to stop myself each time I noticed I was peeling away the layers of my self-esteem.

- A relative or an authority figure criticizing you may have shaped your insecurities.

- Avoid making comparisons; resist comparing yourself to anyone else, including your co-wife. Such comparisons can be emotionally damaging.

- Embrace and celebrate what makes you unique; remember that there is no one else on this planet like you, and that's beautiful.

- Be vigilant about negative self-talk. The conversations we have with ourselves can profoundly impact how we perceive and value ourselves.

To confront my insecurities, I needed to acknowledge them and develop a strategy to avoid self-deprecation. I was determined not to let insecurities defeat me any longer. I consciously moved forward and spoke positively about myself and my aspirations. Every day, I actively celebrated my unique and beautiful attributes.

Positive self-talk became an essential part of my daily life. I was committed to feeling better and putting in the effort to be my best self. Falling in love with our spouses is often easier than falling in love with ourselves. My goal was to wholeheartedly value and love "Fatimah" without hesitation or reservation. This life is mine, and I had only one chance to live it to the best of my ability.

Developing Self-Trust

I remember hearing the story of actor and comedian Jim Carrey from his appearance on *The Oprah Winfrey Show* many years ago. He shared a remarkable tale of believing in his abilities. Carrey recounted when he wrote a $10 million check to himself for acting services, setting a goal to earn it within 3-5 years before Thanksgiving Day of 1995.

Lo and behold, before Thanksgiving of 1995, Carrey had earned $10 million for his role in the movie "Dumb and Dumber." Carrey didn't know precisely how to achieve this, but he had to trust *himself* to believe he could make it happen. I began to reflect on my personal goals and the vision I had conjured for myself. As an ENFP, I had always been a dreamer, but this time felt different. I knew I had much to learn to become the best version of myself. Trusting myself entirely was a skill I had not yet mastered, but my journey was about to commence.

Identifying that I didn't trust myself entirely was the first step. Inner trust issues weren't as apparent as I had expected, but I gained clarity on the signs I had missed earlier as I educated myself.

Signs that you don't trust yourself:

- Constantly questioning your judgment
- Doubting your talents or abilities
- Being overly critical of yourself for making mistakes
- Not fully utilizing your potential
- Forgetting your most significant achievements
- Struggling with feelings of inadequacy or a sense of not accomplishing enough
- Feeling incapable of escaping your problems or issues
- Believing you are unable to solve your problems

I was intimately familiar with this lack of self-trust list. Understanding that I was my harshest critic helped me to pinpoint where to begin my work. My past didn't require my trust, but my future demanded my full attention. Personal development saved me considerable time, but I still had to put in the effort.

We often demand trust from others but rarely question whether we can place confidence in ourselves. I wanted to trust everyone, yet I had not allowed myself the same valuable attribute. Transitioning from monogamy to polygyny introduced new challenges and self-doubts. I had to trust the process if I wanted what was best for me, my marriage, and my family. Rushing personal growth and mental wellness would only lead to setbacks and ripple effects.

I read books, watched videos, and invested in personal development programs.

Through these efforts, I gained insight into the signs of trusting oneself and others:

- I recognize, understand, and believe in my values and worth
- I reject all negative and self-rejecting messages I received in childhood, replacing them with a positive self-narrative
- I am confident in my ability to tackle challenging tasks

- I acknowledge my inner voice and express my wants and needs when necessary
- Self-sabotage has no place in my life
- I refrain from engaging in negative self-talk
- I confront difficult conversations and speak my truth
- I challenge myself by acquiring new skills and am committed to remaining open to learning and coaching
- I practice self-love and self-respect consistently
- I celebrate all my successes, regardless of their size

To develop a trusting relationship with oneself:

- Reflect on past self-perceived flaws and work on overcoming them
- Consistently practice self-trust by reinforcing positive self-narratives and challenging self-doubt

"A man cannot be comfortable without his approval." *Mark Twain*

Chapter 19

Growth Through Vulnerability

Growing up in my grandparents' household, I experienced financial security but lacked emotional security. The toxic nature of my grandparents' relationship led me to perceive vulnerability as a weakness rather than a strength. Their communication, body language, verbal abuse, and suppression of their emotions all reinforced this perception. Witnessing their conflicts, I feared the possibility of their divorce, as any emotion other than dislike, anger, rage, spite, or hatred seemed powerless in their marriage.

While I cannot say whether they fully comprehended the impact of their actions, for us, as their children, it was devastating. I internalized this learned behavior and applied it to my life and marriage. My grandparents divorced in 1989, just as I entered high school and met my future husband. As my grandparents transitioned from a toxic married couple to divorced parents, they became great friends and co-parents to their mentally disabled sons.

My grandfather visited us daily, including weekends, and evenings were enjoyable as he and my grandmother shared dinner and engaged in hours of conversation as close friends. Occasionally, they shed tears while reminiscing about "the good old days." Witnessing them cautiously reveal their vulnerability and fragility to each other, I wished they had been kinder and gentler with their feelings.

While I never aspired to have a marriage like theirs, due to its lack of success, little did I know that a challenge lay just five years in my future that would reshape my life significantly.

My challenge was my difficulty with communication, which left me feeling incredibly vulnerable. It wasn't until I faced the transition from monogamy to polygyny that I began to grasp the idea of vulnerability as a source of strength.

In my pursuit of understanding, I discovered more power within me than I had initially realized. Despite my insecurities, past hurts, traumas, and unresolved parental issues that had emotionally handicapped me, vulnerability unintentionally became my ally. It facilitated my journey toward honesty and self-discovery.

Identifying Vulnerability as a Strength

Discovering my inner courage was a liberating and invaluable experience. The world I had confined myself to **was** filled with limiting actions, thoughts, words, and experiences. I was merely existing within the beautiful cage I called home, with family and friends witnessing my lifeless existence. I withdrew completely from my trusted social circle of friends, effectively deactivating my social life.

Early in polygyny, I disregarded my nutritional needs, making eating a daily struggle. Conversations revolving around my health and weight became the constant soundtrack of my life, whispered among my family and friends. My rapid physical deterioration alarmed my loved ones, and questions of illness loomed, making it a scary period. The self-inflicted turmoil took a toll that my loved ones found unbearable.

Looking in the mirror, I no longer recognized the person staring back at me. While I could regain lost weight, I needed to rediscover my inner strength and courage. I knew precisely where my voice had gone; I had silenced myself mentally and physically. This self-imposed negativity cost me precious time that could have been spent connecting, empowering myself, finding inner peace, and embracing happiness.

However, I eventually permitted myself to reclaim my voice.

Reclaiming your voice involves several steps:

- **Step 1: Reclaim your role in your life.** Ask yourself who you are and who you aspire to become. Reflect on how you show up in your day. Did you start your day with purpose, or did you put meaningful discussions and topics on the back burner? If the answer is the latter, ask more detailed and planned questions.

- **Step 2: Pay attention to your body's language.** Observe your facial expressions, hand gestures, and posture. Is your body language negative or positive?

- **Step 3: Fearlessly speak your truth and practice transparency.** Understand that your story matters. Honesty may not always be straightforward, but being open to the truth is essential. Trust is built when we allow ourselves to share our stories and experiences without fear.

- **Step 4: Set communication boundaries.** Refrain from engaging with people who try to silence your voice. Surround yourself with positive individuals who create a circle of safety. Negative people find problems in every solution, while positive people find solutions for every situation.

- **Step 5: Avoid criticizing your thoughts.** Allow yourself to feel emotions without becoming consumed by them. While not every moment in life will be happy, being proactive in addressing the areas that need improvement is crucial.

- **Step 6: Process information before communicating your experiences.** Remember that we speak to ourselves when we think about topics or issues. Self-talk is essential because it allows us to gather all the necessary facts and information to respond to others.

- **Step 7: Recognize when you feel knowledgeable enough to discuss your chosen topics.** Fostering self-expression is a skill that develops with age—learning how to gather information and understand your feelings about various concerns or challenges for effective problem-solving.

Courage - *The ability to confront and overcome fear.*

It requires courage to embrace "vulnerability" because it means uniting vulnerability with honesty.

"Vulnerability is terrifying, and summoning the courage to reveal your heart is one of life's most daunting yet rewarding experiences. It will set you free."
The Better Man Project

Reflecting on my upbringing and the conditioning I underwent, I realize the profound value of a healthy relationship. This insight wasn't acquired in isolation. Embracing the mindset required for success in my marriage was undeniably frightening but crucial.

Courage, honesty, and transparency were daunting because they demanded change. Confronting my insecurities and uncertain future was something I initially resisted.

During this self-reflection, I posed some fundamental yet powerful questions:

- Do I criticize people who have been in a car accident and are in the process of healing? No, I don't.
- Do I judge women who give birth and require healing time, or do I respect their healing journey? Would I rush them to heal? No, I would never speed up their healing process.

So, I asked myself, "Why would I rush my healing?" Embracing vulnerability allowed me to heal through transparency. Vulnerability became the missing piece for inner peace. I stopped shaming myself for being vulnerable and going through the healing process.

Never Shame Yourself or Others for Healing; it's a Natural Part of Life

Why is it important not to shame yourself or others?

- Shame can foster toxic emotional and psychological relationships.
- Guilt, when combined with exposure, leads to anxiety and overanalysis.

"Overanalysis leads to emotional paralysis." *Unknown*

Shaming another human being can drive a wedge in the relationship. If you want someone to open up to you, they may hesitate if they feel judged.

While healthy relationships are a gift, areas of fragility must be observed and respected.

Connecting with genuine vulnerability in your relationship is vital to its health. How can we connect if we shame others for their experiences and truth? We can't. Stress will be placed on your relationship, rendering you powerless if your goal is to "fix" it.

Be honest about how you feel and share your truth.

Vulnerability is strength, and it will help you become the best version of yourself! It builds a powerful bridge between courage and healing. Resilience and vulnerability go hand in hand.

Chapter 20

MEETING YOUR CHAMPION

YOU HAVE THE POWER WITHIN TO BECOME THE MOST INSPIRATIONAL version of yourself. I was unable and ill-equipped to see that my champion self lay within. I was missing the self-awareness and self-confidence to unearth that part of me. You are aligning yourself with your best self by showing your vulnerable side!

- When you open up and allow yourself to be vulnerable, you position yourself in a place of power
- Self-examination begins as you grade yourself on how you express vulnerability
- Slow down your thoughts when they race and create doubt in your mind
- Connecting with your hardships and struggles equips you with self-awareness to face your challenges. Connecting breaks down relationship barriers and fosters closeness.

To recognize the champion within me, I had to study the lives of others and understand that just because my husband married again, didn't mean my inner champion had to die. For example, consider the journeys of some of the most influential people in personal development. They all have stories of struggle and vulnerability. Tony Robbins, Iyanla Vanzant, Brendon Burchard, and Lisa Nichols — some of the most successful individuals in the world who specialize in the art of healing and finding strength — have stories of struggle woven into their paths to success.

One of the first books I purchased when I embarked on my healing journey was by Iyanla Vanzant, titled "Peace from Broken Pieces." I have vivid memories of feeling apprehensive about her writings because I was aware of some of her stories, and her books confront issues directly.

In this book, she shares personal stories about the death of her daughter Gemmia, her toxic relationship with her ex-husband, and how she fought back to rebuild herself from her brokenness. I was immediately inspired by her story and her effort to heal from her trauma.

After reading Iyanla's book, among others, I told myself, "Fatimah, allow yourself to begin your healing process; your healing is just waiting for you! The only person in control of my healing was me. I was the one delaying my recovery, but I was also the one who could initiate the process. If my husband had the power to heal me, he would have fixed my broken heart. The beautiful lesson from that is knowing how amazing it is to heal myself. And that feeling is priceless!

Think about a weight loss journey, for example. Have you ever expected someone else to lose weight on your behalf? Of course not. Personal trainers can be hired to guide us in our journey, but the blood, sweat, and tears must come from our efforts!

"Personal development is defined as activities that improve awareness and identity, develop talents and potential, build human capital and facilitate employability, enhance the quality of life, and realize dreams and aspirations. Personal development can take place throughout someone's entire life." *Wikipedia.*

Coming to terms with the fact that I don't have all the answers helped me immensely on my journey. Understanding that I was proactive in creating a personal development plan relieved the pressures I had placed on myself as a self-proclaimed perfectionist. Perfectionism no longer served me; it was detrimental to my relationship. Coming from a family that unleashed untreated past traumas on one another, I had undoubtedly experienced what I feared.

When perfectionism inevitably fails, humility often follows. It's normal to desire more than what is given to us, but trying to avoid challenges altogether is unrealistic. Human beings must be tested by hardship, as it is through these trials that our character is built.

One of the significant ways I encountered humility was through the rejection I felt when I could not foster a relationship with my mother. The next major blow was my grandfather's death two weeks after I was married to my young husband. The emotional paralysis I experienced from his death was unparalleled. My grandfather's passing taught me a valuable lesson about mortality and gratitude.

Character building can be closely associated with incredible tragedy. Had I not experienced that heartbreaking loss, I would not have been prepared for the death of my baby sister, Brittany, at the tender age of thirteen. She battled childhood brain cancer for four years.

Feeling as though my grandfather's death was as bad as it could get, I unknowingly drew strength from it. Just seven short years later, I would be faced with more heartbreak. Those two significant losses shaped me and offered their lessons if I was willing to see them. Polygyny entering my life after 15 years of marriage introduced its own brand of humility.

Marriage was not as I had initially planned for me or my husband. However, polygyny served as a critical piece of my journey to becoming the best version of myself I could be. In my wildest imagination, I would have never envisioned my growth and character development taking this particular path. But after losing two of the most valuable people in my life, I now understand why polygyny played such an instrumental role.

Death was something I could explain from an Islamic belief system. People comprehend death more quickly because it makes sense to most people. Monogamy was a topic that I could neither understand nor celebrate because my parents decided never to get married.

Most people in Western society were conditioned to be accepting of monogamy only, including me, however, polygyny was a taboo topic of conversation. It has always been looked down upon or hated by many women I know. Death makes sense to many because it is out of our control and society is accepting of people dying. Unfortunately, polygyny doesn't have the same impact as death, so the subject is either met with hatred or ignored completely.

Monogamy is a social norm, so there is no need for explanations, whys, excuses, or defenses. Polygyny, on the other hand, has been wholly eviscerated regarding it being considered moral, or even acceptable. The societal conditioning that has taken place is unsettling. Naturally, I was one of those people who didn't understand plural marriage.

My goal was never to be in a relationship where my husband practiced polygyny. I feared that particular form of marriage because I had the fear of losing what I had fought so hard to build.

The foundation upon which our family was built was much different than that of our parents before us.

Intellectually speaking, my marriage meant much more than I initially realized. Early in polygyny, I could not see how much negative people affected my mindset. It wasn't until I studied communication, both verbal and nonverbal, that I could comprehend ostracism and the emotions surrounding it.

Some of the most common signs of being ostracized are:
- The sensation of feeling alone
- Not being accepted
- Extreme social anxiety
- Loss of appetite
- Depression
- Self-hatred
- Suicidal thoughts, in some cases
- Increased blood pressure
- Exclusion from social events/gatherings

Ostracism hurts so profoundly because our innate human desire is to be accepted, belong, and maintain a sense of self-worth. Ostracism can shatter our self-esteem and ability to be acknowledged positively, which dehumanizes us. Many people who do not practice polygyny cannot fully comprehend the pain of having their marriage diminished because of another person's involvement.

Women in a polygynous marriage may feel some of the same pressures. Our daughters have experienced negative interactions associated with polygyny. As teenagers, they were asked inappropriate questions about the status of their parents' relationship. People often inquired about whether their father and I were divorced or if we would get divorced.

These questions were typically posed when their father and I were absent, but the damage they caused was immeasurable. One of our daughters' many beautiful attributes is inner strength and a fearless nature. They were ready to defend their family but should not have had to contemplate doing so. Our children have discovered their champion within themselves just as much as their parents have. Personal development is undoubtedly beautiful, but the ability to unite and do what is right feels equally triumphant.

This doesn't mean everything is magically resolved in one moment or a day. Our family had a long way to go, but being on the same page and moving forward together helped tremendously.

Coping with ostracism involves several strategies that aided me in my healing, such as:

- Reconnecting with yourself; not letting others define your identity.
- Speaking your truth, not the distorted narratives of harmful or toxic people.
- Self-soothing and regulating your emotions.
- Reevaluating your social support circle.
- Creating a healthy perspective on what has happened.
- Allowing yourself to feel or grieve relationships that are no longer serving you.

"Give the gift of your absence to those who don't appreciate your presence."
Unknown

To find your inner champion, sometimes you have to let go of people who claim to want you to succeed but wish for the opposite. Throughout my years in a family that practices polygyny, I have personally lost people I considered friends. That's okay because I ultimately discovered that they were not true friends.

The individuals who genuinely love me and my family have remained a significant part of my life. They have consistently supported us through all the ups and downs, witnessing me at my worst and lowest points. Throughout it all, they have proven themselves to be my trusted circle. I am forever grateful to these women whom I consider sisters.

Chapter 21

REBUILDING TRUST IN YOUR HUSBAND AFTER HE MARRIES ANOTHER WIFE

DURING THE EARLY STAGES OF MY FIRST YEAR IN POLYGYNY, I WAS profoundly shaken by the news of my husband marrying a second wife. It was mentally devastating. I use strong language to describe my feelings because I want to express my truth. One of the main factors that deeply affected me was the assumption that, if he were to marry again, we would be prepared as a family. However, he chose not to share many things with me, especially his desire to get married again. He stated that he was not actively seeking another marriage, and I wholeheartedly believed him. If he were, he would have told me.

When I discovered that he was married again, I instantly lost trust in him. My philosophy was that if a man couldn't stand in his truth, he could not be trusted. It seemed that simple to me. His lack of transparency made me question everything he said and did afterward. Trust held a very high position in my hierarchy of values, which remains crucial to me today. Growing up with a father in whom I couldn't place all my faith was traumatic enough. Now, I had to navigate around a man I loved and with whom I had created a beautiful nuclear family as if I had never known him. Countless conversations turned into disagreements and misunderstandings because we both felt misunderstood and mentally wounded.

Like any previous challenges I survived, I knew in the recesses of my mind that this would pass. My issue was that I needed more tools to create the fulfilling marriage I enjoyed. Prayers and personal development ultimately saved my marriage, along with dedication and hard work. Trust is given away slowly and is not so fragile that it cannot be regained.

Placing your trust back into the hands of the person who violated it to begin with is not easy, but it can be a blessing in the end.

Firstly, I had to ask myself several intense questions:

Am I capable of forgiveness? What are the chances that this will happen again? What am I giving up if I leave my marriage? Do we have a future together? Is he apologetic for the part he played? Is this his typical pattern of behavior? Is he trying to punish me?

My concern with asking myself all these questions was the answers I would offer myself. If I asked frightening questions, would I be transparent enough to answer them honestly without bias? For a very long while, I could not see past the influence of my inflated ego. Before anyone else could victimize me, I tormented myself in some of the worst ways. How do you know you are under the influence of your ego?

Here are some warning signs:

- Desire to constantly be "right."
- Demonstrated "solo thought."
- Continually participating in one-sided conversations
- Redirecting attention back to my hurt feelings
- Wanting attention but no connection
- Longing for my husband to "fix" everything because I believed he ruined everything

I came to understand that my ego was not serving my marriage or my family. How could I wish my husband would fix anything when I wasn't willing to work on my attitude? I couldn't demand anything when destroying the fabric of what I used to celebrate about myself. The very personality he thought attractive enough to marry and build a family with was buried under my ego.

I began dismantling my bad ego and vowed never to be that person again. That personality was useless to me, my husband, and my children. One of the most violent instances I regretfully remember was how my ego demolished my husband's character in front of my children. Even if I said nothing, my negative energy was incredibly intense. They knew I was extremely emotionally upset. When I dislike someone or disagree with an action, it's written all over my face.

Instant emotional gratification is unrealistic and is never a starting point to begin trusting again.

Several steps must take place to clear the way for rebuilding trust in your spouse:

1. **Processing Emotions:** Sometimes, we become disconnected from our own emotions, which is not the natural way human beings operate. Identifying the fact that we must feel and have feelings is vital. The first step is acknowledging when we feel emotional or are experiencing emotional difficulty. Processing emotions is paramount to your healing, as this teaches us many lessons on finding understanding, especially in relationships. This process takes time and is crucial for personal growth.

2. **Managing Emotional Triggers Effectively:** Many times, what we are feeling isn't always a knee-jerk response or trigger. We may experience more subtle reactions, such as discomfort and awkwardness. However, you must learn to control these emotions effectively if you find yourself battling intense feelings like rage, hatred, revenge, disgust, anger, or extreme irritability.

    *   Trace the origin of what upset you and why
    *   Reduce or disarm your anger by calming your breathing patterns
    *   Analyze the issues and how they affected you in the moment
    *   Avoid negative conversations or negative people
    *   Contribute or volunteer your time to others. Helping others can foster a sense of connection and accomplishment
    *   Don't push yourself to be "perfect"; there is no such thing as perfect

1. **Choose to Forgive Your Spouse:** Forgiveness occurs when you consciously decide to do so. If you genuinely want to forgive your husband and if he is a good man who deserves forgiveness, then it is healthy to forgive him.

"Forgiveness is not always easy. At times, it feels more painful than the wound we suffered to forgive the one who inflicted it. And yet, there is no peace without forgiveness." Worldtrendblog.com

By following these steps and allowing time for healing and rebuilding trust, it is possible to mend a **relationship** after emotional hurt or betrayal.

- Understand that his position is not easy, even though he decided to marry again. Putting yourself in someone else's shoes can be a game-changer. When we activate empathy, we can see their experience from a different point of view. Then, we can comprehend that they are trying to manage their trauma.

- Commit to working with him on how you can both strengthen the relationship. If each person commits to personal development work, the marriage will become stronger.

- Allow him to come to you and communicate openly so he isn't guarded when he wants to express himself.

- Do not become a "solo thinker" or a person not interested in being a "team player" with their partner. Consider your spouse in your life goals, hopes, and dreams.

- Acknowledge your desire for a flourishing relationship. The success of relationships is significant because we are actively choosing someone who should possess the qualities and abilities to help us build a strong future together. When couples desire a healthy relationship that doesn't work, the damage affects the couple and their family's future.

- Face and overcome your fears. When faced with change or times of challenge, our natural inclination is to feel fear and anxiety. These feelings are often centralized by inadequacy, vulnerability, and uncertainty.

- There are some practical ways to handle these feelings:

- Maintain a positive mindset. Express healthy thoughts and patterns, not negative ones.

- Practice positive communication. When expressing yourself, use firm but positive phrases, such as, "I am concerned, but willing to work together," instead of negative terms like, "This is never going to work because of you."

- Engage in corrective observation. Develop the ability to observe, reflect, and correct miscommunication, lies, assumptions, or behaviors that are not helping the growth of your relationship.

- Continue loving your spouse even if you don't like them.

An example of how we may love someone profoundly but not like them reminds me of times when I interacted with my father. I loved my grandfather and his son (my father). They were the first men I ever loved in my life. I have vivid memories of how we enjoyed time together.

However, they were both functioning alcoholics and didn't practice self-love. In terms of personality, they had some similarities but were different in many other areas. The most potent similarity was that I disliked them both very much when they drank or became inebriated. As an adolescent, I was so confused as to why I felt a strong love for both of them and, at the same time, disliked who they were as drinkers.

Reevaluating the situations and past traumas, I gained abundant knowledge about the psychology of addicts. I especially learned about the people who love and support them. The possibility that I could love them as my father figures made sense. You can love someone and not like what is happening around them. Disagreeing with the actions of our loved ones does not negate the fact that they are still loved.

I began to understand that I did not have to agree that my husband's decision to practice polygyny was okay. I didn't have to agree with his decision. However, I had to understand that just because he committed to another marriage did not mean that love had abandoned our marriage. When we exercise love towards our spouses and that love is reciprocated, we can attach a feeling of entitlement to that love.

Most importantly, we must remember that we can love people and be unhappy with them simultaneously. Love cannot simply be drained from our hearts in one moment. Of course, we can experience trauma, sadness, depression, and other negative emotions, but that doesn't mean we can't recover.

Chapter 22

THE OVERNIGHT NARCISSIST

NARCISSISTS, AS DEFINED, OFTEN POSSESS AN INFLATED SENSE OF THEIR own importance. They crave excessive attention and seek admiration from others, sometimes to the detriment of understanding and caring about the feelings of those around them. This section, titled "The Overnight Narcissist," delves into a belief I've encountered that when husbands, including mine, decide to practice polygyny, they transform into what might be perceived as overnight narcissists.

This transformation is characterized by heightened selfishness, a sense of entitlement, and a shift in their mental health or personality due to their desire to engage in an ancient form of marriage.

Individuals with narcissistic tendencies exhibit various characteristics. They tend to resist agreement with others, often refusing to see another person's perspective, and they strongly desire to be in the right. These traits are accompanied by a propensity to impose punishment and create emotional distance between themselves and those who genuinely care about them.

They often display red flags openly and may engage in love-bombing tactics. One hallmark of narcissists is their constant craving for admiration. They harbor jealousy towards those who achieve more than they ever will. These are just a few of the toxic traits commonly associated with classic narcissism.

Many labeled my husband a narcissist, with the prevailing opinion being, "Coach Fatimah, he only considered himself when he married again; he didn't think about you and your children."

In response, I acknowledged that, while his approach to practicing polygyny may not align with everyone's beliefs, I could attest to his profound love for my family and me. His actions spoke for themselves.

It's easy to believe our husbands no longer love us because they've found new love interests. However, does this mean that our love has become outdated or diminished in any way? Does it render him selfish, or is he merely a man who sought to expand his family for honorable reasons, to help others, or to have more children—desires I may not have shared? Many may argue that he took it upon himself to welcome another wife into his life, to grow his family, and to assume a more significant leadership role.

When caring for multiple individuals, whether they be children, wives, parents, or siblings, we understand that each relationship is unique. I have always been aware of my husband's love for me and continue to feel it intensely. I am loved, valued, and an integral part of the family we've built together. I bore his first child and provided unwavering support when he felt judged by the world, and together, we have put in the effort to nurture our relationship.

Interestingly, many of those who labeled my husband or me as narcissists didn't hold a favorable opinion of us to begin with. Therefore, their judgments and opinions hold no significance in our lives and never will. The positives have consistently outweighed the challenges in our marriage.

Regardless of how unwell I became or how joyful I felt, my husband has always been there, cheering on my recovery and lending a helping hand when it was needed.

He has consistently supported my growth, offering encouragement and enlightenment. He played the role of my coach long before becoming one for anyone else, which holds immense significance to me.

It's a fallacy to believe that the practice of polygyny leads to a husband's overnight transformation into a narcissist. Narcissistic traits and behaviors typically exist within a person irrespective of their actions.

My husband did not undergo such a transformation; he has never been a narcissist. I've extensively delved into the subject of narcissism, studying narcissistic traits and behaviors and narcissistic personality disorder. I've listened to the stories of women who have survived true narcissism and narcissistic abuse. Having heard their challenges and victories, I understand what that entails.

I've approached this with humility, recognizing the distinction between a man who desires to expand his family while continuing to support and lead it, and a true narcissist. A husband contributes to his family meaningfully, celebrating their victories individually and collectively.

The notion of an "overnight narcissist" can be a negative thought that creeps into the minds of wives in polygyny when they are going through difficult times. I've coached women from diverse backgrounds, and many have expressed concerns like, "My husband doesn't love me. There's no way he can." In response, I often ask them if their husbands have explicitly said, "I don't love you." The answer is invariably "no," because it is not valid. These doubts stem from social conditioning, which unfairly portrays men as inherently evil for wanting to practice polygyny.

It's crucial to remember that narcissists typically don't love anyone, not even themselves. They view others merely as sources of supply, projects, or conquests to control and eventually discard. These attributes have never applied to my husband. His character and actions have always been different. Let me share a story to illustrate this point.

Early on, I recounted my healing journey, and the pain I had endured in my polygynous marriage, to a friend who had survived a narcissistic husband. I believed that we had both experienced similar pain. We had both been deeply hurt by our husbands. However, my friend pointed out something crucial.

She said, "Fatimah, while our stories may seem similar, our experiences of pain differ. My ex-husband actively tried to destroy me, but yours never had that intention. Yours didn't mean to hurt you; it wasn't his aim." This conversation made me realize I needed to be mindful of how I spoke to myself and others about my marriage.

I had unintentionally grouped my husband with those who had deliberately caused harm, simply because I felt pain. But the key distinction lies in how we experience that pain and the true intentions of the ones we love.

Throughout our journey, my husband has consistently displayed an admirable track record. There was no reason for him to transform into an "overnight narcissist" because society or relatives labeled him due to his decision to marry again. It's fascinating and revealing to observe how people communicate within their marriages.

I distinctly remember when someone commented, "Your husband, he was doing just fine until now." They questioned what had changed in him. In response, I focused on his overall track record, consistency, and success, rather than dwelling on a period when communication could have been more effective.

I began to shift the questions I asked myself. Instead of wondering how we would get through this, I asked, "What if we succeed? What if this works out?" After all, my husband had demonstrated consistency and determination up to this point. Why would he suddenly stop now because society expected him to fail? Did I need to subscribe to the same belief? Absolutely not. Society had always predicted my husband's failure based on his past, but they didn't truly know him.

This realization brought a smile to my face. They didn't know him as well as I did. They failed to recognize that he would see this through because of the man he had always been and the man he aspired to continue being—someone who constantly sought growth and depth in his actions and decisions.

People must understand that there's no such thing as an overnight narcissist. True narcissism is rooted in a history of intentional destruction of one's own family, spouse, and children. It's an honorable endeavor when our husbands express a willingness to practice polygyny and commit to the hard work required without any intent to harm.

They are willing to work collaboratively with their wives and children, show up, learn, make mistakes, and course correct. There's beauty in a man who commits to this journey and emerges positively from challenging times, while continuing to contribute to his family's ability to thrive.

A good man consistently strives to love, honor, respect, communicate, lead, and understand. He strives daily to become the best husband and father he can be. Society may attempt to pass judgment on a lifestyle like polygyny, especially when pursued within a family filled with love and shared intentions.

However, societal opinions hold no weight within our marriages, families, or relationships. We should embrace growth and recognize that our journey toward success begins within ourselves.

Working alongside our husbands is invaluable when they are willing to do the work. If he is a good man, he will readily embrace the task of making your marriage successful.

Wanting My Husband to Win In Polygyny

I pondered a question: What defined the nature of my relationship with my husband before he decided to explore polygyny? I reflected on it, recognizing that it was characterized by hope, resilience, trust, and kind treatment. While every married couple faces their share of disagreements and challenging days, I always knew that he was someone who would stand by me and protect me.

However, when he chose to venture into polygyny and seek another marriage partner, I couldn't help but wonder if those foundational qualities had vanished. The answer, upon deeper introspection, was a resounding "no."

Trust had become somewhat fragile, but I firmly believed it could be rebuilt. However, I needed to adopt a "me-we mentality" and ask myself a crucial question: *Did I want my husband to succeed?* The answer was an unwavering "yes." I had always rooted for his success because his triumphs meant victories for us all, myself included, regardless of whether that also meant success for my co-wife.

Initially, I entertained the thought that he needed to experience some of the emotions I had been going through. However, was that truly realistic? He wasn't living his life as a woman in a polygynous relationship. He wasn't living life as a woman, period. How could he fully comprehend my experience? The truth was, he couldn't. He could only empathize as a man witnessing the experiences of his wife or wives. And he was committed to doing just that. He was determined to put in the necessary effort for our collective success. While all men and women are unique, I had faith in the man I married, knowing he possessed the ability and determination to make our family thrive. He understood the bigger picture and the significance of our family succeeding together rather than apart. I, too, needed to share that vision.

I asked myself several questions: *Do you want him to struggle? Do you want him to fail? Do you want yourself to struggle? Do you want to fail? Do you want his other marriage or marriages to fail? Do you want your children to fail?* And I kept coming up with the same answer. I said "no" to wanting his marriage to fail because I did not want mine to fail. I unequivocally rejected this feeling because it reflected a sentiment I could not embrace. Holding such a desire went against my principles for myself and others. It was not my place to harbor ill will toward another marriage, even if it meant we shared the same husband.

There was so much I needed to unlearn about wanting my husband to win. So what did I do? How did I overcome my inner feelings of defeat? Again, I had to change the narrative. I had to change the questions. That meant I had to ask myself, what would winning look like in my marriage? It looked like it always did. Healthy communication, positive reinforcement from both partners, the truth, and being able to sit down and talk to one another. It meant allowing myself to be vulnerable in my own way as a woman and affording him the same space to be vulnerable in his unique manner as a man.

While I readily expressed my emotions and didn't hesitate to cry in his presence (a privilege granted to only a select few), I understood that not everyone shared the same emotional intensity. I needed to appreciate his distinctive emotional expression, even if it differed from mine.

Chapter 23

POLYGYNY WIVES: MYTHS VS. REALITY

MONOGAMY IS A FORM OF MARRIAGE, AND POLYGYNY IS ANOTHER FORM of marriage. Of course, monogamy does not share the negative stigma society attaches to polygyny. In its infancy, my marriage never required explanation outside of giving reasons for getting married at such a young age. However, staying with a man who practices polygyny was another matter altogether. After much self-study and active research on polygyny, I uncovered what I had ignored for so long. Because polygyny is not widely researched or taught as a societal norm (or solution), it has been knowingly demonized and buried within many social constructs.

What is the difference between a myth and reality? A myth is a widely held but false belief or idea. On the other hand, reality is the world or the state of things as they actually exist, as opposed to an idealistic or notional idea of them. Making this salient distinction between these words is a must. Breaking down barriers through the use of proper terminology is essential. Words must be understood, and their definitions offer clarification on topics such as polygyny. It is easy to confuse myths and reality, especially when a specific practice is considered taboo, unheard of, or outdated.

Myth number one is that polygyny oppresses women. In reality, polygyny protects women's honor by eliminating mistresses, girlfriends, or side relationships. Another myth is that polygyny is an outdated practice that is irrelevant today. In reality, polygyny has been very successful in contemporary times.

The misconception that the second wife is simply a girlfriend is untrue. When such statements are made, one must consider the historical context and why polygyny continues to be practiced.

Another myth suggests that a man marrying another wife can fix or mend one marriage. In reality, this oversimplifies the complexities of marital issues.

It's also a myth that men only marry other women due to a medical deficiency or illness. Wanting to marry more than one wife is not abnormal for men; it's a personal choice.

Polygyny is not limited to only two wives. In some cultures, like Islam, men may have up to four wives.

Another misconception is that polygyny is only a social solution when the initial wife is sick, dying, unable to bear children, has low self-esteem, or is homeless, widowed, divorced, or desperate. In reality, polygyny can be practiced for various reasons.

A co-wife does not exist to take anything from another wife or wives; she simply wants to expand her family.

The stereotype that women who practice polygyny possess low self-esteem, hate themselves, are weak, uneducated, or home wreckers is unfounded and inaccurate.

Some argue, "Well, she's not his legal wife," but legality may vary depending on the jurisdiction. What's essential is understanding the distinction between lawful and legal marriages and subsequent wives can be considered lawful.

Realities of Polygyny

Sharing time but not solely focusing on your husband is crucial for your mental health and overall well-being. Concentrating on your personal life goals and devising plans to achieve them is not an act of arrogance, selfishness, or self-centeredness; it's a continuous journey of self-improvement.

Maintaining consistency in our best practices and personal development is essential. Neglecting personal growth may lead to an unhealthy cycle of becoming overly preoccupied with your husband. Transitioning into polygyny was far from easy for me, and I vividly remember the relentless thoughts about my husband's whereabouts and activities that plagued my days.

I struggled so profoundly with the unknown that I lost sight of my life. Missed appointments, canceled outings with friends, and a disconnect from the things I once loved became the norm. As an artist, my yearning to create art grew, but I allowed myself to become detached from my natural talents.

Rediscovering my talents and aspirations became possible when I started to revisit what I had lost. With the guidance of my mentors and extensive self-study, I uncovered various steps I could take to regain my sense of self.

Navigating the Realities of Polygyny:

- **Prioritize Self-Improvement**: Take a closer look at your goals and be open to revising or redirecting them to align with your evolving life.

- **Embrace the Inevitability of Life**: Remember that life is inherently unpredictable, and everyone, including your husband, must navigate their journey. Our lives are individual, not owned by others, and we have no control over another person's fate.

- **Love Yourself First**: Prioritize self-love over placing your spouse at the center of your affections. Loving yourself first fosters a healthier relationship, whereas putting your spouse before you can lead to codependency.

- **Recognize Your Intrinsic Value**: Understand that you are a complete person on a personal improvement journey. Self-acceptance is paramount, especially when facing challenges in your relationships.

- **Confront Fear with Purpose**: Fear often arises in the face of uncertainty or intimidation. Managing your response to fear is essential. By avoiding excuses, identifying the sources of anxiety, and gaining insight, you can effectively navigate and overcome what frightens you.

Understanding and Managing Jealousy in Relationships:

Navigating jealousy in relationships can be challenging, as it often carries negative connotations and triggers unpleasant memories. Jealousy, seen as a weakness by many, is an emotion that seldom feels good. Transitioning from monogamy to polygyny as the initial wife, I embarked on a journey of self-discovery and gained insights into the people around me.

When my husband married again, I grappled with intense emotions I had never encountered. My once-solid sense of marital security seemed to vanish, and jealousy became a frequent and unwelcome companion. I often found myself lost in my thoughts, constructing numerous scenarios that often defied reason altogether.

Distinguishing Between Jealousy and Envy in Polygynous Marriages:

Interestingly, as a woman married to a man who practices polygyny, I vividly recall my early days as a jealous young wife. My upbringing exposed me to unfaithful men who exploited women for personal gain, making me particularly sensitive to situations where women "shared" men, especially married ones.

My hypersensitivity stemmed from witnessing the destruction wrought by infidelity, including the arguments, fights, heartbreak, and all the trauma that accompanied shattered marriages. I was not initially a proponent of polygyny, and the idea of having a co-wife was swiftly dismissed.

However, through extensive study and research, I began to understand the naturalness of jealousy, which ultimately made me feel more at ease. Educating myself about the critical distinction between jealousy and envy was pivotal. So, what exactly sets jealousy apart from envy, and how can one effectively manage these emotions?

Managing Jealousy and Envy Positively:

Jealousy and envy are two distinct emotions, each with its own set of characteristics:

- **Jealousy:** This emotion stems from resentment toward someone seen as a rival, enjoying success, or having advantages. It can also manifest as resentment against another's success or benefit.

- **Envy:** Envy, conversely, is marked by feelings of discontent or covetousness regarding another person's advantages, success, possessions, or even their relationships.

Though it is easier said than done, managing these emotions positively can be a noble pursuit. While it's natural to experience jealousy sometimes, the key to overcoming it lies in responding to it peacefully. Understand that you can only control your reactions, not the relationships formed through polygyny, that may trigger these feelings.

Here are some steps to work through jealousy constructively:

1. **Open Communication:** Be transparent about how jealousy has impacted you and your relationship.

2. **Reframe Past Wounds:** Begin reframing and healing past experiences that may have contributed to your jealousy.

3. **Selective Attention:** Control what you pay attention to, focusing on the positive aspects of your relationship.

4. **Self-Compassion:** Refrain from harsh self-judgment, as this can exacerbate underlying insecurities.

5. **Interrupt Negative Thought Patterns:** Employ "negative thought pattern interruptions" to slow down jealousy. Overcoming negative thoughts is a gradual process, and interrupting them helps rebuild what was disrupted. Replace negative self-talk with positive affirmations, such as "I am strong and beautiful. I am capable of creating happiness in my life."

Remember, envy towards others can be dispelled by nurturing and celebrating your unique qualities, as reflected in the quote:

"Don't ever envy anybody. Every person has something no one else has. Develop that one thing in yourself and make it outstanding!" *The Lovely Thoughts*

Shifting from Envy to Self-Improvement and Compassion:

It's not a common practice to replace envy with self-improvement and compassion. Whether a man practices monogamy or polygyny, it shouldn't be the catalyst for women to embark on personal development journeys. Pain, heartbreak, and trauma can push individuals out of their comfort zones in search of solutions. It's natural to desire more for ourselves, but wishing others to lose what is good for them is unhealthy.

Another person's success doesn't equate to your failure. Instead, focus on the abundance in your own life. What do you have that you're grateful for? To facilitate this perspective shift, engage in a "Relationship Abundance Assessment." This assessment comprises a series of questions you can answer individually and, sometimes, with your partner.

Some questions are surface level, while others require more in-depth responses:

- What do you cherish most about your relationship, and why?
- What initially attracted you to your spouse?
- Can you describe your most triumphant moment as a couple? What was it like to experience it together?
- Reflect on your best qualities as individuals and as a couple
- In which areas do you believe your marriage needs improvement, and why?
- What are the top three future successes you'd like to celebrate with your spouse in the next year?

Remember, challenges cannot destroy your marriage as long as both partners stop fighting against each other and start fighting for each other.

A common question I've encountered is how to prevent natural feelings of jealousy from morphing into envy. Transitioning from monogamy to polygyny was one of my most challenging experiences. However, I realized that my marriage didn't end because another began.

Celebrating the beautiful moments and learning experiences within our relationship served as a bridge to appreciate the uniqueness of our marriage. By rediscovering the beauty of your marriage, it becomes challenging to envy another.

Envy often tries to dictate our actions and emotions. It's our responsibility to resist succumbing to these negative feelings.

Here's how to start: Growth Mindset

- Focus on valuing the positive aspects rather than dwelling on the negatives

- Acknowledge the successes of others; celebrating their achievements builds your character

- Be mindful of the company you keep. Surrounding yourself with grateful individuals serves as a reminder to cultivate gratitude

- Broaden your perspective. As relationships evolve, so do our perceptions of challenges, experiences, and our partners, often in a positive light

Putting an End to Emotional Turmoil

Emotional turmoil often arises when individuals feel uncertain, insecure, angry, hurt, or disrespected, among other emotions. The triggers for emotional instability can be numerous and varied. The unfortunate aspect of being caught in an emotional rollercoaster is that it hinders personal growth, and can gradually erode the foundations of a relationship, making it seem irreparable.

Tony Robbins wisely noted, "*Three decisions that we all control each moment of our lives; what to focus on, what things mean, and what to do despite the challenges that may appear to limit us.*" Reflecting on my past self, I recall a time when I experienced frequent mood swings, unintentionally transitioning from one emotional extreme to another. I failed to recognize the hints, clues, and signs causing this behavior.

I couldn't keep up with my actions and reactions. Sometimes, I would utter words out of character, losing sight of who I was. The character I had created had become the antithesis of my authentic self. The vibrant, funny woman I once was vanished. I was overwhelmed by feelings of disrespect, depression, and sheer misery, preventing me from recognizing the goodness in my life.

Recognizing the Symptoms of an Emotional Rollercoaster

Experiencing an emotional rollercoaster can manifest in various symptoms:

- Constant worrying
- Emotional instability, leading to frequent bouts of crying
- Persistent depression
- Irrational thoughts and reactions
- A focus on problems rather than seeking solutions
- Withdrawing and avoiding verbal communication
- Overwhelming feelings of hurt and betrayal
- Persistent feelings of nervousness, irritability, sadness, guilt, exhaustion, or hopelessness could potentially indicate an underlying anxiety disorder, depression, or both

Managing Emotional Turmoil

To manage emotional turmoil effectively, consider these strategies:

- Acknowledge and identify when you are feeling uneasy
- Gradually confront your fears in manageable steps
- Recognize that fear of the unknown can breed uncertainty
- Practice self-soothing techniques, reassuring yourself that feeling this way is okay
- Develop methods for self-management of your emotions

Realizing You're Not Alone

When I unexpectedly found myself in the role of a co-wife, my emotional rollercoaster began abruptly, and I felt like I was spiraling out of control. Recalling old memories was challenging, but the rewards have been remarkable. One of the most significant rewards is the liberating feeling accompanying growth and consistency.

During my darkest moments, I believed I was the only one enduring the trials of heartbreak and relationship despair. Overcoming this obstacle was challenging because I repeated negative words, phrases, and patterns. I had overlooked specific areas that were essential for personal growth. To become a better version of myself, I had to confront the truth, no matter how unattractive it seemed.

There were five key areas where substantial growth was necessary:

- **Resiliency**: The priority was to halt the gradual erosion of my self-esteem and the relationship. Becoming unhinged was different from the lesson to be learned. Shifting my focus towards maturing into a better version of myself first would benefit me and my relationship

- **Responsibility**: Embracing responsibility for my actions and choices

- **Transparency**: Maintaining open and honest communication

- **Optimism**: Cultivating a positive outlook on life

- **Accountability**: Holding each other peacefully accountable for our actions

- **Kindness**: Demonstrating kindness and empathy towards one another

- **Availability**: Being present and available in the relationship

Understanding Relationship Challenges

In all relationships, including polygynous ones, challenges are commonplace. It's a common misconception to believe that we're alone in facing these challenges. Each relationship is unique, with its specific issues and dynamics. Insecurities often make us feel that other people's marriages are better, but our imagination and assumptions drive much of this.

Challenges in relationships serve as opportunities for growth and improvement. They help us become more skilled in areas that need attention, fostering personal and relational development.

Addressing Difficult Conversations

Avoiding or postponing difficult conversations in relationships can lead to resentment and exacerbate existing issues. Addressing these conversations as they arise is crucial to finding efficient solutions. These conversations are necessary to avoid more significant problems down the road.

Continuously Pursuing Your Partner

You must continue pursuing your partner, even within an existing relationship. Remembering what initially drew you to your spouse and revisiting those qualities can reignite the spark in your marriage. Consistency in investing effort into the relationship is vital to maintaining its health. A marriage can't thrive if the individuals within it feel like mere roommates.

Although my husband married again, that didn't mean that our marriage had to be destroyed. Redefining our marriage by falling in love again mattered to us both.

Falling in love with your spouse multiple times throughout your relationship is one of the most inspiring aspects of marriage. Spending quality time together and evolving as your likes and interests change over time can bring freshness and innovation to your relationship.

Flexibility in Forgiveness and Finding Fulfillment

Forgiveness plays a crucial role in maintaining a successful marriage. Forgiving is not just for the other person; it's also for your emotional well-being. Forgiveness may be required multiple times in a marriage, but it doesn't mean accepting unforgivable abuses or unspeakable actions. It means forgiving mistakes, circumstances, or incidents that can be reasonably forgiven.

For instance, if you receive a text meant for a co-wife, you must not overreact or become irrational about it. Healthy intentions should be assumed; small mistakes like texting the wrong person can happen to anyone. Similarly, calling one wife by another's name is an unintentional slip of the tongue.

It's important to remember that husbands, like everyone else, are human and not perfect. Perfectionism should not be expected from them, and it's essential not to jump on every tiny mistake, which can make them feel incapable of doing anything right.

Celebrating Your Unique Marriage

Every accomplishment and victory you experience as a couple should serve as an opportunity to celebrate the uniqueness of your marriage. Reflect on the milestones, achievements, and everything that has positively shaped your relationship.

Questions to Deepen Your Connection:

- What aspects of your marriage are you and your spouse most grateful for?
- Are there any traditions that hold a special place in your relationship?
- Revisit the reasons you got married in the first place and share them.
- Express appreciation for having each other in your lives.
- Remember that your marriage doesn't need to be perfect to be celebrated.

"A fulfilling marriage isn't something you make; it is something you must keep making it." *Unknown*

Marriage should be celebrated regularly, as it's easy to overlook its significance amid the demands of everyday life. Cultivate a healthy marital posture by fostering healthy communication, selflessness, and kindness.

Healthy Communication

Miscommunication often lies at the **heart** of relationship problems.

To foster healthy communication in your relationship, consider the following:

- **Dialogue Without Accusations:** Instead of starting sentences with "You always," begin with "I" to express your thoughts without blame.
- **Maintain Calm:** When engaged in a tense conversation, it's easier to convey your thoughts when you remain calm and composed.
- **Watch Body Language:** Avoid defensive postures like crossing your arms. Make eye contact and actively listen to your partner.
- **Negotiate vs. Manipulate:** Negotiation allows you to express your needs without coercion or fear, while manipulation seeks to control others through guilt or intimidation.

Patience and Forgiveness

Society may suggest that patience is virtuous, yet many struggle with it.

Similarly, forgiveness is sometimes perceived as a sign of weakness rather than strength.

- **Exercise Patience:** Once you've practiced patience, follow through with forgiveness instead of punishing others when you feel wronged.

- **Let Go of Perfectionism:** Understand that your partner isn't perfect, and cease the search for perfection in them.

- **Forgive with Pure Intentions:** If you choose to forgive, do so with genuine intentions rather than hidden motives.

Selflessness

In a relationship, selflessness plays a crucial role in fostering mutual happiness and harmony:

- **Seek Help When Needed:** Don't hesitate to ask your partner for help when necessary; avoiding it can be selfish.

- **Give What You Seek:** Offer others what you desire for yourself, practicing reciprocity in your relationship.

- **Improve Listening Skills:** Be a better listener and speak less, creating space for your partner's thoughts and feelings.

- **Say "Yes" More:** Balance saying "yes" and "no" to your partner's requests. Overusing "no" can lead to resentment and distance in your relationship.

Have Fun Together

Intentionally infusing fun into your relationship can strengthen your bond with your partner. Consider shared activities you enjoy, such as watching movies, dining out, or embarking on adventures. Couples who prioritize fun tend to be happier as they nurture a friendship within their marriage.

Fun and Romance

Fun and romance complement each other, making it challenging to sustain romance without enjoying each other's company. A story about your grandparents illustrates how a lack of fun in a relationship can lead to dissatisfaction and divorce.

KIND TREATMENT

Kindness is a cornerstone of a healthy relationship:

- **Respect and Appreciation:** Cultivate respect and appreciation for each other.

- **Choose Kindness:** Choose kindness over anger, recognizing that your partner isn't your adversary.

- **Lend Strength:** Share your strengths, not your weaknesses, to uplift each other. A story reinforces the importance of avoiding hurtful words in marriage.

Fulfillment: Mind, Body, and Soul

Marital intimacy goes beyond the physical; it encompasses emotional connection and understanding:

- **S.E.X. as Sentimental, Engaging eXchange:** View sex as an intimate exchange that fosters emotional connection.

- **Share Thoughts and Emotions:** Openly express your feelings and stories, emphasizing authentic emotions.

- **Seek Partner's Input:** Encourage your partner's input and avoid assumptions about their feelings.

- **Communication Matters:** Approach conversations with respect and care to prevent misunderstandings.

Fostering a fulfilling relationship requires effort from both partners, with effective communication and genuine emotional connection playing pivotal roles.

Polygyny has posed various challenges and transformations in my life. I've reflected on how vibrant and diverse my life has become, with each role being tested and adapted over time. Initially, I resisted becoming a "co-wife," and my journey toward healing and self-discovery took unpredictable turns.

At first, my coping mechanism involved avoidance and minimal communication. I restricted my interactions to Islamic greetings and simple pleasantries.

This non-communicative lifestyle persisted for over six years but served neither my family nor my marriage well.

One might wonder how my lack of communication with my co-wife affected our marriage—my decision to avoid communication added unnecessary tension and stress to our family dynamic. Compounding negative feelings through non-communication had a profound impact. It made our family environment uncomfortable, especially for the children. They didn't know how to navigate or address the issues between the wives/mothers, and they shouldn't have had to bear that burden.

Recognizing the consequences of my communication choices forced me to confront my core self and the need for personal growth. I had to choose between protecting my ego or fostering a calmer, more manageable environment.

I embarked on a personal development journey, investing in healing myself and repairing my family. The first step was acknowledging the need for a personality makeover. I had to change my negative behaviors and understand the underlying programming that influenced my perceptions.

Early on, I had conditioned myself to believe falsehoods, constructing my narratives and scenarios. These mental constructs created a wall around my emotions. Daily self-study became essential to my routine, complemented by practices like offering salat (prayers), dedicating 30 minutes to reading, and listening to transformative audio materials. Personal development continues to be a vital aspect of my life, facilitating my growth and transformation.

Polygyny initially seemed like a practice meant exclusively for men. I heard stories filled with turmoil, mental abuse, hardship, heartbreak, and failure. These narratives often included extreme jealousy, hurt, anger, and social withdrawal. I knew these experiences were the norm for some, but I had to ask myself, *was being traumatized by polygyny my new normal?*

I realized that I wanted to take charge of my destiny and control what was within my power. While we can't fully control our destinations, we can change how we respond to trauma. Redirecting the negative thoughts, assumptions, and triggers associated with polygyny changed my entire perspective on life.

Co-wives should not be natural-born enemies just because society dictates this.

- Society has conditioned us to believe that women shouldn't share with men, especially in the context of "polygyny." However, we already share our husbands with various people in their lives, including their parents, grandparents, aunts, uncles, siblings, children, or community members. We all share our time with others, and when a husband practices polygyny, a portion of his time is allocated to his other wife or wives. While this relationship is unique, it's essential not to focus solely on "sharing."

- There is also a private physical relationship that may be challenging to ignore, but this aspect should remain a matter strictly between the married parties. Over-sharing or discussing intimate details can lead to jealousy and other negative thoughts and behaviors.

- Setting a new standard for dealing with outside interference in your relationship with your co-wife is essential. People may test your emotions and personal growth, but creating boundaries and controlling the direction of conversations can help prevent gossip or unnecessary drama.

- These boundaries can be seen as goals for the future of your interactions as co-wives. While you may not be best friends, respecting each other is crucial for the family's well-being.

Polygyny doesn't have to be synonymous with conflict and division; it can be an opportunity for growth, understanding, and unity within a family.

Chapter 24

ACCEPTING ANOTHER WOMAN AS A "WIFE" WHEN YOU ARE THE INITIAL WIFE (FIRST WIFE)

ONE OF THE MAJOR LESSONS THAT I LEARNED IN POLYGYNY IS THAT NO matter how hard I tried, this lifestyle was not going to make sense to others. They didn't want to understand. It was like beating a dead horse. I knew something had to change in my mind first before I could explain polygyny to others. These are some areas I had to focus on:

- **Unlearning Societal Norms**: Challenge societal norms emphasizing possession or ownership, such as using phrases like "my husband." Such language can unintentionally imply privilege or exclusivity.

- **Seek Understanding**: You don't have to be best friends but try to understand your co-wife's perspective. Empathy can arise when you consider her life experiences. Avoid making unfounded assumptions, and gather information directly from your co-wife to ensure clear communication.

- **Find Common Ground**: Look for commonality and compromise. Understand each other's positions and be open to her experiences and viewpoints, even if they only partially align with yours. Avoid over-sharing, as this can lead to negative emotions and drama.

- **Respect Privacy**: Resist the urge to focus on past, present, or future intimacies between your husband and co-wife. Their physical relationship is private, just like any other married couple's.

- **Be Genuine and Respectful**: Avoid talking negatively about your co-wife behind her back. If you have nothing nice to say, say nothing at all. Gossip and backbiting serve no one's interests.

Building Sisterhood: The Importance of Positive Connections Among Co-Wives in Polygamy

In these relationships, co-wives often find themselves in a unique and difficult situation. It is important for co-wives to form positive connections with one another. Although this may not happen right away, it is still vital to the overall health of the family.

By fostering understanding, respect, empathy, and cooperation, co-wives can create a harmonious and peaceful family environment. When co-wives communicate openly and respectfully, misunderstandings and conflicts can be minimized, leading to a more pleasant and conducive atmosphere for everyone involved, including the children within the family.

Secondly, common civility and respect among co-wives can contribute to the emotional well-being of each individual. Co-wives can provide a pillar of support for one another, understanding the unique challenges they face. By supporting each other they can navigate their roles and responsibilities with greater ease and confidence.

Moreover, a positive connection among co-wives encourages personal growth and development. They can inspire each other to pursue individual goals and aspirations. Co-wives can become each other's motivators, encouraging continuous self-improvement and contributing to the enhancement of the family as a whole.

Most importantly, children within polygamous families benefit immensely when their mothers share a positive relationship. A united front in parenting enhances consistency, discipline, and love within the family. Children witness their mothers working together, providing a strong model of cooperation and collaboration. This positive environment can have a lasting impact on their understanding of relationships and their overall emotional well-being.

Healthy intentions and connections among co-wives, promotes a harmonious family dynamic. Does that mean the family will not be met with challenges? The short answer is "no." Life will continue to happen. However, by creating a sense of sisterhood, co-wives can become more empathetic and understanding about the complexities of polygamy. They can create a fulfilling and enriching family life if they're willing to see one another as individuals who could potentially benefit from becoming friends rather than enemies.

Positively Connecting with your Co-wife is Essential for the Well-being of your Family as a Whole

- **You Are a Role Model**: Whether you initially accept it or not, you are a role model for your family. Show up as your best self and set a positive example.

- **Influence on Children**: If you have children, they observe your interactions and learn how to treat your co-wife based on your behavior. Your actions can shape their attitudes and behaviors towards her.

Building a positive connection with your co-wife can create a healthier family environment and set a constructive example for future generations.

- **Respect Personal Space:** Acknowledge that each co-wife has her own needs and personal space. Respect each other's privacy and boundaries.

- **Open Communication:** Establish transparent and honest channels of communication. Regularly discuss expectations, concerns, and boundaries to ensure everyone is on the same page.

- **Define Responsibilities:** Clearly define each co-wife's responsibilities within the family. This includes childcare, household duties, and financial contributions. Having well-defined roles can prevent conflicts.

- **Prioritize Respect:** Treat each other with respect and kindness at all times. Avoid disrespectful language, behaviors, or actions that can lead to tension.

- **Conflict Resolution:** When conflicts arise, address them calmly and constructively. Find solutions together rather than resorting to confrontations or arguments.

- **Mutual Agreement:** Reach a mutual agreement on how shared resources, such as your husband's time and attention, will be allocated. Ensure that the arrangement is fair and balanced.

- **Flexibility:** Be open to adjusting boundaries and agreements as needed.

Flexibility can help accommodate changing circumstances and maintain peace within the family.

- **Support and Empower:** Recognize that you may need each other's aid in various aspects of life. Collaboration can strengthen family bonds through co-parenting, emotional support, or sharing responsibilities.

Setting and respecting boundaries can foster a positive co-wife relationship and create a harmonious family environment.

Typically, boundaries are a set of guidelines you agree to live by. These boundaries are essential as they educate others on how you desire to be treated. Setting specific relationship boundaries or goals provides an agreement that each party will mutually respect for the benefit of your relationship.

I love the following quote from Lee Horbachewski, the author of "A Quiet Strong Voice."

"I allow myself to set healthy boundaries. To say no to what does not align with my values, to say yes to what does. Boundaries assist me to remain healthy, honest, and living a life that is true to me."

On many occasions, I have witnessed co-wives neglect to set boundaries for their interactions or relationships. Consequently, their relationships were destroyed and, in some cases, beyond repair. Boundaries are not respected or acknowledged if met with hesitation, making a healthy relationship between co-wives impossible.

In preparation to have a healthy relationship with your co-wife or wives, you should follow some healthy relationship principles:

- **Respecting the Role of Each Wife:** It's essential to acknowledge and respect the unique roles of each wife in a polygynous marriage. Disrespecting any wife can lead to negative responses and reactive behaviors.
- **Avoiding Grudges:** Holding grudges within a polygynous relationship is counterproductive. Grudges harm not only the individuals involved but also the overall growth and harmony of the family. Children can also inadvertently suffer, as trust issues may restrict their interactions.

- **Addressing Issues Promptly:** When conflicts or issues arise, addressing them directly and promptly is crucial. Avoid making unfounded accusations or harsh judgments. Remaining calm and seeking clarity can help collect accurate information and prevent further escalation.

- **Understanding Each Other's Opinions:** Understand your co-wife's opinions on family matters, issues, events, and planning. While co-wives may not share the same mentality, fostering unity is vital, especially when children are involved. Unity benefits the well-being of all children, whether biological or natural.

- **Playing on the Same Team:** Consider your ability to work together as a team within the family. Building a shared history and bonding as a family can facilitate this transition. Simple activities like going out for ice cream together can help strengthen your family bonds.

- **Being Part of the Solution:** Instead of contributing to contention, focus on being a positive force within the relationship between co-wives. Avoid conflicts and disagreements, as they can hinder overall harmony.

- **Rejecting Revenge:** Letting go of any thoughts of revenge or harm towards your co-wife or husband is essential. In some cases, negative emotions may arise due to introducing a new marriage, but seeking revenge is neither productive nor conducive to a healthy family dynamic. Much like hatred, vengeance can not only cause physical violence, but mental violence as well.

- **Co-wives, Not Competitors:** Society sometimes frames wives in polygynous marriages as competitors in an unspoken sister-wife competition. This perspective leads to tracking achievements, brownie points with the husband, and a tally of highs and lows. However, it's crucial to recognize that wives/co-wives don't need to compete for their husband's affection when they already have his love. Men in polygynous marriages love their wives deeply, and there's no need for competition over the love they already share.

- **Co-parenting Bonus Children:** Adjusting to the role of a "bonus parent" is not always a seamless transition, but it's necessary for the mental health and well-being of the children involved. Neglecting the responsibilities of a co-parent can have severe ramifications for a child's emotional development. Children may feel rejected or uncared for when their bonus parent does not participate actively.

- **Respect Each Other's Roles as Mothers:** In a polygynous marriage, it's essential to recognize that each wife has her unique role as a mother. If you and your co-wife have children, neither set of children seeks a replacement mother figure, especially if you're both already great mothers. Children generally aren't looking for new mother figures either.

I recall an incident involving one of my daughters, who was initially hesitant about interacting with my co-wife. She wasn't prepared for it. However, this situation marked a turning point in their relationship. My co-wife made a profound statement to my daughter: "I'm not trying to be your mother."

This statement resonated with my daughter and addressed her concerns directly. It broke the ice and became a springboard for their relationship. As a mother, I appreciated the transparency in that first conversation. My daughter also felt a sense of relief, and this openness allowed them to connect positively. Young adults and adolescents often don't warm up to a bonus parent just because they exist, and that's entirely normal.

However, my children could sense my co-wife's good intentions and positive energy, which was encouraging. Human beings are sensitive to vibes, and experiencing positivity during times of awkwardness or challenge fosters hope for the future. My co-wife's support and honesty with my daughter helped me to trust her more.

This conversation, independent of our husband's role as an intermediary, was a liberating and triumphant moment for our family.

"Bonus parents deserve the same respect a biological parent would receive. They pour their time, energy, and love into a child they don't even create. Bonus parents don't do it because they have to; they do it because they want to." *Unknown*

Nurturing Relationships as Co-Wives and Bonus Mothers:

As a co-wife and a bonus mother, I fully understand that building these parenting relationships doesn't always happen **overnight**. In many cases, it takes years of effort and bonding, which has certainly been true for my family. We faced numerous trials and challenges while striving to create a strong bond within our family. However, our commitment and dedication have borne fruit on many levels. Our journey as co-wives was significantly influenced by our shared fundamental goals, particularly within the context of our faith, Islam. Our religion held us accountable for how we treated each other. Together, we aimed to heal and find reassurance in our roles as wives and mothers.

Emotions are a natural part of being human. While some emotions are positive, it's crucial to manage negative ones and avoid them spiraling out of control. I recall an incident that occurred overseas involving two wives. The first wife remained quiet when the husband announced his intention to marry a second wife. However, tension escalated when the second wife prayed while the first wife sat. In response, the first wife attacked the second wife.

As Muslim women, a positive approach to handling such situations involves offering sincere prayers and seeking refuge with Allah Ta'ala. Engage in a constructive conversation rather than planning an attack. Remember that you can control the outcome by taking the proper steps and remaining open to learning and growth.

I also want to share an inspirational story I heard many years ago about two co-wives who supported each other. One wife babysat the other's children while the other pursued her education. Both earned their college bachelor's degrees. When the husband passed away, they chose to live together and have grown old together, raising their children as their own. This story illustrates how two women can collaborate for the greater good and the well-being of their children.

Polygyny should not be about isolation or personal suffering but about expanding family and community. While the story I mentioned is an exceptional case, it highlights the importance of respecting each member's role in your relationships' mental health and wellness, especially within a family striving to thrive.

Chapter 25

WHY I CHOSE TO STAY IN MY MARRIAGE

OVER THE PAST DECADE, I'VE ENCOUNTERED NUMEROUS INQUIRIES ABOUT my decision to remain in a marriage with a husband who practices polygyny. Early on, the answers to these questions were not crystal clear. I needed to reevaluate the value of my marriage, looking beyond the roles of friend and mother. This shift was essential because evaluating my marriage based solely on raising a family and companionship would be unbalanced.

It's easy to resort to blanket statements like, "Where else could I go with six children? Who would want to marry me now? I'm damaged goods. I can't financially support myself."

Designing a set of probing questions about my marriage left me feeling exposed and fearful. Fear was not new to me, as I knew it stemmed from my apprehension of facing the truth. Delving into my "why" was crucial but required peeling back layers I hadn't realized existed.

I began by questioning why I wanted a husband in the first place and, subsequently, why I wanted to remain in a marriage with my husband. This marked the beginning of my introspective journey.

Marriage Evaluation Questions:
- What positive qualities initially attracted me to my husband?
- Does my culture support his decision to enter into another marriage?
- Would I find greater happiness if he were no longer part of my life through divorce?
- Do I feel mentally, emotionally, physically, and spiritually safe within this marriage?

- Is my husband committed to doing the necessary work to heal our relationship?

- Does he possess the patience required to support my healing?

- Am I considering divorce out of a desire to hurt him, or is it genuinely warranted for the well-being of our marriage?

- Is my unhappiness primarily caused by my spouse or myself?

- Did my spouse enter into this marriage to get divorced?

- Have we exhausted all efforts to salvage our marriage before contemplating divorce?

This process was daunting, as it meant confronting my fears and peeling back layers I hadn't realized existed. I recall the advice of a dear friend who had gone through a difficult divorce. She warned me that divorcing my husband wouldn't mean he'd be entirely out of my life. We would still cross paths at graduations, community events, during times of illness, weddings, and funerals.

She asked, "Are you prepared for that, especially when you have a good husband?" My answer then, and still today, is "no." I wasn't ready for a life where we'd pretend we never knew each other, where nothing that had mattered would have any significance.

I meticulously examined and scrutinized my answers to each question, replaying them in my mind repeatedly. The conclusion was the same: wanting a divorce had become an emotional decision rather than a logical assessment of who I was married to and what he was willing to sacrifice for the greater good of our future as a couple.

Instead of scrutinizing his every move after he married again, I decided to invest back into my marriage. I embraced the belief in matching energy, but now channeled it positively. One significant decision was to allow my husband time to grow, heal, and learn the lessons he needed to become the best version of himself. I had sought perfection, but even my monogamous marriage wasn't perfect. How could I demand perfection from his life while we practiced polygyny?

I understood that having the right skills to avoid divorce, such as communication, compassion, conflict resolution, listening, care, and humility, would set us on a much better path. Personal growth had to precede any demands from others. While I could ask for kind treatment and financial support, ignoring my husband's work was the most disrespectful thing I could do.

Self-education couldn't be rushed; it needed time to develop.

I longed for instant results, but like anything worthwhile, timing was essential. Honoring my marriage was a practice, and I realized that a fulfilling marriage wouldn't happen without us working together. Asking and answering difficult questions honestly became my goal. It wasn't easy to be honest with myself, but the truth lay within the wreckage of my ego.

The man I married demonstrated his willingness to work with the right tools and refused to procrastinate. I witnessed his dedication. My ambition propelled us forward positively to heal our marriage. That doesn't mean we're always pleased with each other; we're human beings with limitations. Consistency became my closest ally as I engaged in personal development every day.

I crafted a detailed list of what I wanted in my marriage and why. My "why" to stay married had to be powerful enough to evoke emotion. Transitioning from monogamy to polygyny enlightened me about myself and who I needed to become. Divorcing because of plural marriage would feel surreal at this point in my life.

Polygyny happened when it was meant to, not a moment sooner. The trials our marriage endured were not merely about a man and a woman; they were about two individuals becoming more than they ever saw in themselves. When facing a struggle in marriage, it can become a story, either of divorce or working together to build a stronger marriage. I chose the latter, and we found our truth.

Chapter 26

INITIAL WIFE INITIATIVE: WHAT'S YOUR PLAN MOVING FORWARD?

INITIATIVE IS DEFINED AS HAVING THE POWER OR OPPORTUNITY TO ACT or take charge before others do. The Initial Wife Initiative is a philosophy that calls for initial wives to take charge in various areas of life while in polygyny. As an initial wife, I needed to establish a guiding principle for my everyday life. Participating actively in my personal growth and development as an individual, initial wife and mother was crucial for my successful transition from monogamy to polygyny. Changing my mindset had a profound impact on my life in many ways.

I created an acrostic, *I.N. I. T. I. A. T. I. V. E.* Each letter representing a meaningful word, and began implementing these principles, each with its own unique significance and power.

I	= Illuminate
N	= Numerous
I	= Inspirational
T	= Thought Patterns
I	= Intentionally
A	= Affirming
T	= Teamwork and Togetherness
I	= Increasing
V	= Valuable
E	= Effectively Each Day

Implementation is crucial when healing from trauma or marital discord is the goal. I reflect on when I felt at my lowest in my relationship. I was trapped in a fatalistic, solitary mindset. However, as I started making changes to eliminate what wasn't serving me, I gained valuable insights into becoming a better person overall.

Monogamy provided a sense of security, but I found a different kind of security in polygyny. I grew into my new self by recognizing my worth as a woman and striving to evolve further. My new motto became "best practices for best results."

Here are some best practices to consider:

- Set daily goals and construct a calendar for your goals, focusing on areas where you can take more initiative

- Discover new aspects of yourself

- Embrace self-reinvention and personal development

- Cultivate self-love

- Engage in continuous personal development

- Actively promote your growth

- Go above and beyond what's required of you; it will help build your character

- Seek self-education in areas where you need clarity

Understanding Polygamy: A First Wife's Experience

Polygamy is a practice seen in many cultures and religions, where a person can have more than one spouse. Sometimes it's due to tradition or personal choice. My story is about being the first wife in such a marriage and the unique emotions, challenges, and growth that came with it.

Living in a polygynous marriage is like navigating a map of many different feelings. In all honesty, when I first heard my husband had another wife, I felt scared, angry, and sad. It made me question my worth our relationship, and his intentions.

As time passed, I tried to understand why polygamy was important in our culture and religion and to him. I realized life throws unexpected challenges at us, and it's how we handle them that shapes us.

Being the first wife meant sharing my husband's attention and love with another woman. Sometimes, I felt jealous and unsure. But talking openly with my husband and sharing my feelings was crucial for our relationship and a successful marriage. I knew the real work of overcoming my challenges had to begin with me. It was my responsibility to make myself a better person; a happy person who had more good days ahead.

Despite the difficulties, this experience taught me a lot about life and love and especially growth. Love can grow and change, even when it involves more than one marriage. I learned to love in a more mature and understanding way by allowing myself to evolve into a better woman. Ultimately, through much personal development, I became a relationship coach and counselor to women from all walks of life.

In challenging times, I found strength in connecting with my co-wife and bonus children. We supported each other, forming a special bond that went beyond what society expected. This support helped us embrace our unique situation wholeheartedly. I am forever grateful to all the members of our beautiful family.

Being a first wife in a polygynous marriage is a journey filled with complex emotions, challenges, triumphs, and societal expectations. It requires self-reflection, honest communication, and a commitment to growth and understanding.

Although your journey into polygyny may not have an easy start, working through the challenges can make you more compassionate and strong, teaching you important lessons about love and adaptability..

Polygyny became our unexpected blessing and trusted friend.

"Polygyny is not about the destruction of family. It is about the expansion of family and our family is priceless." *Coach Fatimah*

PART 3

Let's Talk Polygamy with Coach Nyla

INTRODUCTION

"You know that they can have more than one wife, right?" These were the words I heard constantly when I would mention to family and friends that I was studying Islam. Growing up in the West, polygyny is not and was not a typical topic of discussion.

If a man you were with thought about another woman or even complimented a woman on television, you were taught to believe he didn't love you and would cheat on you. No one in my life ever mentioned anything about marrying more than one person and what that would look like. I didn't officially hear anything about it until I was in my early 20s when I went on my Islamic journey.

I decided to read the only book I knew about it, titled "Polygamy in Islam," and I was intrigued. I had to read it. I wanted to know about this marrying more than one wife thing that everyone told me Muslim men could do. Surprisingly, the book made much sense to me as it explained the institution of polygyny and how it was laid out.

Being a woman raised by a single mother, who was also raised by a single mother, I already had a negative view of men and their purpose in a relationship. Even though the book helped me understand and even appreciate the concept of polygyny it didn't discuss the intricacies that come with practicing polygyny and how to deal with them.

Well, we'll talk about that in this section. I will walk you through a man's polygynous nature, and the resulting difficult feelings it can provoke in wives, such as jealousy, loneliness, bitterness, and feelings of betrayal that may rear their ugly head in some marriages.

I will also discuss why one would want to marry a married man, as well as how to look out for predators, losers, and bums who may wish to use polygyny as a way to collect and demean women. I would be selling you short if I didn't also discuss co-wife connections in addition to building and blending your family for success in a polygynous family dynamic.

While polygyny may be a deeply ingrained cultural and historical norm in some societies, it remains a subject of intrigue and controversy in many others, especially in the West. Let's talk more about polygyny, shall we?

Chapter 27

UNVEILING THE NATURE OF POLYGYNY

"MEN ONLY WANT POLYGYNY FOR THEIR LUSTFUL DESIRES." "ISLAM degrades women by allowing polygyny." "The Bible doesn't condone this practice." "Men who love women, especially their wives, would never do this."

These are some of the many emotionally charged statements that float around when the topic of polygyny is discussed. Let's get into some of the history as well as how polygyny is practiced today so we can dispel these myths. Why? Because knowledge beats ignorance any day, and we don't want to spew ignorance when it comes to a form of marriage that is an ancient solution to modern-day relationships and familial problems.

On our platform, we encounter a number of people who have very strong opinions about polygyny. Many use their emotions at the expense of their intellect and like to tell us how my co-wife and I are brainwashed, being used, and don't know our worth as wives. That our husband is "benefitting much more than we are through a religion that oppresses women."

Maybe this is because my husband, co-wife, and I are practicing Muslims, and we don't shy away from letting that be known. We unapologetically discuss the regulations that Islam puts in place for polygyny. However, many things Islam teaches, that are against the immoral practices we have been led to believe to constitute freedom, have been downplayed and rejected through societal conditioning in the West. However, I digress.

Islam is not the only religion that allows polygyny, and it didn't start polygyny. There are many religions and reasons why men have practiced and still practice polygyny. Here are some examples:

Ancient Egypt: Polygyny was common among the pharaohs of ancient Egypt. For example, Ramses the Great (Ramses II) is believed to have had multiple wives, including the famous Nefertari and another named Isetnofret. These marriages were often used to strengthen political alliances and consolidate power.

Biblical Times: The Bible contains several references to polygyny, particularly in the Old Testament. King Solomon (Prophet Sulayman), known for his wisdom, had 700 wives and 300 concubines, as described in the Bible (1 Kings 11:3). This symbolized his wealth, power, and wisdom. Prophets Abraham (Ibrahim), Jacob (Yaqub), and others also practiced polygyny, being married to at least two wives simultaneously.

Medieval Africa: In some African societies, such as the Zulu Kingdom, polygyny was practiced by nobility and elite individuals. Shaka Zulu, the famous Zulu warrior king, had multiple wives, as did other Zulu leaders, to strengthen their alliances and expand their lineage. Expansion of lineage is still very important, especially for men. Legacy building is an essential factor in the practice of polygyny. More on that later.

Islam: In Islam, polygyny is allowed with specific regulations. Prophet Muhammad (Peace be upon him) had multiple wives. These marriages sometimes served political, social, and humanitarian purposes, such as caring for widows or forging alliances with various tribes. There were other reasons that the Prophet Muhammad (peace be upon him) practiced polygyny. The above are just a few.

Mormonism in the 19th Century: In the early days of the Church of Jesus Christ of Latter-day Saints (LDS), also known as the Mormon Church, some members practiced polygyny. Church leaders like Brigham Young had multiple wives. However, the church officially abandoned the practice in 1890 due to increasing pressure from the U.S. government.

Modern Polygynous Societies: Polygyny is still practiced in various societies today. It remains a common practice in some parts of Africa and the

Middle East. For example, wealthy men often have multiple wives among the Maasai people in East Africa. These marriages are usually arranged for economic, social, or cultural reasons.

Polygyny in the Fundamentalist Church of Jesus Christ of Latter-Day Saints (FLDS): Some splinter groups of the LDS Church, such as the FLDS, continue to practice polygyny. Warren Jeffs, a former leader of the FLDS, had multiple wives and was involved in controversial cases involving child brides. I will delve more into predators, losers, and bums later, as this man, in my opinion, fits into that category.

Not everyone who practices polygyny is moral and ethical, and I will also cover that later in the book.

Polygyny in the Fundamentalist Mormon Communities in the United States: Despite the mainstream LDS Church's abandonment of polygyny, some fundamentalist Mormon communities in the United States continue the practice. These communities, often living in isolation, practice polygyny as part of their religious beliefs.

Polygyny in Indigenous Cultures: Some indigenous societies in North and South America practiced polygyny before European colonization. For example, certain Native American tribes in the southwestern United States engaged in polygynous marriages for various reasons, including kinship ties and societal organization.

These examples demonstrate that polygyny has been a part of human history and has been practiced for a variety of reasons, including social, economic, political, and religious factors. Although these are not prerequisites for practicing polygyny, it does dispel the myth that polygyny is "only for men's lustful desires. It's crucial to recognize that the practice and acceptance of polygyny have varied widely across different cultures and time periods. Moreover, it is gaining acceptance as an "ancient solution to modern-day problems and challenges," particularly in response to evolving notions of the nuclear family.

Can we acknowledge the fact that men are genuinely polygynous by nature? It can be a complex concept to grasp, but let me break down a few things to help get that point across.

One fundamental piece of men's biological makeup is the desire for reproductive success, which is measured by one's ability to pass on genes to the next generation. Men can potentially increase their reproductive success by mating with multiple females. This is because each additional woman can lead to more children, increasing the chances that their genes will be passed on. I know that this might seem obvious, however, it is an important topic that should be addressed.

Women have a limited number of eggs and a defined period of fertility. Men do not have that problem as they typically produce a large number of sperm throughout their lives. I know I don't have to give you a biology lesson, but stick with me here.

This difference can create an incentive for men to seek multiple opportunities to maximize their reproductive output, so to speak. Even though men may not understand it or know how to explain this, it's a biological fact that makes them very different than we are as women and gives partial insight into how and why they are polygynous by nature.

Parental investment may play another role in men's conscious or sub-conscious drive to practice polygyny. Coach Nyla, what do you mean by parental investment? I'm glad you asked. Well, it refers to the resources, time, and effort we invest in raising our children or offspring. Mothers provide more parental investment through gestation, lactation, nurturing, etc., so much so that men may desire multiple women to maximize their reproductive success (remember what I said earlier?) while maximizing the parental investment of the offspring. (Think, "it takes a village to raise a child.")

When it comes to polygyny, there is the moral account of being married, and with marriage comes responsibilities and regulations. So, being more than twice the man is required as it is not just about sexual reproduction and spreading one's seed everywhere. However, the practice and acceptance of polygyny have been heavily influenced by cultural, social, and individual factors, making it a complex and multifaceted phenomenon that extends beyond a man's biological makeup.

I know I explained the biological reasons men are polygynous, and it may seem that they are just robotic creatures. However, men are capable of experiencing deep emotional connections and love for multiple women simultaneously.

Sometimes, women do not want to hear that a man can love multiple women when they come from a society that has engrained the "Disney Princess, happily ever after in monogamy" ideals into their psyche.

However, it's a fact that men can love more than one woman, and a polygynous marriage can be just as successful and fulfilling as a marriage in monogamy. It's about the people involved, not the form of marriage.

Let's talk about some of the key aspects to consider when we are trying to understand the concept of our husbands loving more than one wife. Yes, we must seek first to understand so that we can also be understood, right?

Women are not the only ones who can connect emotionally; men have the emotional capacity to love and form meaningful connections with multiple people as well. The belief that you can only love one person at a time is a societal construct, and many men find that they are capable of loving multiple women in different ways. Women know this as well. Our issue usually lies with whom he loves most. Yes, I said it, and you may have thought it.

It is essential to understand that love can take on various forms and intensities, making it possible for our husbands to love multiple wives without diminishing each individual's quality or depth of love. For some men, loving more than one wife can provide the emotional fulfillment they may not find in a monogamous marriage. Different wives can meet different needs and desires, leading to a more holistic sense of satisfaction in the individual marriage as well as within the family environment.

While men are polygynous by nature; women are not so much. I'm referring to their natural biological makeup, rather than anomalies or societal conditioning. Responsibilities come with being married, and being married to multiple spouses is no exception. In fact, it increases your responsibility without the addition of children.

Would women truly want to care for multiple husbands? Marriage isn't solely about our satisfaction as wives; it's also about our ability to please our husbands and meet their needs. The kicker is that men can successfully take care of multiple wives more naturally than a woman can take care of multiple husbands with or without the addition of children into the mix.

Fill in the following sentences.

I will do _____ to understand my spouse's wants and needs.

It is essential for me to educate myself on polygyny because…

A husband's decision to pursue polygyny can be influenced by a variety of factors, some of which may not be directly related to his existing marriage. Some factors can heavily influence his desire to pursue polygyny, which can also come from challenges in the union as well.

It is crucial to understand that polygyny is not a remedy for a bad or troubled marriage. However, it does give a husband the option to stay married to his existing wife and work on their marriage while he morally fulfills his needs by marrying again.

Each marriage is its own separate entity, In most cases, a husband staying married while marrying again, shows that the husband wants his existing wife and sees that there is a possibility for growth and reconnection. If he didn't feel this was possible, he could end the marriage.

It's essential to understand that polygyny is a complex and deeply personal choice, often influenced by a combination of emotional, cultural, and practical considerations.

Emotional Fulfillment

For some husbands, polygyny can provide a sense of emotional fulfillment that extends beyond their existing marriage. They may believe that forming additional relationships can enhance their overall well-being and bring them happiness and, more importantly, peace. While it may seem counterintuitive to seek happiness outside of an existing marriage, it's essential to recognize that love and emotional connections are not finite resources. Husbands may genuinely feel that their capacity to love and connect with multiple spouses enriches their lives and contributes to their emotional well-being.

Cultural and Religious Beliefs

In certain cultures and religious traditions, polygyny is not only accepted but encouraged. Some husbands may choose polygyny as a way to adhere to their cultural or religious values and fulfill their duties as providers and protectors of their families. These cultural and religious beliefs can be deeply ingrained and may shape a husband's perspective on marriage and family dynamics.

It's crucial to respect and understand the significance of these beliefs in a husband's decision-making process. Communicating about the goal for the family and what plans and ideas each spouse has is essential to being able to foster that respect and understanding. It is important to be honest and upfront from the beginning, and if anything changes, make sure that is discussed so that trust is not severed and one is not blind-sided.

Practical Considerations

From a practical standpoint, polygyny can serve as a means to expand the family, share responsibilities, and build a robust support system. Husbands may pursue polygyny to provide for and protect their loved ones more effectively. In many cultures, having a large and interconnected family is seen as a source of strength and security. Husbands may view polygyny as a way to build a robust family network that can weather life's challenges and offer support in times of need.

Chapter 28

NEGATIVE RESPONSES TO POLYGYNY AND FORCED MONOGAMY

The Role of Manipulation

While the desire for polygyny may be rooted in various motivations, it's essential to acknowledge that unhealthy dynamics can harm any marriage, including polygynous ones. Manipulation, when used as a tool to control and coerce, can lead to the deterioration of trust and love within a marriage. Recognizing the signs of manipulation is crucial for maintaining a healthy marriage. That goes for both husbands and wives.

Later in this book, I will explore how predatory men can employ manipulation in ways which can be detrimental to the marriage and all parties involved. But for now, let's explore the common ways manipulation is used, mainly by women, to negatively affect a marriage.

Using Sex as a Weapon

Sexual manipulation is a destructive tactic that can destroy trust and intimacy in a marriage. When one partner uses sex as a means of reward or punishment, it creates a hostile and unfulfilling environment. In a polygynous marriage, such manipulation can have far-reaching consequences, as it can lead to jealousy, resentment, and emotional distance among spouses.

Children as Pawns

Using children as pawns in marital disputes can have devastating effects. When a husband or wife manipulates the relationship with the children, it damages the marriage and harms the emotional well-being of the children involved. In polygynous families, children are an integral part of the dynamic, and their well-being should be a top priority for all spouses.

Having to fight for custody of his daughter, my cousin had to deal with some highly manipulative tactics from the mother of his child. It went as far as child services having to be called to investigate my cousin as the mother accused him of heinous acts against his young daughter.

The woman who conducted the investigation saw right through the mother's lies and manipulation, as she had years of experience in what she does. Not only was the investigation closed, the findings provided my cousin with enough evidence to get his daughter away from a potentially harmful upbringing and, in turn, allowed the daughter to grow up resenting and losing trust in her mother for the vindictive nature of her actions.

Weaponizing Love and Affection

The weaponization of love, where one partner withholds affection or love to control the other, can cause deep emotional scars. Love should be freely given and received in a healthy relationship. We can be upset with one another and still love and display love for one another. I never let my negative emotions hinder my love for and duty to my husband. I can be upset with him, and he will still get a nice meal. I will still ensure things are well with him even if we may not see eye to eye on particular things.

In polygyny, it's essential for spouses to nurture their emotional connections and ensure that love is not used as a tool for manipulation or control.

Answer the following:

To me, weaponizing love looks like_____, and if I experience this or find myself doing this, the steps I'll take are…

It is important to keep children out of adult decisions. However, it is also important to keep them informed on matters that can affect them.

Explain how you will include/inform your children on important matters while refraining from using them as pawns.

The Power of Understanding, Communication, and Submission

Dealing with the various energies in polygyny can be challenging. That's why understanding, communication, and submission can be invaluable tools for maintaining harmony and building strong bonds among husbands and wives.

Understanding

We must work to understand each other's needs, desires, and motivations in polygyny. This practice is crucial if we value success when it comes to marriage in polygyny. By taking the time to comprehend the reasons behind a husband's desire for polygyny and the emotions of all parties involved, spouses can cultivate empathy and compassion towards one another.

It's important to recognize that every member of the family brings unique perspectives and experiences to the family, and husbands and wives bring unique perspectives and experiences to their own individual marriages. Understanding these differences can lead to greater harmony and integration within the unit.

I remember when this was challenging for me. Thinking of others before myself and trying to understand them. I hoped that this will show them that I wasn't a threat, but someone that they could like, connect with, and build with. Despite my efforts, I was the one expected to jump through hoops, to make others comfortable or happy and to not have issues when these efforts not reciprocated. This caused me to become cynical over time.

I was told that I should be happy that my co-wife finally acknowledged me and said my name when she had struggled to do this in the beginning. That bothered me because I intentionally worked on building success in my marriage and family from the start. I tried to be understanding about others' feelings, emotions, and actions only to be told that I don't understand, will never understand, and should go above and beyond to be accepted as though I wasn't struggling and needing others to understand me.

Understanding the bigger picture and learning to embrace my position in my marriage and family, as well as learning to practice courageous communication, helped me to start to feel better about my choice, my family, and my life.

Answer the following:

I will "seek first to understand, then be understood" by _____
with my spouse on …

I embrace my place in my family through…

Communication

"I thought we were better than that. If you feel that you are unable to talk to me about what is bothering you, then I have to wonder about where we are in our marriage." Yeah, those were words that stuck with me after having an "uncomfortable conversation" with Coach Nazir about how I'd been feeling and the reasons why I was bottling up the many things that were troubling me.

I was fighting with my own issues with polygyny. I was not connecting with my co-wife or bonus children, and was seen as the outsider, homewrecker, and many other hurtful names because I had married a married man.

Truthfully, it was difficult to know where we stood when I didn't know how to communicate effectively. I started to believe the noise of the "vocal minority" that said I shouldn't have a voice when it came to the challenges I was facing in polygyny. That was reserved only for my co-wife.

Open and honest communication is the cornerstone of any successful relationship. Spouses should foster an environment where they can freely express their thoughts, concerns, and feelings. Healthy communication can help address issues, build trust, and strengthen emotional connections. In polygyny, communication is even more critical, as multiple individuals are navigating complex emotions and relationships in their own way. Regular family meetings and one-on-one discussions can provide a platform for effective communication.

"Practice Courageous Communication" ~From our family's Code of Honor

Submission

Submission in the context of polygyny does not imply subservience or inequality but rather a willingness to cooperate and compromise for the greater good of the family. All spouses, including the husband, should be willing to submit to the greater good of the family. This means prioritizing unity, understanding, and fairness. Submission involves making decisions that benefit the family as a whole, even if it requires setting aside personal desires or ego.

Submission does not make you less than, and it's not about submitting directly to a person but to a higher cause/power. For me, it's to the Most High. Because we, as Muslims, submit to Allah, it makes my submission to my husband and his leadership that much easier. As long as he follows Islam as his way of life, then through ups and downs, good times and bad, I trust that he will do what's right, fair, and just.

In polygyny, submission is more than obedience. It's about humility, trust, and seeing past our own noses to embrace the bigger picture.

Answer the following:

I see submission as…

My thoughts about it are beneficial/detrimental to my marriage because…

It's important to note that not all men are interested in or capable of practicing polygyny. There are a variety of factors. However, I felt it was necessary to shed some light on men's desire to practice polygyny (from what has been shared with us from men- Coach Nazir included) because we know a large number of women who demonize men or question their love, loyalty, and legitimacy when they discover that their husbands or the men in their lives want to pursue polygyny.

So, let's talk more about how we as women can enjoy our marriage, trust our husbands, and stay away from destructive thoughts and behaviors when they are married to or desiring to be married to someone in addition to us.

Chapter 29

MINDING YOUR MARRIAGE

What if he does the things he does to/for me to/for her?

I wonder what they are doing right now.

What if he likes her cooking/cleaning/movements, etc., better than mine?

How are any of those thoughts benefitting you? Correct, they are not serving you in any way, shape, or form. However, many wives in polygyny are feeling this way. In my programs and coaching sessions, I challenge those who think or speak these thoughts to tell me how this level of thinking benefits them. We can agree that these are destructive thoughts that can make a person feel lower than low.

Sometimes, being low or being a victim is beneficial to some women because then they will receive attention. And if they receive attention from the one they want, their husband, then the attention is taken away from the other wife. Score!

On the flip side, the sabotaging nature of that wife will be exposed and can cause problems in her individual marriage. So, let's talk about how minding your marriage is better than sabotaging it through manipulation.

Embracing Individuality

In polygyny, a complex interplay exists between personalities, desires, and expectations. It's vital to understand that each wife brings her own experiences, aspirations, and challenges to their marriage. These differences are not obstacles but rather opportunities for growth and learning.

As a wife in a polygyny, one of the first lessons to remember is that each marriage is unique. The dynamics between your husband and his other wife/wives may vary, as will the dynamics between you and your co-wives. Resist the temptation to compare your marriage to others, as this can lead to unnecessary jealousy and insecurity.

I will deal with jealousy and insecurity in a little more detail later, but first, let me let you in on a little story about how I let my insecurities and jealousy affect the way I felt about my marriage by not embracing my individuality and what I had to offer:

What am I here for? What do you want from me? How am I important to you when you already have a wife that you love and have a family with? I played these questions in my head over and over in the scenario of how I would present them to my husband.

I didn't know him since we were teenagers. I wasn't his "high school sweetheart." Heck, I didn't give him his first daughter or first son. I always felt that I came second. Second string, second fiddle, second class.

Even though I knew I was kind, loving, beautiful, ambitious, caring, intelligent, and a host of other things, they didn't seem like enough to deserve my husband's heart, respect, and desire in my mind. I harbored so many insecurities for the man that checked the boxes for me (I'll get into that a bit more later in the book).

The insecurities fueled jealousy, especially when he would replay the "love story" of his and my co-wife during their anniversary when he ran a business promotion. The green-eyed monster reared its ugly head when I was told that I would never catch up to Coach Fatimah.

I found out later that this statement had to do with time as my timeline was something I could not control and would never be able to change. However, I didn't see that in his meaning. I saw it meaning something else.

I felt my husband had all that he needed, and even though I wanted the connection of my husband and the blending of the family, I felt many times that I just didn't belong.

I never desired to replace my co-wife, despite what others said or thought. In fact, I saw us as friends, sisters in Islam, building, bonding, and being one big happy family. However, insecurities, poor communication, jealousies, comparisons, and many other relationship-wrecking balls kept tearing through our lives before the strong foundation could be built.

I let so many things get in the way of my being confident in myself, in my marriage, in my place in the family. I felt I had to learn to be what I thought people liked, instead of just embracing and embodying the person I was and let them love, or leave. I learned that my uniqueness brings much to me and those around me, and when I keep that in mind, my relationships, especially my marriage, became much fuller.

Learn to embrace the uniqueness of your own marriage. Take the time to understand your husband's individuality, as well as your own. What drew you both together? What are your shared interests and values? What differences do you have that can create opportunities to learn from one another?

Coach Nazir teases me about the words that I've "taught" him and how my different experiences in life have opened him up to things that were just "corny," "bougie with a mix of country," and just unique. I, too, have learned so much and continue to learn much from him.

By focusing on what makes your individual relationship special, you can build a stronger connection that transcends the complexities of polygyny. Every time I think about the things that make the connection between Coach Nazir and me unique, I can't help but smile and embrace the fact that I didn't have to be my co-wife, nor did Coach Fatimah have to change and be like me in order to establish and build a fulfilling marriage with our husband.

The following are several commitments I encourage clients to practice when they are working to connect on a higher level within their marriage: For information on my coaching programs, visit CoachNyla.com.

Set Personal Goals: Encourage each other to set and pursue personal goals. These goals can be related to career, education, hobbies, or personal development. Having individual goals not only fosters a sense of purpose but also contributes positively to the family's overall well-being.

Respect Boundaries: It's crucial to respect each other's boundaries and personal space. Understand that there may be times when a spouse needs some time alone or with friends to pursue their individual interests. Encourage and support these moments of self-discovery and "me time."

Celebrate Differences: Embrace the differences between one another. Celebrate each individual's unique qualities, talents, and interests. Recognize that these differences can enrich the family dynamic and bring new perspectives.

Quality Time Together: While it's essential to nurture individuality, don't forget to spend quality time together as a family. Engage in activities that everyone enjoys, fostering a sense of togetherness and unity. We love to get together for "family game/family movie night". I encourages bonding as a unit. I discuss this more later in the book.

Chapter 30

THE FOUR SELFS

EMBRACING INDIVIDUALITY WITHIN POLYGYNY STARTS WITH THE "FOUR Selfs." It's crucial for each spouse to understand and cultivate these in their lives. I had to learn the power of being intentional with the Four Selfs through trial and error. My clients have the privilege of not having to go through what I grew through to possess this knowledge. So do you. Here's what they are and why these aspects are so vital within marriage:

Self-Awareness: Self-awareness involves understanding your own emotions, needs, and desires. It allows you to communicate effectively with your spouse(s) about what you require to feel happy and fulfilled. Self-awareness also enables you to identify and address any insecurities or challenges that may arise.

Self-Love: Self-love is about nurturing a positive relationship with oneself. When spouses practice self-love, they are better equipped to love and support each other. It prevents the development of unhealthy dependencies and encourages personal growth.

Self-Discovery: Self-discovery is an ongoing process of learning about oneself. It involves exploring new interests, passions, and facets of your personality. Self-discovery is very powerful for maintaining a strong sense of individuality within a polygyny. Constant, never-ending growth comes from the continuous practice of self-discovery.

Self-Care: Self-care is the practice of taking time to prioritize your mental, emotional, and physical well-being. It includes activities such as exercise, meditation, pursuing hobbies, and seeking moments of relaxation. Self-care is not selfish; it's a necessary part of being a healthy, happy spouse. Well, I call it being selfish for the greater good!

Answer the following:

I will spend _____ per week learning about myself, nurturing and caring for myself by doing …

Chapter 31

FOSTERING THE FOUNDATION
OF TRUST AND SECURITY

TRUST AND SECURITY ARE FOUNDATIONAL ELEMENTS OF ANY SUCCESSFUL polygynous marriage. When we feel secure in our relationships, we are more likely to embrace our individuality and support each other's personal growth. Here's how trust and security play vital roles in polygyny:

Open and Honest Communication: Trust is built through open and honest communication. Spouses should feel comfortable discussing their feelings, concerns, and desires without fear of judgment or rejection. Creating a safe space for such conversations is essential.

This seems to be challenging in polygyny, especially for husbands. The judgment they receive for wanting to marry and being responsible for more than one wife is beyond degrading and discriminating. That, in turn, takes away the safe space to have the challenging/uncomfortable conversations that can create closeness and understanding vs. condemnation and distance.

I'm not choosing sides on this; I'm just addressing one of the significant challenges reported when having open and honest communication in polygyny.

Consistency and Reliability: Consistency in actions and words helps build trust for both husbands and wives. Spouses should be reliable in fulfilling their commitments to each other. Notice that I didn't say promises. Although keeping our promises is important, I've found that they are not considered to have as much importance as commitments.

Former NFL tight end Shannon Sharpe gave a quote that summed it up beautifully, and I like to use it to remind myself to make commitments and not promises.

"Make commitments instead of promises. Promises are like pie crusts, thin and easily broken."

Trust grows when spouses know they can depend on each other, and depending on one another happens when commitments are honored.

Respect and Empathy: It's essential to show respect and empathy toward each other and consider one another's feelings and perspectives. Even if you don't fully understand your spouse's point of view, acknowledging their feelings and experiences is a significant step toward fostering trust.

Active listening helps when trying to understand perspectives. Gaining clarity and knowing that your spouse may not always see things the way you do and vice versa gives you the opportunity to learn from and respect the differences between each other.

Transparency: Being transparent in financial matters, family decisions, and future plans is crucial. When all spouses are informed and involved, it reduces feelings of insecurity and promotes a sense of ownership within the family unit.

Being transparent doesn't mean that every little detail is discussed or laid on the table. It's more about addressing the important and beneficial matters so the unit can run smoothly. We must be mindful of acknowledging the husband as the leader and, with that being said, knowing to trust his decisions. If there are any issues or discrepancies, these should be discussed without drama.

Suppose we, as wives, are confident in our decision to be married to a man who is capable, responsible, a great provider, and maintainer. In that case, we must support his leadership and his role as a husband. This is true no matter how many wives he has.

Conflict Resolution: How conflicts are handled can significantly impact trust and security. Spouses should work together to develop effective conflict resolution strategies that promote understanding and compromise rather than escalation.

Having a code word, special touch, or look to use when conversations get heated, or drama ensues keeps conflicts from escalating to the point of no return or from allowing us to say or do things that will break trust or respect that we may regret later.

"I said a beef hotlinks!" A smile creeps across my face every time I hear that from my husband. As corny as it is, this sentence and the way it is said by Coach Nazir reminds me to relax and have fun, and it's not that serious. It also helps interrupt a negative pattern and redirect us to a better one.

The Importance of Privacy

In any marriage, monogamous or polygynous, maintaining a level of privacy is essential. While it's natural to seek support and advice from friends and family, some matters should remain within the confines of your relationship. This includes intimate details of your marriage, conflicts, and disagreements. Sharing these private matters with others can harm trust and intimacy.

I tell clients that they must "be careful not to give others ammunition to blow holes in their marriage. "That means that they must set boundaries and respect their marriage even through challenging times. If you need someone to talk to, get a trusted coach or counselor or keep a journal. Many times, biases can come out from those who are close to you when you start to complain about your marriage.

In polygynous marriages, the need for privacy becomes even more significant. Conflicts and challenges may arise between co-wives or with your husband. These issues should be addressed and resolved within the family unit. Outsiders may not fully understand the complexities of your relationship and can unintentionally exacerbate tensions.

Privacy also extends to social media and public spaces. It's essential to exercise discretion when discussing your marriage online or in public. Oversharing can lead to unwanted attention and potential harm to your family's reputation. Remember that not everyone will be accepting or understanding of your lifestyle choices.

We knew that before we started Outstanding Personal Relationships, and we discussed the pros and cons of being in the public eye as coaches who are Muslim and practice polygyny. There are challenges. However, the benefit we provide outweigh any problems that we may come across.

Focusing on Your Connection

As a wife in a polygyny, our primary relationship is with our husband. He is the common thread that ties all the wives together. While it's natural to form bonds with your co-wives and build a sense of sisterhood, remember that your husband is the one practicing polygyny. Your connection with him is unique and essential.

Nurturing this connection involves open and honest communication. Discuss your feelings, needs, and expectations with your husband regularly. Be attentive to his feelings and concerns as well.

Our husbands appreciate our support, comfort, and compassion. They go through their own dramas in a world that expects so much of them. We, in turn, can be their solace and peace. Maintaining strong emotional ties with your husband can help to build a stable and fulfilling family structure with trust, respect, and a deep connection.

Set aside quality time for one-on-one interactions with your husband. These moments can deepen your connection and provide a sense of intimacy that is specific to your relationship. Whether it's sharing a hobby, going on dates, or simply engaging in heartfelt conversations, these moments contribute to a stronger bond.

Wives as Equals

One fundamental principle to uphold in a polygynous marriage is that each wife is equal in value and importance. There should be no hierarchy in wife status. All wives deserve love, respect, and consideration from their husband. In short, All Wives Matter! The success of a polygynous marriage is not measured by who holds a superior position but by the quality of the relationships within the family and individual marriage.

I see a lot of online battles about who deserves the higher position, the highest level of respect, love, and honor, and hands down, the initial wife is the one brought to the forefront. The argument includes the initial wife's sacrifices for the husband.

It focuses on the fact that she has been there from the beginning and helped to make him who he is, and their life together what it is, only for another woman to come and benefit from it.

We must understand that the husband took part in his growth, and the initial wife benefited from that growth. Don't get me wrong, it is understandable that initial wives were first, and no one will debate that. However, it is usually by timeline and not that the husband had a choice between which wife he would have married first. When we humble ourselves and let go of the ego, we can enjoy our marriages without comparing ourselves to our co-wives and competing with one another.

No matter how tough it can be at times, talk of sacrificing, building, and going through the actions, to make a marriage succeed doesn't usually come up as a problem until the husband chooses to practice polygyny. When that happens, there becomes a need to showcase why other wives cannot, and should not be at the level of an initial wife, due to the timeline.

This observation is not to discredit or to throw shade, It's so we can be aware and stop looking at things from such a biased view. When we learn to practice this with sincerity, relationships can thrive on a higher level.

The idea that a wife is a wife is a wife, regardless of her position in the order of marriage, should be embraced by all involved. Yes, the initial wife was around longer. Yes, she and the husband built the family that existed before the husband married again.

However, once the family dynamic has changed, any additional wives have rights as wives, regardless of when they came into the picture. A family can still be built, changed and grown, with the presence of another wife and any other additions to the family. Do we discredit new children that are added just because they came later?

Husbands should encourage mutual support and cooperation among the wives and not feed into the timeline rhetoric. Jealousy and competition can be destructive forces, but unity and sisterhood can make the family stronger.

Suppose there are issues where it seems as though a wife is getting preferential treatment at the expense of the family and/or the other wife or wives. In that case, it's essential to communicate openly with your husband about these feelings regarding equality within the marriage. Ensure that he understands your desire for fairness and equity among all wives. A strong and compassionate husband will strive to create an atmosphere of equality and harmony within the family.

Answer the following:

My biases have affected my marriage and family dynamic by…

I will replace my biases in order to improve my marriage and family connections by…

Minding your marriage in polygyny helps quell the biases that can come from societal conditioning because it involves recognizing the uniqueness of each relationship, respecting privacy, focusing on your connection with your husband, and upholding the principle that all wives are important.

By practicing these principles, you can navigate the complexities of polygyny with grace, understanding, and harmony. Remember, it's not about the structure of the marriage but the love, respect, and unity within it that truly matters. Polygyny can be fulfilling and harmonious when approached with open hearts and minds, as well as recognizing the beauty in diversity and the strength in unity.

Chapter 32

NAVIGATING SOCIETAL CONDITIONING AND RELATIONSHIP DYNAMICS

WE DISCUSSED SOCIETAL CONDITIONING AND HOW IT CAN AFFECT HOW we view ourselves, our relationships, and our marriages. When it comes to polygyny, especially in the West, we must understand the importance of the delicate balance between social esteem and self-esteem.

Let's talk about the influence of societal conditioning, the dynamics between initial and additional wives, and the impact of family and friends on the polygynous dynamic.

Societal Conditioning and Expectations

"Why would you not consider the feelings of your co-wife before you married HER husband?"

"Why would you think that that would be ok?"

"You are nothing but a pick-me, home-wrecking, selfish snake that doesn't care about anyone but yourself."

"I hope your husband marries again so you can see how it feels.

"You are just trying to take someone else's life because you can't have one of your own."

*"Your self-esteem must be really low to marry someone else's man." ~**A few of the many statements I heard after marrying into polygyny**.*

We just discussed biases in society and how that can show up in polygyny and our other relationships. I just have a quick question for you to ponder: if those statements were hurled at you, would you say, "Yeah, I deserve that," or would it touch you in a way that may cause some shakiness in the way you view others and their degree of fairness? Would you question whether you were wrong for doing something that allowed, even if others didn't understand it?

How do you think that questioning may affect how you operate with others and how you navigate through your relationships, let alone your marriage?

Societal conditioning plays a significant role in shaping our beliefs and expectations, especially when it comes to the structure of romantic relationships. In many societies, monogamy is the prevailing norm, and any deviation from this norm, such as polygyny, can be met with judgment, stigma, and misunderstanding.

As a wife in polygyny, it's essential to recognize that societal conditioning can affect your self-esteem. The pressure to conform to societal expectations can lead to feelings of inadequacy or self-doubt. It's crucial to differentiate between the values and expectations imposed by society and your own sense of self-worth.

Societal norms that may be immoral, biased, and downright wrong can create a mentality of war within the natural dynamic of the nuclear family structure. We are pro-morals, so we understand this war can affect monogamous and polygynous marriages. In polygyny, it creates a versus between wives.

Chapter 33

Initial Wife vs. Additional Wife Dynamics

In polygyny, there can be challenges and conflicts between the initial wife (the first wife) and additional wives (those who enter the marriage later). These conflicts often stem from a sense of competition for the husband's attention, resources, or affection.

Understanding these dynamics requires empathy and open communication. The initial wife may grapple with feelings of insecurity or territoriality, while additional wives may feel like outsiders trying to find their place within an established family. It's essential for spouses to address these emotions openly and collaboratively.

Recognizing that your husband's decision to practice polygyny does not diminish your value or importance is crucial for initial wives. Your unique bond with him remains intact, and your role in the family remains vital. Nothing or no one but you can change that. Each wife is an integral part of the family unit, contributing her strengths, love, and support.

Similarly, it should be understood that additional wives are not "add-ins" but cherished members of the family. They are equal in importance and deserving of love, respect, and openness from both the husband and their fellow wives, in order for the family dynamic to reach a high level of success and fulfillment.

Embracing unity and sisterhood within the family fosters a harmonious environment where each member can thrive and feel valued. In order to do that, we must learn how to properly maintain balance when it comes to social esteem and self-esteem.

Balancing Social Esteem and Self-Esteem

Balancing social esteem, which is how you're perceived by others, and self-esteem, which is your own sense of self-worth, can be challenging in polygyny. It's essential to prioritize self-esteem and maintain a strong sense of self-worth regardless of external judgments or opinions.

Building self-esteem involves self-reflection and self-acceptance. It is essential to understand that your worth as an individual is not defined by your relationship status or the structure of your marriage. Your value lies in your character, your abilities, and your contributions to the world.

While it's natural to seek social esteem and acceptance, prioritize your self-esteem above all else. Surround yourself with individuals who support and respect your choices. Seek out communities and support networks that are inclusive and understanding of polygynous relationships.

Navigating social esteem versus self-esteem in polygyny requires a strong sense of self-worth, open communication, and resilience in the face of societal conditioning and external influences. By recognizing the influence of societal norms, addressing conflicts within the family, and preserving self-esteem, you can build a resilient and harmonious marriage in polygyny that thrives despite external challenges. Remember that your self-worth is not defined by the structure of your marriage but by the love, respect, and mutual understanding within it.

Polygynous marriages are inherently complex, characterized by multiple individuals with unique feelings and needs. It's essential to recognize that emotions play a significant role in any relationship, and in polygyny, they can be especially intense and intricate.

Jealousy, insecurity, and loneliness are a few of the emotions that regularly show up in wives in polygyny. Whether initial, additional, or a potential wife, your timeline doesn't matter when it comes to these emotions showing up in your life or marriage.

Jealousy: The Green-Eyed Monster

Jealousy is a powerful and often overwhelming emotion that can surface in any relationship, monogamous or polygynous. In polygyny, jealousy can manifest when we feel threatened or insecure due to the attention or affection another spouse receives. This doesn't have to be jealousies between wives.

In some marriages, wives are jealous of their husbands. They become jealous of what they have, what they can do, and the differences that exist between men and women. It's essential to acknowledge that jealousy is a natural human emotion, but how it is managed can make all the difference in how a marriage grows or dies.

Loneliness: The Isolation Within

Loneliness can be a pervasive and isolating emotion in polygynous relationships. Spouses may experience moments when they feel disconnected or distant from their partners due to the complexities of shared affections and responsibilities. Loneliness can lead to emotional detachment and strain within the family unit when it's not addressed properly.

Did you know that even those who understand and agree with being in polygyny encounter the feeling of being lonely? Wives may go through moments of thinking that the husband doesn't care about her or is too busy with his other wife or other household (if there are separate dwellings).

Husbands can feel the strain of loneliness in their marriage as well. When they are working hard to provide, protect, and deal with the outside world for the betterment of their family, it can be difficult to face complaints, disrespect, and manipulative actions from a wife or wives who lack control of how they handle any of the complexities that can come with polygyny.

Insecurities: The Self-Doubt Struggle

Insecurities often stem from feelings of inadequacy or self-doubt. In polygyny, wives may compare themselves to their co-wives and even their own husbands. This can lead to a sense of inferiority or the belief that they don't measure up. Insecurities can erode self-esteem and hinder personal growth.

Chapter 34

CONFRONTING JEALOUSY

JEALOUSY IS A NATURAL HUMAN EMOTION, BUT IT CAN BECOME PROBLEMATIC if left unchecked. In polygyny, where multiple wives share affection and attention from a common partner, jealousy can be particularly challenging. However, it is possible to confront and manage jealousy constructively.

Self-Reflection and Self-Awareness

Recognizing and acknowledging jealousy is the first step in managing it. Take time to reflect on the root causes of your jealousy. Is it triggered by fear, insecurity, or a sense of competition? Self-awareness can help you understand why you feel the way you do.

Open and Honest Communication

Communication is key to addressing jealousy in polygyny. Engage in open and honest conversations with your spouse(s) about what is triggering you and feeding into your jealousy. Share your concerns and fears, and actively listen to their perspective. Constructive communication can lead to a deeper understanding and help alleviate jealousy.

Self-Compassion

Be kind and compassionate to yourself. Understand that feeling jealous does not make you inadequate or unworthy. It makes you human. Embrace self-compassion as you work through your emotions, knowing that you are on a journey of personal growth and emotional development. However, don't excuse bad behavior from yourself or others.

Combating Loneliness

Loneliness can be a pervasive emotion in polygyny, particularly when communication falters or when individuals feel isolated within the family unit. Feelings of not belonging or losing one's place can make tense or uncomfortable situations worse. To combat loneliness, consider the following strategies:

Scheduled Family Time

Create designated times for family meetings or activities that encourage interaction and bonding. These moments can help combat loneliness by fostering a sense of togetherness and unity within the family.

For years, we have been holding weekly family meetings. They've evolved over the years, and they were a little rocky at the outset. Getting used to meeting once a week, learning about one another, and sharing input on different family activities, events, etc., was awkward, to say the least.

However, with open minds and strong leadership guiding the way, we became closer as a family, and the family meetings became less awkward. They later became the catalyst for family dinners, movie and game nights.

Individual Attention

As a husband, dedicate quality one-on-one time to each wife. These personal moments can alleviate loneliness and provide a platform for deeper emotional connections. Whether it's a heartfelt conversation, a shared hobby, or a romantic date, prioritize these moments to nurture your relationships.

Be mindful if you decide to take your wives to the same movie, show, or event at different times. I may cause them to feel that you don't see them as individuals, or special, and that they are just part of some "buy one, get one" deal.

I remember when I discovered that I was attending some of the same movies and events that my co-wife attended with our husband. At first, I felt hurt. I didn't look at the time spent as quality time with my husband. I saw that I was getting the replays of what my co-wife was enjoying.

Because she was his first wife, I felt like the "leftover wife," "second fiddle," "not the real wife," and any other title other than a wife that is loved in her own individual right. I couldn't help but think that with everything we did together, every restaurant, every movie that she had experienced it first, and, I only experienced it so I wasn't "left out."

I eventually expressed my feelings about it, and we had an eye-opening, heartfelt conversation. I will spare you the details. However, he understood why feeling special was important.

He understood how actions like that (at the time I was trying to figure out where I fitted into his life, and family), could cause insecurities and doubts within me. I was also able to appreciate his thought process behind it all, and we came to a healthy place of understanding and resolution.

Now, before you all start to jump up and complain about how men should not be so insensitive and take women, especially their wives, to the same places, understand that we all have been to the same places at some point in time. It's not the place but the experience that makes it different.

We tend to favor a lot of the same things, so should we miss out because someone was there before we were? If we keep up that type of petty, immature mindset, we will miss out on so many fun, exciting, and beautiful moments in life and relationships and loneliness will be an ongoing occurrence.

Seek Support

Loneliness can intensify when you feel isolated from external support networks. Reach out to different off and online pro-polygyny communities where like-minded individuals share similar experiences. Connecting with others can help combat feelings of isolation and provide valuable insights and advice. You can find ours at PolygamyEducation.com and LetsTalk-Polygamy on Facebook.

Contesting Insecurities

Our insecurities can chip away at our self-esteem, which can lead to discontent and lack of fulfillment in our marriages. However, there are ways to overcome and combat insecurity when it arises in our relationships. Self-awareness and being proactive in conquering the negative self-talk and self-defeating thoughts or practices are important steps to use to keep insecurities at bay. To confront insecurities that may arise in polygyny, consider the following strategies:

Communication and Vulnerability

Initiate conversations with your husband about your insecurities. Sharing your vulnerabilities can lead to a deeper understanding and mutual support. When spouses communicate about what triggers insecurities in the marriage, they can then work together to confront, combat, and conquer those triggers to strengthen the trust and connection as well as encourage growth in the marriage.

Focus on Self-Growth

Use your insecurities as motivation for personal growth. Set goals and work on self-improvement to boost your self-esteem. Remember that personal growth is an ongoing journey, and progress is a sign of strength. This takes a significant amount of self-awareness because never-ending improvement can only happen when we look inside and admit that we are always a work in progress.

If we were perfect or complete the way we are with no need for growth, that would be a sad state to be in as we would shut off any opportunity to learn, improve, and connect with others.

Positive Self-Affirmations

Practice daily affirmations to boost your self-confidence and self-worth. Remind yourself of your unique qualities and contributions to the marriage and to the family. Positive self-affirmations can help counteract negative self-talk and foster a more positive self-image.

The emotions we go through in polygyny can be complex and varied. Jealousy, loneliness, as well as insecurities can test the bonds between spouses, but with self-awareness, open communication, and a commitment to personal and relational growth, these emotions can be transformed into opportunities for deeper connections and emotional resilience. Remember that polygyny is a journey that involves navigating a wide range of emotions, and how we address and learn from these feelings is what truly matters.

Answer the following:

I will actively focus on self-growth by...

Chapter 35

The Impact of Family and Friends

Family and friends can have a significant impact on the polygynous dynamic. Their reactions and attitudes may range from curiosity and support to judgment and disapproval. Navigating these external influences requires a delicate balance between preserving your self-esteem and maintaining healthy relationships with loved ones.

I didn't discuss the challenges that I was having in the early years of polygyny with my family or with many others. I had one friend who knew that I was having some issues with the adjustments of polygyny and the issues that my marriage to Coach Nazir brought about.

She was very understanding, did not insert any bias, and did not encourage any slander, negativity, or drama in our conversations or our time spent together. I liked that, and it increased our bond and showed me that I had a true friend in all of this. We just focused on having fun, relaxing, or taking my mind off any troubles I was going through.

I didn't want to tell anyone in my family about the feelings I was experiencing in polygyny, nor did I inform them of the rough transition period. I did not want them to impose their thoughts and biases on the situation nor did I want them to look at my family or my religion in a negative way because of their desire to protect me or "have my back".

When discussing your polygynous marriage with family and friends, it's essential to set boundaries regarding what you're willing to share. While open communication is vital, not all details of your marriage need to be disclosed to external parties. Respecting your family's privacy can help prevent unnecessary conflicts and judgment.

It's common for family and friends to have concerns or reservations about polygyny. They may fear for your emotional well-being or question the stability of your marriage. In such cases, calmly and confidently asserting your position and choices can help ease their concerns. Explain the reasons behind your decision and emphasize the importance of mutual respect within your marriage.

Having the Right Support System

Navigating the intricacies of polygyny can be both rewarding and challenging. So, establishing a solid support system is crucial to ensure emotional well-being, effective communication, and the overall success of the family unit.

Let's talk about the importance of building a strong support system that includes those who are non-biased, genuinely care about your well-being, and know how to provide the support needed for those in polygyny.

The Need for Support in Polygyny

The dynamics of polygyny can be complex as it deals with multiple individuals with their own unique personalities and experiences. As with all relationships, you have your ups and downs, highs and lows; polygyny is no exception, and it's not uncommon for spouses to encounter situations that require outside perspectives and guidance.

Emotional Well-Being: The emotional well-being of each spouse is paramount in a polygyny. Emotions such as jealousy, loneliness, and insecurities can surface, and having a support system can help individuals navigate and manage these feelings effectively.

Each person's support system may be different, consisting of various friends, family members, and professionals. Just because you are a part of the same family does not necessarily mean that you will utilize the same resources all the time.

Effective Communication: Open and honest communication is crucial in polygyny. Having a support system that encourages and facilitates communication can prevent misunderstandings and conflicts from escalating.

Personal Growth: A strong support system can encourage personal growth and self-improvement among spouses and family members. With the proper guidance and encouragement, individuals can work on their insecurities and develop a more positive self-image.

Family Harmony: Supportive individuals can help maintain harmony within the family unit. They can provide guidance on conflict resolution, family planning, and other important aspects of family life.

Building the Right Support System

Creating a strong, solid support system in polygyny involves carefully selecting those who can offer non-biased, caring, and effective support. We need care, love, and support throughout our lives, and having those whom we trust is paramount, especially when we are facing challenges in polygyny.

Below are characteristics of a strong, solid support system, and the individuals who are chosen to be a part of them should possess these in the highest regard.

Non-Biased Individuals: Seek out those who can provide objective advice and perspective. They do not take sides or favor one spouse or family member over another. This neutrality is crucial in polygynous families to ensure fair treatment and equitable solutions to conflicts.

Genuine Care and Empathy: Your support system should consist of people who genuinely care about your well-being and the well-being of the entire family. They should have a deep sense of empathy and be willing to listen and understand your concerns without judgment.

Effective Listeners: Effective listening is a vital skill in a support system. Individuals who can actively listen to your thoughts, feelings, and concerns are better equipped to offer meaningful guidance and support. They should be patient and attentive without adding any biased feedback.

Effective listeners can be that shoulder that you may need to cry on or that soundboard from which you can bounce productive ideas. Yes, building a successful family dynamic requires productivity in order to grow.

Experienced Advisors: Seek out individuals who have experience in polygynous relationships or have expertise in relationship dynamics. Their knowledge can be invaluable in helping you navigate the unique challenges that may arise.

Confidentiality: Confidentiality is essential in a support system. Spouses should feel comfortable sharing their thoughts and feelings without fear of breaches of trust. Ensure that your support system understands the importance of discretion and won't abuse their position to impart information.

Types of Supportive Individuals

Your support system can consist of a variety of individuals, each offering different forms of support.

Trusted Friends and Family: Close friends and family members who are non-biased and genuinely care about your well-being can provide emotional support and a sense of belonging.

Therapists, Counselors, and Coaches: Professional therapists, counselors, or coaches can offer expert guidance on emotional and relationship issues. They can help you develop effective coping strategies and improve communication within the family.

Coaches can assist you in taking your relationships to higher levels. They will stretch you and give you the tools to grow within yourself and consequently, grow within your relationships. We offer coaching at OutstandingPersonalRelationships.com

Support Groups: Joining a support group for those in polygyny can provide a sense of community and understanding. Groups allow you to connect with others facing similar challenges. This can be on or offline.

Religious or Spiritual Leaders: If your polygynous marriage is religious or spiritually based, seek guidance from leaders or mentors within your faith community. They can provide both spiritual and practical advice.

Online Communities: Online forums and communities dedicated to polygyny can be valuable sources of support and information. They offer a platform for sharing experiences and seeking advice from like-minded individuals. You can check out our various online communities at PolygamyEducation.com and on Facebook at LetsTalkPolygamy.

The Role of a Support System

Supportive individuals can offer fresh perspectives on challenges and conflicts within the family. They can help spouses see situations from different angles and make informed decisions.

During times of emotional distress, a support system can provide a safe space to express feelings and receive comfort. Knowing that you have someone to lean on can alleviate stress and anxiety.

Those in your support circle can offer guidance on resolving conflicts and improving communication within the family. They can act as mediators or facilitators in discussions. They can also encourage personal growth and self-improvement among spouses by motivating each other to work on their insecurities and develop healthier self-esteem.

Having a source of encouragement and positivity within your support system can also increase the success of the family dynamic through celebration of achievements and milestones within the family.

Cultivating and Maintaining Your Support System

As much as it is needed and essential for fulfillment and success, we must understand that building a strong support system takes time and effort.

Below are tips to help you in choosing the type of support system that will offer the best benefit to you throughout your journey.

Identify Your Needs: Consider what types of support you need when it comes to navigating through your polygynous marriage. Do you require emotional support, conflict resolution guidance, or personal growth assistance?

Seek Out Supportive Individuals: Actively seek out individuals who meet the criteria of being non-biased, caring, and effective supporters. Reach out to friends, family, or professionals who align with your needs.

Nurture Relationships: Once you've identified supportive individuals, invest time and effort in nurturing these relationships. Keep the lines of communication open and let them know how much their support means to you.

Regularly Engage with Your Support System: Engage with your support system regularly. Attend support group meetings, schedule therapy sessions, or maintain contact with friends and family who offer support.

It's okay to ask for help and embrace the assistance that is beneficial. Don't feel like a failure or that something is wrong with you because you sought out assistance and support. It makes you proactive, intentional, and wise.

Be Open to Feedback: Remember that your support system may offer constructive feedback or advice. Be open to receiving input and considering different perspectives.

Navigating through the waters of polygyny can be complex and challenging at times. However, a strong support system can make a huge difference. Having that winning support team that understands what it means to be there for you emotionally, mentally, and spiritually is essential for maintaining harmony, fostering personal growth, and resolving conflicts effectively.

It's important to cultivate and maintain your support team with care and embrace the positive impact it can have on your polygynous journey. Teams win when they work together.

Chapter 36

CHOOSING TO BE MARRIED
TO A MARRIED MAN

LET ME LET YOU IN ON SOMETHING YOU MAY NOT SEE IN ANY OF THE other polygyny books that are out there, or at least not in those that have been released before this one. It is, why would someone choose to share their husband?

We hear different stories about initial wives and the struggle of accepting their husbands marrying again. However, we don't really hear why one would choose to become an additional wife or why one would want her husband to practice polygyny. So, let's talk about it.

Some women find themselves drawn to the idea of marrying a married man. Some women actually encourage their husbands to marry other women. Despite being looked at as women with low self-esteem or women who do not love or desire their husbands, mature women in polygyny display the characteristics of confident, loving women who understand the desires of men as well as the benefits of a healthy polygynous family dynamic.

Of course, as a Muslim woman who married a married man and who coaches women on polygyny (initial wives, additional wives, and potential wives), I believe it's only proper that I share my story of how and why I decided to marry a married man as well as explaining a few of the challenges that came my way and how they were lessons for myself and others.

This may clear up some of the rhetoric that comes from those who don't understand women in polygyny or who like to impose their projections on another's experience.

After the failure of the relationship with my son's father, I became how I was raised, a single mother, raised by a single mother.

"Mom, what if I just want to have a baby and just kick the guy to the curb? Can I do that?" I asked as a curious 14-year-old with some experience in caring for children as I was the oldest child helping my mom who was a single mother and caring for her children as well as her young brother, nieces, nephews and cousins from time to time.

"You could, but why would you want that?" asked my mom, looking at me in confusion. I answered, "Because I can deal with and guide my children, but I don't want to have to deal with the drama of the man."

I felt that my mother was doing a great job raising me, my younger sister, and my two younger brothers on her own. She did have assistance from my grandmother (who I lovingly call, Gram-ma), who was also raising her youngest son, on her own as well.

As much as I loved my pop-pop (my younger siblings' father), he and Mom were on and off again for a short time, and even though he helped out and treated me like his own, the drama of their union didn't scream relationship goals to me.

Throughout my latter teenage years, I realized I wanted more than what had been offered in the relationships I'd had. It wasn't until meeting and fostering a relationship at 17 with my then boyfriend and giving birth at 20 to our only child together, that I thought I was going to have a stable family life. We talked about getting married after college and grow the family we had started.

To cut a long story short, he cheated, and it didn't work out the way we had discussed. I became a single mother to my son, struggling emotionally, mentally, and, after a while, financially.

The crazy thing was that, for a while, I had so much animosity towards the one with whom he had cheated and realized that I was angry at her, but hurt by him. Eventually I had to live, learn, and let go.

Several years later, I became an entrepreneur and started my first business in a network marketing company. Through that company, I met Coach Nazir and Coach Fatimah and was impressed and inspired by them. As I worked to grow my business and improve my life, I learned so many things. I later converted to Islam in my journey towards success and fulfillment that I desired for myself and my young son.

Years later I met a Muslim man who would become my husband and the father of my second child. Things didn't work out for us as he was drawn to a lifestyle that was much removed from what I wanted and saw for my family. We divorced, and I was once again a single mother, this time raising two children on my own.

As the years went by, despite focusing on building my business and raising my children, I knew I wanted more. I desired a better dynamic for myself and my children.

I remembered a book I had read on polygamy in Islam, and I saw the family dynamic and leadership qualities that I desired in Coach Nazir and his family. I was never against the thought or practice of polygyny, and as a practicing Muslim, I understood and respected the regulations and wisdom behind it. I was attracted to the idea, thinking it would be a good fit for what I was looking for.

After settling the nervous thoughts and going through the what ifs in my mind, I finally expressed my interest to my wakeel and he reached out to Coach Nazir. I still don't know all of the ins and outs of the conversations, however, I do know that he said yes when he could have said no and took on the commitment of honoring me as his wife.

The beginning was not what I expected or desired, as it was a rocky start. However, with work, education, and growth, we became and are still becoming the family I envisioned we would be.

There are things that I would have liked to have been prepared for or at least known about prior to diving into marrying a married man. Of course, the dynamics are different from monogamy, and there were no books, programs, or the like to prepare me for what was in store. Prayerfully, we are changing that.

Checking the Boxes: What Women Seek in a Husband

When contemplating marrying a married man, it's crucial for a potential wife to evaluate her expectations and ensure that the man she's looking to marry meets her criteria for a husband.

In Islam, these discussions happen through the guardian of the potential wife (known as the wakeel or walee) and the potential husband and family. It is up to the guardian to do the leg work to make sure the potential husband is compatible, and the leadership and financial qualities are in place.

There is so much wisdom behind this, as women can overlook things based on feelings. We tend to be seduced by our ears, while men are seduced by their eyes.

The potential wife does have a say in what she is looking for, and she brings that information to her guardian, who can be her father, uncle, or other male Muslim she cannot marry who has her best interest in mind. He can take that information and add other vital elements that may have been overlooked, and seek out a potential husband who meets those characteristics to see if they are a suitable match. This is the same process whether practicing monogamy or polygyny.

As in any other marriage, certain fundamental aspects should be considered:

Compatibility

Compatibility is the cornerstone of a successful marriage. Potential wives should assess whether their values, beliefs, and life goals align with those of the married man. Open and honest conversations about expectations, lifestyle, and future plans are essential.

Emotional Connection

Emotional connection and intimacy play a vital role in any relationship. It's essential for a wife to feel emotionally fulfilled and secure in the relationship with the married man. Trust and communication are critical factors in nurturing this connection.

Respect and Support

Respect and support are non-negotiable elements in a healthy marriage. The married man should demonstrate respect for his wife's feelings, aspirations, and boundaries. Supportive actions and words should be part of the relationship dynamic.

Financial Stability

Financial stability is a practical aspect that needs to be considered. Potential wives should discuss financial arrangements and responsibilities to ensure that both parties are on the same page regarding their financial future.

Legal and Social Considerations

It's vital to be aware of the legal and social aspects of marrying a married man, as these can vary significantly depending on the jurisdiction and cultural context. Additional wives should understand the potential legal and social implications of their choice to marry a man who is already married. Having wills and contracts in place is essential in making sure rights are fulfilled and enforced.

The Wife, Her Support, and Her Role in Maintaining a Successful Family in Polygyny

What is the role of a wife when it comes to success in polygyny? Should the success of a man being married to multiple women depend on the women involved? As adults, we should understand that we must take responsibility for our part in success as well as failure in our marriage, even if that marriage is in polygyny.

As wives, we are monogamously married to our husbands, and being an attractive wife to a mature, compatible man who practices polygyny can and will increase our chances of success and fulfillment in it. What does being an attractive wife look like? Let's talk about it.

Femininity: Embracing one's femininity as a wife provides a proper balance within the marriage. Being feminine doesn't mean being weak or not having a voice. It means knowing how to influence with a soft nature. It means being nurturing and comforting, as that is in our natural makeup as women.

I told the story of being raised by a single mother who was raised by a single mother and becoming a single mother myself after some time. Being a woman who had to nurture, protect, provide, and maintain things mostly on my own, I began to lose my femininity as my masculine energy increased. Men are built to fight through the pressures, strain, and madness in the world.

Women can tackle these stressors, but we aren't created for it. Therefore, we start to take on a masculine identity that feeds unhealthy relationships, breeds confusion in roles and family dynamics as well as problems in our genetic makeup through fibroids, cysts, and hormonal issues.

There was a study that concluded the further a mother is away from the home, the worse off the children will be. Women are built to nurture and care as wives, mothers, and outstanding friends.

We do not have the same genetic makeup as men, and that is a great thing. It allows us to complement one another and not compete with each other.

When we embrace our femininity and embody our soft nature, we attract and feed our husbands' masculinity, and he becomes a better leader, protector, maintainer, and provider for his entire family, including his wives.

When we fight nature and try to change what the Most High created and allowed, we become the problems that destroy the nuclear family and relationship structure. That includes the option of polygyny.

Femininity consists of being classy, soft-spoken but firm, taking care of your health, body, and mind. It also includes embracing that nurturing muscle and being submissive as well as a solid pillar of support for our husbands and family.

Submission: Submission is a beautiful and humbling way to have peace in your life and marriage. What are you talking about, Coach Nyla? Yes, I know that in these "modern" times, it seems as though being submissive is looked at as being weak by a lot of women, including wives. However, it shows trust, support, and acceptance of our husbands' leadership.

There are women today who state that they would like to be submissive. Then they add on, "to the right man." A woman who embraces her femininity is naturally submissive to the leadership of her husband because it is in her nature.

However, the blurring of the lines and switching of the roles, paired with single motherhood, feminism, and the growth of what is known as "boss bitches", have made it a normal phenomenon to buck at what is natural.

It doesn't help that women feel the need to protect themselves from predators, losers, and bums. This increased masculinity does not pair well with the masculinity of a husband who takes his role of protecting, providing, and exuding personal power seriously for the growth and success of his family as well as himself. That is why the wisdom of having a guardian such as a walee or a wakeel is important in Islam and should be important whether one practices Islam or not.

We must learn that submission is not a bad word, nor does it make us weak. We also have to understand that we must be mindful of who we choose to lead our family because women are built as solid supports and men are built for the toughness of what it takes to lead his team (family) to success and take care of that team along the way.

When we fight that, we blur the lines and add confusion which adds to the disruption and destruction of a strong, stable family unit.

Support: Supporting the leadership of the family is an amazing superpower. Don't get me wrong, sometimes it can be overlooked. However, we must understand that there is nothing small about being the support of a well-oiled machine known as your family.

Think of a building. The strongest one you can think of. What do you think holds it up? The support, paired with a solid foundation. A solid foundation, worked on by the leadership of the husband and the support and influence of the wives, can create and maintain an unstoppable, unshakable family dynamic in polygyny.

Maturity: As adults, we must establish higher levels of maturity in order for our relationships to thrive, especially in polygyny. In his relationship program, Tony Robbins stated that many of us come into our marriages/relationships with the maturity/emotional level of a 5-year-old.

At the time of writing this, my youngest son with my husband is 5-years old. He is not yet emotionally or mentally mature enough to lead or conduct any type of relationship without the assistance of his parents.

That says a lot about relationships that are started without assistance and preparation. Emotional and mental maturity are essential to healthy, successful, and fulfilling marriages and relationships—especially those in polygyny.

Emotional: Being emotionally mature means that you can handle challenges that can come your way with poise. You can look at all angles and not fly off the handle when things don't go your way.

Mental: Being mentally mature is a little different from being emotionally mature. In being mentally mature, you believe in your ability to figure things out. You know how to seek the answers you need and can understand the logical reasons why things may occur. That is within life as well as within your relationships.

Confidence: Confidence is believing in yourself and the ability to figure things out. Knowing what you possess and not being afraid of compassionately speaking your piece for your peace, and knowing what you bring to the marriage and the family to help it run, grow, and succeed, is a large part of exuding confidence in your marriage.

Being confident is essential for your well-being as well as the well-being of the family. Confidence does not harm, so don't confuse it with cockiness or arrogance.

The Husband, His Leadership, and His Role in Maintaining a Successful Family in Polygyny

We have discussed embracing our individuality to foster a healthy support system. We have also gained clarity on the polygynous nature of men as well as why women would want to marry a man who is already married.

While working to understand these topics may account for doing our own work for success in our individual marriage, we must also understand that we are not alone in this. Questions arise, such as:

"What is the husband's role in all of this?"

"Do they just marry other women with no regard to how the wives feel?"

"What about conflicts that may arise?"

The husbands that are worth having are those who can live and thrive in their masculinity as a protector and provider as well as being a beacon of support to their wives.

Polygyny can be emotionally challenging at times for all parties involved, including the husbands. However, understanding and addressing the needs and emotions of each wife is crucial for maintaining a harmonious and balanced family dynamic.

Here's how husbands in polygynous relationships can empower their wives to embrace their individuality:

Open and Honest Dialogue: Initiate and maintain open and honest conversations with each of your wives. Encourage them to express their feelings, concerns, and desires without judgment. This communication can foster understanding and trust in your marriage.

Respect for Individuality: Recognize and respect the individuality of each wife. Understand that they have unique personalities, needs, and aspirations. Encourage them to pursue their interests and goals, and provide support in their endeavors. Be mindful not to compare them to each other or project one's personality onto the other.

Celebrate Achievements: Acknowledge and celebrate the achievements and milestones of each wife. Whether personal or professional accomplishments, showing appreciation reinforces their self-worth and helps foster a positive atmosphere within the family.

Address Jealousy and Insecurity: As discussed earlier, jealousy and insecurities can naturally arise between wives in polygyny. It's crucial to address these emotions empathetically and constructively. Encourage open discussions about these feelings and work together to find solutions that help to alleviate them.

Encourage Sisterhood: Promote a sense of sisterhood among your wives. Encourage them to support and be there for each other. When your wives have strong relationships with one another, it can create a more harmonious family environment.

I know that this may take time and careful navigation, depending on the maturity of the wives and the individual dynamic. However, success and the goal of an outstanding family unit depends on it.

Nurturing the Marriages: Contributing to Growth and Flourishing

In polygyny, nurturing each marriage individually is essential for maintaining a healthy and balanced family structure. Here are ways husbands can contribute to the growth of each marriage to enable it to flourish within the polygynous framework:

Quality Time with Each Wife: Dedicate quality time to each wife separately. This allows you to strengthen your bond with each wife and create meaningful memories together.

Shared Goals and Aspirations: Encourage the development of shared goals and aspirations within each marriage. Discuss plans for the future, such as family, finances, and personal growth, to ensure that each relationship has a sense of direction and purpose and that it's going in the right direction. Creating your Marriage Mission Statement is an extremely useful tool for this. You can grab your marriage mission statement prompts at by checking out our resources at the end of the book.

Clear Communication: Establish clear lines of communication with each wife. Regularly check in with them to discuss any concerns, joys, or challenges within your marriage. Effective communication helps prevent misunderstandings and conflicts.

Conflict Resolution Skills: Develop strong conflict resolution skills to navigate challenges that may arise in each marriage. Approach conflicts with empathy, active listening, and a willingness to compromise to find mutually satisfying solutions.

Be aware of proper timing, emotions, hormonal issues that can play a part in communication, as well as misunderstandings that can arise. Have a code word, touch, or phrase in case things get off track.

Maintain Romance: Keep the romance alive in each marriage. Surprise your wives with thoughtful gestures, date nights, and expressions of love and appreciation. Romance can help maintain the emotional connection in each relationship.

Women desire connection and to feel special with their husband. Although it's understood that men are protectors, maintainers, and providers, they must realize that emotional connection and maintenance is just as important as the financial aspect.

Equal Financial Consideration: Ensure that financial considerations are fair and equitable within each marriage. Transparency in financial matters is crucial to avoid feelings of neglect or favoritism. However, as previously touched upon, we must understand that transparency does not mean disclosing every detail.

Creating separate banking accounts or using a budgeting system can make it easier to distribute funds equitably. In Islam, husbands are to be equal with time and money between wives.

Maintaining Transparency: The Importance of Open Communication

Polygyny demands a high degree of transparency and communication to maintain trust and harmony within the family. From the husband's perspective, here's how to emphasize the importance of open communication in a polygyny:

Regular Family Meetings: Schedule regular family meetings where all members can come together to discuss important family matters. This practice allows for transparency and ensures everyone has a voice.

Individual Check-Ins: In addition to family meetings, have individual check-ins with each wife. This private time provides an opportunity for them to share their thoughts and concerns openly.

Financial Transparency: Establish an effective and efficient method to handle finances equitably. Family meetings, separate accounts for each wife, budget tracking, and such can help keep things organized and just.

Understand that not everything is up for disclosure. As crazy as that may sound, having too many hands or immature feelings or emotions in important financial dealings can negatively impact the stability and growth of family wealth and security.

Conflict Resolution Mediation: If conflicts arise between wives, act as a mediator to facilitate open and respectful communication. Encourage each wife to express her perspective and feelings while emphasizing the importance of finding common ground. Be mindful not to be biased and lean towards any wife.

Respect Boundaries: Recognize and respect each wife's boundaries when it comes to privacy and personal space. Ensure that they feel comfortable discussing their needs and preferences openly with you.

Emphasize Family Unity: Reinforce the idea that the family unit is built on unity and cooperation. Encourage your wives to work together, support one another, and resolve differences amicably for the sake of the larger family's well-being.

We must understand that the husband's role in polygyny is one of immense responsibility and complexity. In addition to protecting, providing, and maintaining the needs of the family, it requires a delicate balance of supporting and empowering each wife, nurturing the growth of individual marriages, and maintaining transparency through open communication. By actively engaging in these aspects, husbands in polygyny can contribute to the overall harmony and well-being of their family.

Chapter 37

Predators, Bums, and Losers: What to Avoid When Seeking a Husband in Polygyny

It's essential to remember that successful polygyny is built on mutual respect, trust, and a commitment to ensuring that each wife's individuality is cherished and valued within the family structure, as we discussed earlier in the book. Of course, there are men out there who are not husband material, whether it be through monogamy or polygyny.

Let's talk about what I call Predators, Losers, and Bums; PLB, not to be confused with PB&J but can be just as messy and sticky if you find yourself dealing with one.

Polygyny, like any form of relationship, can attract individuals with less than honorable intentions. Unfortunately, there are individuals who exploit the concept of polygyny to collect and mistreat women for their own gain. Here are the warning signs of predators, losers, and bums in the realm of polygyny and what women should look for so they can avoid falling into their traps.

Rushing into Marriage

Beware of men who rush into polygynous marriages without taking the time to get to know you, your needs, and your desires. Predators often push for quick commitments, ignoring the importance of building trust and understanding.

Lack of Transparency

A lack of transparency regarding personal finances, existing family obligations, and emotional availability is a red flag. Honest communication should be a cornerstone of any marriage, including polygyny.

Isolation and Control

Predators may attempt to isolate you from friends and family or exert undue control over your life. Healthy polygynous marriages respect the autonomy and independence of all parties involved.

Disregard for Consent and Boundaries

Any disregard for your consent and boundaries is unacceptable. Predators may pressure you into situations you're uncomfortable with, violating your autonomy and well-being.

History of Failed Relationships

Be cautious of individuals with a history of failed polygynous or monogamous relationships. While everyone can experience relationship challenges, serial failed relationships may indicate a pattern of unhealthy behavior.

Lack of Ambition and Responsibility

Losers and bums may display a lack of ambition and responsibility in various aspects of their lives, including financial stability, employment, and personal growth. A partner should contribute positively to your life. A husband should be the leader and exhibit the qualities of a protector, maintainer, and provider for his family.

Dependence on Others

Men who are married and who are consistently depending on others for financial support, housing, or basic necessities may not be ready for polygyny. A stable husband should be self-reliant.

Disrespect and Irresponsibility

A lack of respect for your feelings, aspirations, and boundaries is a major red flag. Losers and bums may exhibit irresponsible behavior, such as neglecting financial obligations or family responsibilities.

Unwillingness to Grow and Improve

Husbands who resist personal growth and improvement may hinder the progress of a marriage, especially one in polygyny. Seek out those who are open to self-improvement and committed to personal development.

PROTECTING YOURSELF - WHAT TO LOOK FOR

Transparency and Open Communication

Demand transparency and open communication from any potential husband. A marriage requires candid discussions about expectations, boundaries, and shared values.

A Proven Track Record

Evaluate a potential husband's history of relationships and commitments. You will want a husband who has demonstrated stability and commitment in his current marriage and relationships with family and others.

Financial Responsibility

Assess a potential husband's financial responsibility and independence. Ensure that they can contribute to the well-being of the family and meet their financial obligations.

Respect for Boundaries and Consent

Establish clear boundaries and consent within the marriage. A spouse should respect your autonomy, seek your consent when it comes to your personal things, and value your emotional well-being. That holds true for husbands and wives.

Shared Values and Goals

Aligning values and life goals are essential for marriage in polygyny to be successful. Ensure that you and your potential husband share common values, aspirations, and future plans for your marriage and family.

Being knowledgeable about the ins and outs, what to do, and what to look out for as a wife in polygyny is all fine and dandy, however, we must be able to apply what we know for the success and fulfillment in our lives and relationships.

As wives, we must be responsible for our journey and how we embrace ourselves, our husbands, and our family (including our co-wives) through it. It will be filled with changes and sometimes challenges, however, how we choose to navigate through the waters of polygyny is up to us, and our success depends on how we guide ourselves to the right information and proper actions. For information on courses and coaching, visit OutstandingPersonalRelationships.com.

Chapter 38

THE JOURNEY TOWARD CO-WIFE CONNECTION

OUR JOURNEY IN POLYGYNY IS A DYNAMIC AND EVOLVING PROCESS. Whether as an initial wife or an additional wife, navigating the complexities of polygyny requires embracing self-confidence, building sisterhood, and cultivating emotional resilience. Let's talk about the unique challenges and opportunities that each wife may encounter along her path.

I will share some of the story of my co-wife connection with my beautiful co-wife, Coach Fatimah.

"I had to send this before my nerves got the best of me..." ~***Part of my initial message to Coach Fatimah***

Finally, I sent the message that has taken way too long to send. Many times, in many ways, I wanted to reach out, establish a relationship, and get to know my co-wife as a friend as a sister.

Before marrying Coach Nazir, I envisioned my would-be co-wife as a friend, a person with whom I could connect and who could teach me things about Islam and her life. She was then and is now a beautiful spirit and an amazing artist, and I was impressed by her.

I never wanted to be her nor replace her. However, when others interfere with things that are none of their business or if the information sought is given by the wrong person, misunderstandings and roadblocks can form. This can make it challenging to build the bridge to a good relationship, let alone an outstanding one with your co-wife, as it did for me and mine.

It took a while, but through gifts sent through Coach Nazir as the liaison and a message that was typed, retyped and retyped again before it was finally sent, my co-wife reached out to me to take me on the "date"* that would be the first of many "girl outings." Outings, get-togethers, and gatherings that would grow our connection and get us to a place where we weren't just "wives of Coach Nazir,"

These helped us to stop feeling like we had to hold on to or prove ourselves for some coveted spot in his life or family, but be ourselves as women who shared many things in common and were able to learn from and embrace our various differences.

Let me get something clear, we are co-wives, and we are in polygyny, not polyamory. We are NOT with each other. We are married to Coach Nazir only. The "date" I mentioned was just a fun play on the word that just meant we went on an outing, just the two of us, to get to know one another.

Now that I cleared that up let's talk about what we can do as wives to foster a connection that can improve our family dynamic. It's about our personal growth and winning as a team, right?

SELF-CONFIDENCE: INITIAL WIVES

Self-Identity and Acceptance

For initial wives, it can be challenging to adapt to the idea of sharing your husband with another woman. The journey towards self-confidence begins with self-identity and acceptance. Remember that your worth is not defined solely by your role as a wife but by your unique qualities, aspirations, and individuality. Take time to rediscover and appreciate yourself outside of the marriage.

Open Communication

Effective communication is the cornerstone of any successful marriage in polygyny. As an initial wife, it's vital to openly express your feelings and concerns to your husband. Share your expectations, boundaries, and desires honestly. Open communication can help alleviate the uncertainties that often accompany the introduction of an additional wife.

Be mindful of timing, tone, and temperature. Is it a proper time? Meaning, can both be receptive to the information, or is there a lot going on at the moment? How's the tone? Is the conversation sarcastic, demeaning, loud, or boisterous? How's the temperature? Are you in a heated mood? Is the vibe between you both off? Those things are very important to consider when communicating with one another.

Self-Improvement and Independence

Investing in personal growth and independence is a powerful way to build self-confidence. Engage in activities that ignite your passion, pursue educational or career goals, and cultivate your own hobbies and interests. By focusing on self-improvement, you can strengthen your self-worth and sense of purpose.

We have several resources that can assist at *OutstandingPersonalRelationships.com/resources*

Boundaries and Self-Care

Establishing clear boundaries and practicing self-care are crucial aspects of self-confidence. Determine what boundaries are essential to your emotional well-being and communicate them to your husband and co-wives. Additionally, prioritize self-care routines that promote your physical and emotional health.

Positive Self-Image

Maintaining a positive self-image is essential. Avoid comparing yourself to your husband's additional wife or wives, as each wife has unique qualities and strengths. Practice positive self-talk, and remember that your husband's choice to engage in polygyny does not diminish your value as a person nor as a wife.

EMBRACING SELF-CONFIDENCE: ADDITIONAL WIVES

Self-Respect and Boundaries

As an additional wife being married to or looking to marry an already married man, self-confidence can be a rocky journey for some, especially when you are dealing with societal bias and conditioning that is against polygyny or strongly favors a hierarchy position between wives.

It's essential to respect the boundaries of your co-wife as well as set boundaries of your own. Respecting the boundaries of one another demonstrates maturity and can help establish trust within the family unit.

Self-Exploration

Before fully embracing self-confidence, take time for self-exploration. Understand your own desires, strengths, and weaknesses. This self-awareness can help you navigate the complexities of polygyny more effectively.

Open Communication

As with initial wives, open and honest communication is key. Express your feelings and expectations to your husband and co-wives, whether they are challenging or celebratory. Also, be mindful of timing, tone, and temperature. transparency can foster understanding and can mitigate any potential conflicts.

Support from Co-Wives

Leverage the support of your co-wife/wives. They can offer guidance and understanding based on their own experiences. Building a network of emotional support can assist in your journey toward self-confidence. I know this is not always easy, and some may want to keep their lives separate. However, building a sisterhood is essential, as you never know when you may need one another.

Focus on Individual Growth

While polygyny can involve shared responsibilities and family life, it's crucial to focus on your individual growth. Continue pursuing personal interests, education, or career goals. Maintaining a sense of independence and self-worth can boost your self-confidence. You have an identity outside your marital one. Don't forget that.

BUILDING SISTERHOOD: INITIAL WIVES

Empathy and Understanding

Initiating a sisterhood with an additional wife can be challenging, but it begins with empathy and understanding. Recognize that she may be experiencing her own set of emotions and insecurities. Extend compassion and support to help her feel welcome. Yes, it works both ways, and maturity is the key.

Collaborative Efforts

Engaging in collaborative efforts can foster sisterhood. Participate in activities with your co-wife that you both enjoy, such as meal preparation, childcare, homeschooling, or shared hobbies. These shared experiences can create bonds and break down barriers, as you can see the benefit each has on the family as a whole.

Conflict Resolution

Conflict may arise when establishing a sisterhood, but it can be managed constructively. Develop conflict resolution skills and aim to find common ground rather than dwelling on differences. Seek mediation if necessary.

Celebration of Differences

Celebrate the differences between you and your co-wife/wives. Embrace the diversity each of you brings to the relationship and family dynamic. Recognize that your husband values both of you for your unique qualities, and neither one has to be like the other.

Regular Communication

Maintain regular communication with your co-wife. Check-in with each other, ask about each other's well-being, and offer support when needed. Building a foundation of trust and respect is essential for a strong sisterhood and a successful family structure.

BUILDING SISTERHOOD: ADDITIONAL WIVES

Contribution and Support

Offer your contribution to the family and to the building of a sisterhood. Show your willingness to support both your husband and co-wife/wives in their endeavors. Be proactive in building connections with your co-wife.

Don't take it personally if it is not quickly reciprocated. Continue to improve on your personal development and focus on your skills and hobbies. Allow space for reflection and keep an open mind.

Open Dialogue

Maintain open and honest dialogue with your co-wife. Share your feelings and concerns while actively listening to hers. Mutual understanding can pave the way for a strong sisterhood.

My co-wife and I keep our lines of communication open and make it a point to be there for one another as we know how important it is to be positive role models, solid pillars of support, and caring individuals in our family. We work together to create and host events, educate the children, and hold each other up if and when challenges come our way.

Shared Experiences

Participate in shared experiences that allow you and your co-wife to bond. Find common interests or hobbies, and use these opportunities to strengthen your connection. Painting, baking, or just watching something you both enjoy can foster a connection of friendship and help remove any insecurities and jealousies that can come from speculations and imaginary thoughts. Shared experiences also creates a safe environment to talk and get to know one another, outside of just being wives.

Collaboration in Co-Parenting

When it comes to raising and caring for the children in the family, it can be helpful to collaborate with your co-wife to ensure a supportive and nurturing environment for the children. Joint efforts in parenting can forge a deeper sisterhood.

I know for some, co-parenting can cause problems, and jealousy can ensue. However, that happens when levels of maturity are not where they are supposed to be, and pettiness becomes the focus. Collaborating with one's co-wife is for those who are ready to win as a family and leave a positive impact on the children about the benefits of growing up in a polygynous family.

Chapter 39

CULTIVATING EMOTIONAL RESILIENCE

Self-Awareness and Self-Regulation

Cultivating emotional resilience begins with self-awareness and self-regulation. Recognize your emotions, especially jealousy and insecurity, when they arise. Develop strategies to manage and process these feelings constructively. Don't hesitate to seek guidance and support from trusted friends, therapists, or support groups. Sharing your feelings with others who understand the complexities of polygyny can provide valuable insights and coping strategies.

Personal growth and self-care are important to bolster emotional resilience, so be mindful of that. Pursue your own goals and interests, and prioritize activities that promote your well-being. A healthy, balanced life can help you better manage challenging emotions in polygyny. Especially when times get tough and nights may feel lonely.

Cultivate Gratitude

Gratitude can shift your focus from feelings of jealousy and insecurity to appreciation for the blessings in your life. Make that your daily practice. Reflect on the positive aspects of your relationship and the growth it has brought you. Utilize gratitude journals and mindful meditation as well as affirmations to solidify your peace and fulfillment.

I know that this may sound ridiculous to some, especially those who have been conditioned in a society that pushes the "need no man" or "I don't need to bring anything to the table, I am the table" mentality. It helps to engage in check-ins with your husband regularly and, your co-wife/wives when you feel ready. Create a safe space to discuss concerns and emotions openly. Collaboratively seek solutions to issues that may arise.

It's much easier to blend and bond as one big family when you get along with your co-wife/wives. Let's talk about what it looks like to get the negative societal conditioning out of the way.

Connecting with your co-wife in order to build a mature, connected family structure through personal development, proper communication, and parenting on purpose can be highly beneficial. This is especially true when that connection involves rearing healthy children and building a lasting legacy through polygyny.

Understanding the Importance of Connection

Building a connection with your co-wife is essential for the well-being of everyone involved in a polygyny. Why? Because it can help create a supportive and harmonious environment where mutual respect and understanding thrives between husbands, wives, and children (biological and bonus), as well as through the parent and child dynamic. Here's why connection matters:

Emotional Support

A strong connection can provide emotional support in times of need. Co-wives who feel connected are more likely to empathize with each other's challenges and offer a helping hand.

We are a species that likes to reciprocate, so lending a helping hand in times of need can just about guarantee that you will have one waiting for you when you need it.

Conflict Resolution

Effective communication and connection can facilitate conflict resolution. When co-wives have a bond built on trust, they are better equipped to address issues and find mutually agreeable solutions.

Shared Responsibilities

In polygynous households, responsibilities are often shared. A strong connection between co-wives can streamline household tasks and childcare, making daily life more manageable.

This also works in polygynous families in different households. The organization of tasks and responsibilities can be easily executed through proper communication and connection.

Emotional Well-Being

Feeling connected to your co-wife can enhance your emotional well-being. It is a bond fosters a sense of belonging and reduces feelings of isolation or exclusion within the family structure.

REACHING OUT TO YOUR CO-WIFE

Start with Empathy

Empathy is the foundation of any meaningful connection. Put yourself in your co-wife's shoes and try to understand her perspective, experiences, and emotions. Recognize that she may have her own concerns and insecurities within the practice of polygyny. This holds true for both initial and additional wives.

Respect Her Space and Boundaries

While it's essential to reach out to your co-wife, it's equally crucial to respect her need for personal space and boundaries. Not everyone is ready to connect immediately, and that's okay. Allow her the autonomy to decide the pace at which she feels comfortable to build a connection.

Extend a Genuine Invitation

Extend a genuine invitation to connect. This could be a simple message expressing your desire to get to know her better or an invitation to spend time together. Ensure that your approach is friendly, non-threatening, and free of any expectations.

Offer Support and Understanding

Let your co-wife know that you're there to support and understand her. Reassure her that you're interested in her well-being and that you respect her role within the family. Be a listening ear when she needs someone to talk to.

Shared Activities and Interests

Identify shared activities or interests that you both enjoy. Engaging in activities together can be an excellent way to build a connection. It could be as simple as sharing a meal, going for a walk, or pursuing a hobby you both appreciate.

Practice Active Listening

Active listening is a powerful tool for building connections. When your co-wife speaks, listen attentively, ask questions to show your interest, and validate her feelings and experiences. Don't interrogate or push your own narrative. By actively listening and being open minded, you are demonstrating that you value her perspective.

Show Respect and Appreciation

Respect and appreciation go a long way in fostering a connection with your co-wife. Acknowledge your co-wife's strengths, contributions, and the unique qualities she brings to the family. Showing genuine appreciation can create a positive atmosphere.

Respecting Rejections with Grace

Not every attempt to connect with your co-wife may be met with enthusiasm, and that's perfectly normal. It's crucial to handle any rejections gracefully and not take them personally. Here's how to do it:

Understand It's Not About You

A rejection is not necessarily a reflection of your character or worthiness. Your co-wife may have her reasons for not being ready to connect, and these reasons may have nothing to do with you.

Respect Her Choice

Respect your co-wife's choice to decline your invitation to connect. Understand that she may have her own timeline for building relationships, and that's her prerogative.

Avoid Pressure or Guilt Trips

Refrain from pressuring your co-wife or making her feel guilty for rejecting your invitation. Coercion or guilt-tripping can strain the relationship further.

Give Her Space

After a rejection, give your co-wife space and time to process her feelings. Continue to be respectful and open to a connection if and when she is ready.

Maintain a Positive Attitude

Maintain a positive attitude and approach future interactions with an open heart. Over time, circumstances may change, and your co-wife may become more receptive to building a connection.

Fostering Connection with Respect

Reaching out to your co-wife and building a connection within polygyny is a valuable endeavor that contributes to the overall well-being of the family unit. It requires empathy, patience, and a deep respect for personal boundaries of everyone involved.

Importantly, handling rejections or setbacks with grace and understanding is key to maintaining a positive atmosphere within the family. Remember that building connections takes time, and each individual's journey is unique. By fostering connections with respect and sensitivity, you contribute to a harmonious and supportive polygynous family structure.

Chapter 40

PROTECTING THE HONOR AND INTEGRITY OF THE FAMILY IN POLYGYNY AND BUILDING A LASTING LEGACY

BEING ABLE TO WORK TOGETHER, EVEN THROUGH DISAGREEMENTS OR mixed emotions, shows a level of maturity that is needed for the success of the total family dynamic. When disconnect and discord are prevalent, it causes a level of hardship on everyone involved. Let's talk about properly protecting the honor of the family by honoring all members of the family.

Blending families in polygyny is a multi-faceted journey that requires careful consideration, empathy, and a strong sense of unity. In this chapter, we will explore the dynamics of blending families, with the husband as the head and leader. We'll also discuss the concept of complaints going up while compliments go down, the importance of "one for all and all for one," and the implementation of a family code of honor to foster unity and harmony.

The Husband as the Head and Leader

In a polygynous family, it's common for the husband to take on the role of the head and leader. This role involves making important decisions, ensuring fairness, and maintaining the overall well-being of the family. Here's why this role is significant:

Maintaining Balance

The husband's role as the head helps maintain balance within the family structure. His leadership can provide stability and direction, especially when navigating the complexities of a polygynous relationship.

Decision-Making

The husband is often responsible for making decisions that affect the family as a whole. This includes financial planning, resolving conflicts, and addressing any challenges that may arise.

Ensuring Fairness

As the leader, the husband must ensure fairness among his wives and children. This entails treating each wife equitably, both emotionally and financially.

Fostering Unity

The husband's leadership plays a crucial role in fostering unity within the family. By being a fair and just leader, he can encourage a sense of belonging and cooperation among his wives and children.

Complaints Up, Compliments Down

In many families, there is a common dynamic where complaints tend to go up the chain while compliments go down. We do not complain to the children and expect them to assist us as adults to work out our problems.

Although the saying includes, "compliments go down," it doesn't mean that compliments only go down. It means that if anything is to go down the chain, it should be in the form of positivity, not negativity.

The following can help shed light on what this means in detail and how to address this concept.

Open Communication

Encourage open communication within the family. Wives and children should feel comfortable expressing their concerns and grievances directly to the husband without fear of reprisal.

Addressing Concerns

The husband, as the leader, should take the responsibility of addressing the concerns and complaints of his wives and children. This may involve mediating conflicts, finding solutions, or making necessary changes to improve the family's well-being.

Promoting Positivity

It's essential to promote positivity and appreciation within the family. Encourage wives and children to express their compliments and appreciation for one another. This can help balance the dynamic of complaints going up and compliments going down the chain.

Establishing a Feedback System

Create a feedback system within the family where constructive criticism is welcomed and compliments are encouraged. This system can help ensure that everyone's voices are heard and valued.

"One for All and All for All Y'all" Concept

The concept of "one for all and all for all y'all" is a fundamental principle in creating unity within the family. It signifies that the well-being of one family member is interconnected with the well-being of all.

When one wins, we all win. If we are all in this together, then when one loses, we lose as a team. So, being there for one another is paramount. Here's how to apply this concept:

Mutual Support

Encourage mutual support among wives and children. Emphasize that when one member of the family succeeds or faces challenges, it impacts the entire family. Show empathy and offer assistance when needed.

Shared Responsibilities

Distribute responsibilities within the family, ensuring that everyone plays a part in contributing to the family's well-being. This can include household chores, childcare, or financial responsibilities.

Celebrating Achievements

Celebrate each other's achievements and milestones. When one family member succeeds, acknowledge and celebrate their accomplishments as a whole family.

Addressing Challenges Effectively

When the family is facing challenges, or a member is having issues that can affect the overall well-being of the family unit, work to approach them as efficiently and effectively as possible. Encourage open discussions and brainstorming sessions to find solutions that benefit the entire family.

Establishing a Family Code of Honor

To promote unity and harmony within a family in polygyny, consider establishing a family code of honor. This code should outline the values, principles, and expectations that all family members agree to uphold. Every week during our family council meetings, we recite our code of honor together and provide examples of how they were implemented throughout the week.

Here's how you can implement and enforce your own:

Collaborative Development

Involve all family members in the development of the family code of honor. Encourage open discussions and consensus-building to ensure that everyone's perspectives are considered.

Clearly Defined Values

The code of honor should clearly define the values and principles that the family holds close and cherish. This may include respect, fairness, honesty, and cooperation.

Accountability Mechanisms

Establish accountability mechanisms to ensure that the code of honor is upheld. This may include regular family meetings to discuss adherence to the code and address any violations.

Memorization and Practice

Encourage all family members to memorize and put the code of honor into practice in their daily lives. Lead by example as the husband and leader, and ensure that the code is an integral part of family life.

Navigating as One Unified Family

Blending families in polygyny requires a commitment to unity, effective communication, and a strong sense of shared values. With the husband as the head and leader, complaints can be addressed, compliments can be encouraged to flow, and the concept of "one for all and all for all y'all" can be embraced.

Implementing a family code of honor can further reinforce the principles that guide the family's interactions and decisions. By navigating as one unified family, the challenges of polygyny can be met with cooperation, understanding, and love, leading to a harmonious and fulfilling family life.

Answer the following:

I embrace and contribute to being a part of my family's team by...

Chapter 41

OUR FAITH AND HOW IT HAS
AFFECTED OUR FAMILY DYNAMIC

THERE ARE A NUMBER OF THINGS TO CONSIDER WHEN IT COMES TO practicing polygyny, or being married to a married man. Earlier, I discussed different societies and religions that have practiced polygyny throughout time, and I would be remiss if I did not speak about how Islam played a part in my understanding of polygyny as well as my appreciation for how it is regulated.

As you may now know, if you haven't before, my family are practicing Muslims, and maybe this section will shed some light on the justness that Islam provides and the honor it gives to wives, especially in polygyny.

Earlier, I spoke about how my studying Islam triggered those around me to inform me that men in Islam can have multiple wives. That wasn't something that I was aware of until I started my study of why people follow this religion.

I was brought up Christian and baptized at about ten years old. We weren't overly religious, but we went to church on Sundays and read the Bible from time to time. I did believe that there was a God and that there was only one, and that we are here through God, our Creator.

The sense that I had something in my life that I knew was more powerful than anything on the planet that kept me grounded was always inside me, it just wasn't guided in the way that it should have been. I didn't find that true guidance and understanding until I studied and converted to Islam in my early 20s.

I share this to help some understand that I was not always a Muslim. Neither was my husband or co-wife. However, being practicing Muslims has helped ground us and has increased our understanding of divine decree, wanting for each other as we want for ourselves and increasing our connection with the Most High, known as Allah. We are grateful for Allah when things get challenging, and we are grateful for what is put in our lives whether it be a lesson, a liberation, a stepping stone, or success story.

There are rules and regulations to follow, and it is laid out for us, whether it be in the Quran or the sunnah of the Prophet Muhammad (Peace be upon him). The sunnah is described as the thoughts, words, and actions of the Prophet Muhammad (Peace be upon him). We believe that we are accountable for how we live our lives, how we treat others, and how we follow what the Most High has intended.

Nurturing a family through polygyny in Islam also comes with rules and regulations and consists of understanding the following for success in the family unit:

Honor of Family

In Islam, the status of parents is extremely high, and their rights are considered among the most important of all within the family dynamic. Children are required to be obedient to their parents, show respect, and fulfill their needs. The Prophet Muhammad (peace be upon him) said: "He who wishes to enter paradise through its best door must show kindness to his parents." This shows how important it is to honor and respect our parents in Islam.

The Quran stresses the importance of treating one's parents with kindness and respect. For instance, Allah says in the Quran:

"And your Lord has decreed that you not worship except Him, and to parents, good treatment. Whether one or both of them reach old age [while] with you, say not to them [so much as], 'uff,' and do not repel them but speak to them a noble word." (17:23)

This verse highlights the significance of treating one's parents with kindness and love, regardless of their behavior or attitude.

This has helped us in raising our children as well as being role models for them in how we treat our parents. What we put out, we get back. This establishes the honor and integrity of the family dynamic.

Husband as Leader

"Men are the protectors and maintainers of women because Allah has given the one more (strength) than the other, and because they support them from their means." (Qur'an 4:34)

Men are required to protect, provide, and offer maintenance for their families. They were created to handle all that it takes to do so, and in that regard, they should be respected as the head and leaders of the family and household.

Fairness of Wives

"You are never able to be fair and just as between women, even if it is your ardent desire: but turn not away (from a woman) altogether, so as to leave her (as it were) hanging (in the air) ..." (Quran- Surah al-Nisa, 129)

This verse of the Quran has been described as that, a man must be fair in his external treatment of his wives, where he should spend equal time with all of them; spend money on them equally, etc. However, if his heart is inclined towards one or he has more love for one wife over the other, then that is not blameworthy, for it is beyond his control.

The Prophet Muhammad (peace and blessings be upon him) would treat his wives equally and justly and then say: *"O Allah! This is my distribution according to my capability, thus do not hold me for what you own and I don't."* (Sunan Tirmidhi, no. 1140, Sunan Abu Dawud, no. 3133 & Musnad Ahmad)

This was stated to mean to not hold him against what is in his heart as Allah is the controller of the heart.

This can sometimes be a problem for some women in polygyny because they desire to be favored or want to know that they are loved more or that no one is loved or desired more than them. If this is a problem that can affect the family dynamic, then that wife should truly question if she will thrive in the family and her marriage and if the family and marriage will thrive with her and that mentality.

There are many benefits that reside outside of just the desires of the heart, however, as polygyny is not for everyone, this is usually the challenge for women, especially in the West.

Rights of Spouses

Spouses have rights over each other in Islam. For men, it included the supervision, protection, and maintenance of the wives as well as just treatment among the wives. For women, it includes being submissive and obedient as long as what the husband desires is not against the rules of Islam. That includes being sexually available for him when he desires.

It must be understood that men and women operate differently and are created differently. Anomalies do not change that fact. We submit to the Creator and the divine wisdom of our Creator first and foremost, and if the creation receives submission, it's because our Creator commanded it.

We believe we are living an open-book test and because we will be questioned and will be held accountable. So, we work to live our lives and nurture our relationships with the guidance of our faith. Our faith in Islam is what keeps us grounded as individuals as well as a part of this family.

No, we are not perfect! It was not easy in the beginning, and challenges still tend to show up along the way. However, as long as we are here on this planet and in this life, we can improve ourselves, increase our connection in our relationships and intensify our influence in a positive way so we are able to grow intentionally, love fearlessly and connect on a higher level, every single day!

Answer the following:

When challenges arise in my marriage and in my relationships, I ground myself by...

How does my faith/spirituality play a part in the success of my marriage and family dynamic?

Chapter 42

MY FINAL THOUGHTS

As I look back on the incredible journey we've undertaken together in this book, I'm overwhelmed with a sense of gratitude and transformation. Our exploration of polygyny, its intricacies, and the strategies we've uncovered for nurturing love, empathy, and unity within our family dynamic has been nothing short of remarkable.

Throughout these pages, I've shared my own experiences, vulnerabilities, and the valuable lessons we've learned as a polygynous family. We've delved into the critical aspects of building self-confidence, fostering sisterhood, and cultivating emotional resilience, all of which are vital for a thriving polygynous family.

Our faith, Islam, has been a guiding force in shaping our family dynamics. It's provided us with a strong moral foundation, helping us navigate the complexities of polygyny while reminding us of our duties to honor our parents, treat our spouses fairly, and uphold the principles of justice and equity. Our faith has been our unwavering anchor during trying times, and a source of strength, connection, and growth.

Our journey has been illuminated by open and honest communication, empathy, and an unshakable commitment to supporting one another. We've celebrated each other's victories and faced challenges together, embodying the idea that we're all in this as a unified team, "one for all and all for all y'all."

Our family code of honor has been our compass, reinforcing the values and principles that guide our daily lives. It's served as a roadmap for navigating the complexities of polygyny with grace and integrity.

We've come to understand the pivotal role of the husband as the head and leader of our family. His leadership has provided stability, balance, and direction, ensuring fairness among his wives and nurturing unity within our family.

Through Islam, we've discovered not just a set of rules and regulations, but a profound sense of justice and honor. We've embraced the significance of honoring and respecting our parents, upholding the rights of spouses, and recognizing the unique qualities and interdependence of each family member.

Our challenges have been transformative experiences, and our successes have fortified our bonds. We've learned that polygyny, while challenging, can be navigated with faith, understanding, and unwavering commitment, resulting in a harmonious and fulfilling family life.

In conclusion, I want to emphasize that our journey is ongoing. Although we are successful coaches who have navigated fairly well through the complexities of polygyny, we are not perfect, and we continue to learn and grow each day. But we face each day with intention, striving to love fearlessly, connecting on a deeper level, and nurturing our relationships with the guidance of our faith.

I hope that our story has provided you with insights, encouragement, and a deeper understanding of polygyny. May it serve as a reminder that, even in the face of challenges, we have the power to grow intentionally and love fearlessly. Thank you for being a part of this incredible journey, and may your own path be filled with love, unity, and growth.

~ Coach Nyla

In Conclusion

Your Journey Awaits: Next Steps to Outstanding Personal Relationships

As you close this book, know that it's not the end, but rather a stepping stone to the next chapter of your relational journey. The complexities of love, partnership, and the ancient yet ever-relevant practice of polygyny require more than theories and anecdotes. They call for actionable tools, guided help, and a community that understands the unique blend of joys and challenges that come with this lifestyle.

Our mission is to arm you not just with knowledge, but with the practical skills and emotional intelligence required to forge and maintain outstanding relationships. Words on a page can only take you so far. It's real-world application and ongoing support that truly makes a difference. So let's continue this journey together.

Want to Dive Deeper? Here's How You Can Work With Us.

If you found the insights and guidance in this book invaluable, imagine what more you could achieve with personalized coaching, advanced courses, and live events tailored to your unique relationship dynamics. Head over to our website for resources designed to elevate your relationship game to the next level.

- For one-on-one coaching sessions with myself and my experienced team, visit: (https://outstandingpersonalrelationships.com/coaching)

- If you're interested in comprehensive courses that take a deep dive into everything from communication to the psychology of polygyny, head to: (https://outstandingpersonalrelationships.com/resources)

- If you're Want to be part of an immersive experience? Check out our Polygyny Education Campus or upcoming live events where you can engage with experts and community members who share your relationship goals, visit PolygamyEducation.com

Our tools are meticulously crafted to offer both breadth and depth, equipping you with a holistic understanding and practical skill set that empower you to build, nurture, and sustain the kind of relationships you've always wanted.

Take the Leap

If there's one thing I want you to take away, it's this: The most extraordinary relationships are not just dreamed, they're built. They're crafted through conscious effort, guided by informed choices and empowered by actionable strategies.

The door to your best life, best love, and best relationships is wide open. All you have to do is walk through it. The support, the resources, and the community you need are all just a click away.

So what are you waiting for? Seize the opportunity to transform your relationships and, by extension, your life. We are here to support you every step of the way.

Your journey to Outstanding Personal Relationship starts now.

ABOUT THE AUTHORS

Meet the Outstanding Personal Relationships Team: Coaches Nazir, Nyla, and Fatimah. Together, they don't just talk the talk; they've walked the walk—investing tens of thousands of dollars into becoming the best versions of themselves. And now they're poised to catapult your life to levels you've o dreamed of.

Initially united by a 15-year monogamous marriage, Coaches Nazir and Fatimah broadened their horizons by embracing polygyny when Nazir married Nyla. This wasn't a casual shift; it was a calculated decision anchored by substantial investment in self-education and growth.

Why did they invest so heavily? Because they understood a fundamental truth: excellence isn't stumbled upon; it's cultivated. Coaches Nazir and Fatimah were committed to family excellence from day one. They welcomed mentors, coaches, and wisdom-filled elders into their lives, absorbing invaluable lessons in leadership, entrepreneurship, art, interior design, and nurturing a family.

Fast forward almost 15 years: Coach Nazir expanded his family with the addition of Coach Nyla, embarking on a challenging but rewarding polygynous journey. They faced trials, yes, but each obstacle was an opportunity for growth—an opportunity they seized because they had already made a monumental investment in becoming better human beings.

The Return on Investment

What has this significant investment in themselves yielded? A robust, blended family of twelve children. Expertise in relationship development,

renting, business strategy, mindfulness, and wellness. And the ability to reach and transform the lives of over a million people on YouTube alone.

While their coaching emanates from a foundation of Islamic principles, they've successfully guided people from every conceivable spiritual background—Muslims, Hebrew Israelites, Mormons, Christians, African Spiritualists, Jews, and even those with no religious affiliation.

Their message is universally resonant: You can drastically improve your life and relationships, but you must be willing to invest in yourself.

Remember a *WISH* changes *NOTHING* but a *DECISION* changes *EVERYTHING*!

ACKNOWLEDGMENTS

First and foremost, all praise and thanks belongs to Allah and we submit to the One through Al Islam. Any mistakes or shortcomings are ours and we accept full responsibility for them and seek the forgiveness of the Most Loving, The Most Gracious, Allah, The Most High, ameen.

To our mentors and coaches who guided us in life and challenged us when we felt pain, thank you, your advice and encouragement has been invaluable.

We also want to acknowledge our family, especially our children who have been some of our greatest teachers and students. Keep us in your prayers and pass on the wisdom to our descendants.

Our friends and supporters who have been our cheerleaders, sounding boards, and occasional reality-checkers, thank you.

Our incredible daughter Faatimah, The Family Artist, who has helped with manifesting our imaginative designs so well in print and video. Our incredible editor Claire who worked diligently from the UK on a time crunch. Your encouragement has made this book possible.

To those who have believed in our vision and the importance of this book as a service to humanity, thank you for standing by us especially with the topic of this book which is so often misunderstood.

Last but not least, a word to our detractors, skeptics, and haters: Thank you as well. Your doubts and criticisms have only fueled our determination to write this book and lay out our perspectives for the world to see. You've given us the fire to press on, making this work not just an answer to a question but a clarion call for understanding, choice, and respect in human relationships.

We sincerely hope that "Let's Talk Polygamy UNCENSORED" serves as a resource that enlightens, challenges, and aids all who come across it.

"Ready to elevate your understanding of polygyny and unlock the keys to a fulfilling polygamous marriage?

- Schedule an Exclusive Coaching Call: Get personalized guidance and breakthrough strategies.

- Become a Member at PolygamyEducation.com: Access an ever-expanding vault of resources, and connect with like-minded individuals.

- Dive into Group Coaching: Immerse yourself in collective wisdom, supported by our seasoned experts.

- Enlist in a Signature Online Course, Challenge, or Workshop: Engage in curated content that addresses your specific needs and aspirations.

- Experience a Live Event or Retreat: Be part of transformative experiences that will challenge, enlighten, and empower you.

- Invest in Our Library: Grab another one of our groundbreaking books for further insights and tools.

All of this and more awaits you: OutstandingPersonalRelationships.com.

Take decisive action now and reshape your destiny!"

OPR

OUTSTANDING
PERSONAL RELATIONSHIPS